"Now into the third decade of the twenty-first century, Christians find themselves wandering in a discursive wilderness full of bitter streams and toxic waste. This timely book offers a cup of water for the parched and a signpost for the weary. Editors Wood and Connable have brought together a qualified group of scholars to tackle the thorny issue of Christian responsibility regarding civility in a grossly uncivil society. When some of the most uncivil members of society identify as Christian, the issues grow exponentially complex. In exquisite fashion, this collection practices the very Gospel it preaches. More symposium than book, the interlocutors disagree at times, but their disagreements are framed by a deep appreciation for one another and for the subjects they discuss. No simple answers are presented, no glib solutions proffered. Instead, these scholars engage in earnest dialectic that mingles incisive scholarship with compelling personal experience. This distinctive approach succeeds in filling out extraordinary dimensions of Humility and Hospitality—some of which may take the reader by surprise. In the end, the reader comes away with practical tools for realizing the important call of historian Jemar Tisby in *The Color of Compromise* to awareness, relationship, and commitment in a divisive world."

—**Matthew Melton**, Dean, College of Arts and Sciences, Lee University

"This book is an engaging, interesting, and even provocative look at the need for hospitality and humility in society and Church if we wish to recover private as well as public civility in today's world. It humbly offers the language we need to engage in conversations that just might set the scene for a rebirth of one of the most ancient practices, namely, the love of one's neighbor as self. Highly recommended."

—**Quentin Schultze**, Professor Emeritus, Communication, Calvin College

"Kristin Kobes Du Mez's *Jesus and John Wayne* offers a diagnosis of the arrogant and inhospitable expression of evangelical Christianity at large in the U.S. The chapters in Naaman Wood and Sean Connable's *Humility and Hospitality: Changing the Christian Conversation on Civility* offer a prognosis for this expression of Christianity. Their book unleashes the humane expressions of Christianity for students and scholars committed to biblical frameworks and readers seeking the touchstones of civility in the Christian tradition. Intended for readers in Christian colleges, seminaries, pastors, and lay leaders, scholars outside the Christian tradition will find the authors of these chapters well-versed in the academic literature. To illustrate:

John Hatch, in his chapter, offers a splendid analysis that draws from René Girard and Walter Brueggemann to effectively deconstruct, using biblical principles, the "royal consciousness" fueling the dominant theology of White American Christianity. This excellent book offers an effective Christian antidote to one interpretation of Christianity that is cruel and crude."

—**David Frank**, Professor of Rhetoric, University of Oregon

"In the world of academic inquiry, one of the great benefits is the presentation of ideas and the ensuing discourse that emerges in response to that inquiry. What Wood and Connable have done in this text is not only to create an opportunity for discourse and dialogue, but also they have set up critique and evaluation as a necessary part of that interaction. One of the challenges among evangelical Christians today is that there is a recognition that our discourse is not healthy. However, the attempts to address that unhealth have often only scratched the surface of what has caused the decline in our communication climate. What the contributors of this text do, as guided by Wood and Connable, is to address the inherent illness in evangelicalism that prevents our assessments from addressing the heart of the challenge and limiting our correction to surface level fixes that never get to the real issues. Often, evangelicalism and evangelicals are called upon to address the lack of self-critique in the movement. What this book does is begin that self-critique and allow the community to begin to really get to the heart of the matter. If we are to ever heal our communication climate, this work will be considered a seminal work that enabled that healing to begin."

—**Joy Qualls**, Associate Professor and Associate Dean, Division of Communication, School of Fine Arts and Communication, Biola University

"Readers may note the conversational metaphor at the center of Wood and Connable's edited volume and breathe a sigh of relief. Here, surely, is a shelter in this polarizing season of late-modern society. But heads up! This book offers much more than a conversation about the uncanny disagreeableness of our time. It does that. But the book's notably diverse contributors transform what might have been a merely sedate exchange into a robust and omnidirectional colloquium. Come for the dialogue, stay for the multilogue."

—**Craig Mattson**, Professor of Communication Arts, Department Chair, Co-director of the Honors Program, Trinity Christian College

Humility and Hospitality

Humility and Hospitality

Changing the Christian Conversation on Civility

EDITED BY

NAAMAN WOOD *and*
SEAN CONNABLE

FOREWORD BY Janie Marie Harden Fritz

Integratio Press

HUMILITY AND HOSPITALITY
Changing the Christian Conversation on Civility

Copyright © 2022 by Naaman Wood and Sean Connable. All rights reserved. Except for brief quotations in critical publications or reviews, no part of this book may be reproduced in any manner without prior written permission from the publisher. Write: Permissions, Integratio Press, 11503 Easton Dr., Pasco WA, 99301.

Integratio Press
An Imprint of Christianity and Communication Studies Network
11503 Easton Dr.
Pasco, WA 99301

www.theccsn.com

Cover design: Carol O'Callaghan and Ashley Knight
Interior design: Carol O'Callaghan
Image: Depositphotos

PAPERBACK ISBN: 978-0-9991463-5-4
EBOOK ISBN: 978-0-9991463-6-1

Library of Congress Control Number: 2022946285

Dedication

For NAIITS: An Indigenous Learning Community. May I continue to listen to the wisdom Creator God has given you. — Naaman

To Christina who walked with me in the valley, and to Gideon, Amelia, and Liam, may you leave the world better than we left it. — Sean

Table of Contents

Acknowledgments   *xv*
Contributors   *xvii*
Foreword   *xxi*
   Janie Marie Harden Fritz

INTRODUCTION

   INTRODUCTION   3
   Changing the Christian Conversation on Civility:
   Contextualizing Calvin Troup's Call for Humility and Hospitality
     Naaman Wood and Sean Connable

PART I   Changing the Conversation on Civility

   CHAPTER 1   19
   Humility and Hospitality: Two Conditions Necessary for
   the Possibility of Civility
     Calvin L. Troup

PART II   Foundations for Civility

   CHAPTER 2   33
   Substantive Discourse: Love, Justice, and Hierarchy as the
   Basis for Civility
     Mark A. E. Williams

   CHAPTER 3   47
   Endeavoring Hospitality as Interaction: Reflections on
   Subtle Enactments of Empire
     Michelle Shockness

TABLE OF CONTENTS

PART III   Lived Challenges of Civility

> CHAPTER 4   63
> Reverse and Covenantal Hospitality: Expanding the Paradigm of Giving and Receiving in Cross-cultural Christian Mission
> *Susangeline Y. Patrick*
>
> CHAPTER 5   77
> On the Limits of Love: Entanglements with Colonialism in the Sixties Scoop and the Christian Reformed Church in North America (CRCNA)
> *Naaman Wood*
>
> CHAPTER 6   95
> There Is No Civility without the Recognition of Power: How Perceived Persecution, Hostility, and Unilateral Conditions Impact Christian Calls for Civility
> *Jaime Harris*

PART IV   Opportunities for Civility

> CHAPTER 7   111
> On Regulating Civility: The Directing Meta-virtue of Integrity and the Barmen Declaration
> *Annalee R. Ward and Mary K. Bryant*
>
> CHAPTER 8   127
> Suffering and Civility: Rethinking the Role of the American Evangelical Tradition in Public Discourse and Public Life
> *Mark Allan Steiner*
>
> CHAPTER 9   143
> Marginally Persuasive: Recovering the Cruciform Power of Prophetic Witness
> *John B. Hatch*

TABLE OF CONTENTS

CONCLUSION

    CONCLUSION   161
    For God, All Things are Possible: A More Substantive
    Christianity for the Twenty-first Century
      Naaman Wood and Sean Connable

Endnotes   179
Index   207

Acknowledgments

WE ARE HAPPY TO THANK a number of friends, colleagues, and institutions that have nurtured us along this long process. The book began in conversations in the summer of 2017, at the Forum 4:15 Unconference, supported in part by Spring Arbor University. Those in attendance, in some way, touched us as we talked over dinners, chatted in people's homes, or walked across campus. That nurturing and encouraging environment was essential to lay the groundwork for this book. While we were initially hesitant to edit this book, our peers from the conference, several of whom appear in this book, encouraged us to do so. Without their belief in us and their support, we do not think we would have been able to begin much less persist and finally finish this volume.

I (Naaman) would like to thank two institutions that were vital in supporting my contribution to this book. First and most importantly, NAIITS: An Indigenous Learning Community is a tertiary school of theological studies accredited by the Association of Theological Schools (ATS). They are a unique community in that they are designed and delivered by and primarily for Indigenous peoples of the world, primarily serving students and practitioners in settler colonial states like the USA, Canada, Australia, New Zealand, and across Latin America. In a world where profound injustices persist, their insights are, to my mind, laying the groundwork for what Christian faithfulness looks like. If we, as white settler Christians, want to say anything meaningful in the twenty-first century, we must listen long and hard to Christians like those who lead and learn at NAIITS. Redeemer University also supported this project. In the Winter of 2021, they offered me release time to work on this and other projects. They also offered generous funds in aid of publication for the proofreading of the manuscript, which Sean's colleague, William Duffy, provided so wonderfully and promptly.

Much of this project was completed during the COVID-19 pandemic, and it took us longer than it likely should have to finish. We

Acknowledgments

did not feel, as we entered the crises of 2020, that pushing our authors into revisions was the best choice. So, we essentially halted the project for about a year. We are not sure the delay was the wisest choice, but we do want to thank everyone involved—authors and publishers especially—for their patience and understanding. Erring on the side of giving everyone (perhaps a bit too much) room to navigate the traumas of these years, was the choice we ultimately made. We wish everyone healing and peace as we, hopefully, begin the long process of imagining our post-pandemic future together, a future in which we, Christians especially, might listen more deeply to those not like us.

Contributors

Mary K. Bryant is Assistant Director of Programming & Media for the Wendt Center for Character Education at the University of Dubuque. She enjoys her work with Annalee R. Ward in support of the Wendt Center's mission to promote lives of purpose and excellent moral character. Above all, she is delighted to serve students and tackle creative projects such as editing the Center's annual journal and producing videos, animations, and podcasts. With a BA in Biology, Theatre Arts, and German, along with an MFA in Comparative Literature—Translation from the University of Iowa, she pursues of variety of interests, including music, crafting, and gardening.

Sean Connable is a Senior Lecturer at Christopher Newport University in Newport News, Virginia, where he teaches courses in rhetorical theory and criticism, as well as dialogue. He has a BA, MA, and PhD in communication from the University of Memphis. In addition to his work in the classroom, he researches the intersection of rhetoric, religion, and politics. When not in the classroom, he spends his days with his wife and three children.

Jaime Harris is a sociologist and Senior Lecturer at Christopher Newport University in the Department of Sociology, Social Work, and Anthropology. Harris's research emphasizes the role of religion on conflict, policy, and organizational processes, and he has also written about religious conflict and terrorism. He earned his BA from Texas A & M University-College Station and his MA and PhD from Pennsylvania State University.

John B. Hatch is a Senior Fellow for the Christianity and Communication Studies Network (www.theccsn.com). His previous academic roles include Wendt Ethics Professor at the University of Dubuque and Chair of Communication Studies at Eastern University. He has published extensively on race relations, public apology, reconciliation, religious discourse, and popular/contemporary Christian music. His articles appear in *Rhetoric &*

Public Affairs, Quarterly Journal of Speech, Journal of Communication and Religion, and other scholarly journals and edited books. His volume *Race and Reconciliation: Redressing Wounds of Injustice* received the 2009 Top Single-Author Book Award from the Communication Ethics Division of the National Communication Association. Hatch is also the author/editor of an anthology of speeches titled *Speaking to Reconciliation: Voices of Faith Addressing Racial and Cultural Divides*. Hatch earned a PhD from Regent University. Captivated by the grace of God, the beauty of nature, and the ancient liturgy of the Church, John and his wife, Christie, enjoy traveling, hiking in the mountains, leading worship music, and being "parents" to their lovable beagle.

Susangeline Y. Patrick is Assistant Professor of World Christianity at Nazarene Theological Seminary in Kansas City, MO, and faculty member at NAIITS: An Indigenous Learning Community. Her research interests are Asian Christianity, history of First Nations Christians, and women in World Christianity. She is the author of the upcoming book *Christians in the City of Shanghai: A History Resurrected above the Sea* (London: Bloomsbury). Patrick earned a PhD from Asbury Theological Seminary.

Michelle Shockness is a nonprofit organizational specialist and consultant in Toronto, Canada. Her more than 30 years of experience in the nonprofit and social service sectors include former roles as a community worker, social worker, program director, and therapist, and in recent years, roles as a lecturer and professor in organizational leadership and applied social sciences, respectively. Her practice over the years has focused primarily on the needs of marginalized and racialized groups, and has included work with children, youth, and women, often in economically disenfranchised communities in Canada. Her practice has also included volunteer, teaching, and research experiences with communities abroad. Shockness earned a PhD from Eastern University, and her research has included a focus on women's leadership, and on organizational values and member experience, which speaks to her broader interest in organizational inclusivity. She describes her mission as working to contribute to a safer nonprofit organization and a fairer world, and through her various endeavors, she aspires to live this mission consistently and practically.

Contributors

Mark Allan Steiner is Associate Professor of Communication at Christopher Newport University in Newport News, Virginia, and is a past president of the Religious Communication Association. His areas of research and scholarship include rhetorical theory and criticism, religious rhetoric, public discourse, and the relationship between mediation and religious identity. He is the author of *The Rhetoric of Operation Rescue: Projecting the Christian Pro-Life Message* (2006) and has published a range of articles and book chapters on evangelical Christian rhetoric, media and religion, undergraduate communication pedagogy, and rhetoric education at the primary and secondary school levels. He earned a PhD from Indiana University.

Calvin L. Troup was inaugurated in 2016 as Geneva College's twentieth president. He earned a master's degree and a PhD from Pennsylvania State University. He served on the faculties of Penn State-University Park and Indiana University-Bloomington before teaching in Communication and Rhetorical Studies at Duquesne University, where he directed the university's nationally ranked Rhetoric PhD program. His scholarly work resides in rhetoric and philosophy of communication and media ecology. His books include *Temporality, Eternity, and Wisdom* and *Augustine for the Philosophers*. He has edited the *Journal of Communication and Religion* and is a past president of the Religious Communication Association.

Annalee R. Ward directs the Wendt Center for Character Education at the University of Dubuque in Iowa. The Initiative works campus-wide to promote excellent moral character and lives of purpose through a multi-pronged programmatic outreach that includes fifty Character Scholars engaged in curricular work and off-campus volunteering, a community lecture series, general curricular work throughout the university, athletics, and faculty support. Her background in communication, theater, and theology informs the work. Along with Mary K. Bryant, she produces a digital journal called *Character and . . .* in which faculty write on a particular topic each year. In addition, they produce a podcast called *Character Explorations*. Her research and writing falls in the intersection of culture, rhetoric, and ethics with work on Disney films, Christian theme parks, and tourism as well as work that investigates moral character in conversation with current issues. Ward earned a PhD from Regent University.

Contributors

Mark A. E. Williams is Professor of Rhetoric at California State University-Sacramento, where he teaches courses in rhetorical criticism, rhetoric and religion, and the history of rhetoric. Williams earned a PhD from Louisiana State University and is a former research fellow of Oxford University and of L'École Biblique et Archaéologique de Jérusalem. His publications include "Saint Socrates, Pray for us: Rhetoric and the Physics of Being Human" in *Rhetoric in the Twenty-first Century: An Interactive Oxford Symposium*, "From Here to Eternity: The Scope of Misreading Plato's Religion" in *Communication and the Global Landscape of Faith*, and "Saint Anselm of Canterbury" in *Words and Witnesses: Communication Studies in Christian Thought from Athanasius to Desmond Tutu*. Left unsupervised, he will read Tolkien, bind books by hand, watch the shadows change in the back yard, fret vaguely about the world, and write just for fun.

Naaman Wood is Instructor of Communication at Saint Paul College in St. Paul, MN. After earning an MA and a PhD from Regent University, Wood received an MTS and ThM from Duke Divinity School. His interdisciplinary scholarship has been published in the journals *Symbolic Interaction* and *Jazz Perspectives*, and the books *Prophetic Critique and Popular Media: Theoretical Foundations and Practical Applications*, *More than "Precious Memories": Critical Essays on the Rhetoric of Southern Gospel*, and several chapters for the *Critical Companion to Popular Directors* series at Lexington Books. He has forthcoming monograph in that series titled *A Critical Companion to Sofia Coppola*, which he coauthored with musicologist Christopher Booth. He won the *Journal of Christian Teaching Practice's* 2018 Quentin J. Schultze and Paul A. Soukup Faith-learning Integration Award for Outstanding Christian Scholarship in Communication Studies for his essay, "Analogy as a Strategy for Faith-learning Integration." He also coedited *Words and Witnesses: Communication Studies in Christian Thought from Athanasius to Desmond Tutu*.

Foreword

THIS VOLUME, *Humility and Hospitality: Changing the Christian Conversation on Civility*, generated in response to the June 2017 address by Calvin L. Troup, president of Geneva College, at the Forum 4:15 Unconference in Spring Arbor, Michigan, is an important contribution to the conversation on the nature and role of civility in the practice of Christian faith in a moment of narrative and virtue contention. Troup, drawing on the work of Saint Augustine, identified humility and hospitality as conditions that make civility possible. The vigorous conversation that ensued from this address raised questions that confront us in these chapters. We would do well to take heed and meditate on these authors' thoughtful responses as we consider our responsibility to invite and live out a Christianity that listens to and suffers with those on the margins, embracing and enacting a civility that resists imposition and listens with an attentive ear to the cries of those long ignored from the past and the present.

The editors, Sean Connable and Naaman Wood, have done an outstanding job of gathering contributors to address difficult, often painful, issues that have emerged with stark clarity as the Christian community reflects on its conflicted engagement with life in a pluralistic society and its historical struggles with the temptation to pursue the Kingdom of God through purely human means and to define success in earthly terms—political and material. Drawing from historical and contemporary events and concerns, these authors seek to texture and reconfigure our understanding of civility and incivility, integrity, faithful witness, caring presumption, empire and hospitality, justice and injustice, orthodoxy and orthopraxy, colonialism, concern for God's creation, Christian nationalism, suffering, similarity and difference, individualism, consumerism, tribalism, and the sins we are willing to overlook. These authors hold up a mirror to members of the Christian community; their gift is an honest reflection of where we fall short and how we might find a way forward to embrace a civility grounded in genuine love and respect for all.

Foreword

The first chapter, Calvin L. Troup's address, lays the foundation for changing the conversation on civility. In response, the authors in this volume model a civility that keeps the conversation going, each finding a constructive entry point through which to explore implications of Troup's remarks. The chapters unfold through three sections—(1) Foundations for Civility, (2) Lived Challenges of Civility, and (3) Opportunities for Civility—all focused on a common center of concern for Christian participation in public life, sometimes correcting entrenched views that have little basis in fact, and always providing insights that inform and persuade us of more helpful ways to think about and enact Christian witness in and to the world. The contributors to this volume have worked hard to provide excellent scholarly treatments of their topics that are accessible for a general readership. In this sense, the work engages in humble and hospitable academic discourse.

These authors remind us that through the lens of our present understanding, events of the past take on very different contours. The substance of justice has not changed, but our understanding and recognition of it has. The realization that we, as Christians, bear a legacy of injustice and violence as we have sought to carry out a mission of mercy and peace is deeply unsettling. The wounds we have inflicted have injured us, as well. The current moment carries the residue of the past; before healing begins, we must call ourselves out and bear witness to our own complicity in oppression and our refusal to acknowledge the image of God in all human beings. These chapters, together, urge us to develop a prophetic sensitivity to the pain of others, to listen to the voices of those unheard, to enter into suffering with those who suffer, and to remain rooted in an ongoing narrative while being responsive to new understandings and insights emerging from the lives of the forgotten and overlooked. We are called neither to dominate and colonize the culture in triumphalism nor to retreat and hide from culture, but to stand with it and in it and engage it, welcoming the disruption and interruption that emerge from the encounter.

This volume is a prophetic call for the Christian community to reflect, repent, and reconsider how to live out our witness in a turbulent moment with a civility that listens, learns, responds, and, finally, takes a stand. Not all will agree with each perspective presented here, but all should value the opportunity to consider these entry points into the ongoing conversation. I thank the editors and authors for a book that opens new spaces for conversation and constructive civility, inviting a

FOREWORD

Christianity that embraces, in the words of the editors, God's good future, one that is diverse and pluralistic.

    Janie Marie Harden Fritz
    Professor and Chair of Communication & Rhetorical Studies
    Duquesne University
    Past President, Religious Communication Association

INTRODUCTION
CHANGING THE CHRISTIAN CONVERSATION ON CIVILITY

Introduction

Changing the Christian Conversation on Civility

Contextualizing Calvin Troup's Call for Humility and Hospitality

NAAMAN WOOD AND SEAN CONNABLE

Introduction

THE CONFERENCE THAT BIRTHED THIS BOOK took place in the summer of 2017, and those days were nestled amidst a tumultuous period of American history. In July of 2016, many across the U.S. would come to know the names Philando Castile and Alton Sterling, both unarmed Black men killed by police. Some would come to know their names through the news, through Black Lives Matter protests, or in the case of Castile, through a Facebook live video. Many names came before these. Many would follow. In November of 2016, the U.S. saw the election of a new president, Donald Trump, in what could only be described as a surprising and contentious election. On the day after his January 2017 inauguration, the Women's March on Washington became the largest single-day demonstration in U.S. history, drawing the nation's eye toward women who stood in direct opposition to the recently elected administration. In August of 2017, millions of Americans would watch as white supremacists marched on Charlottesville, Virginia, in a "Unite the Right" rally. Participants marched with torches at night and with Confederate and Nazi flags by day. In October of 2017, the #MeToo movement would shine a light on the horror and widespread impact of sexual assault, starting most notably with the survivors of film producer Harvey Weinstein.

In June of 2017, I (Sean) remember stepping out of a warm but pleasant summer evening into a large multi-purpose room that served as the home to the Forum 4:15 Unconference, a time for students, teachers, and scholars of communication and religion to engage in the daunting task of exploring the question of "Civility and Virtue in a Multi-cultural Public Sphere." As if that topic were not daunting enough, I (Naaman) remember—though no one mentioned it—that I could feel the events of the previous year pressing on nearly every conversation. But, before we get too far, as a matter of clarification, a word about the aforementioned term unconference is in order.

An unconference emerges out of the experiences of many scholars who attend academic conferences. The centerpiece of those conferences is the formal academic presentation. It is a speech, delivered for about fifteen to twenty minutes. It is usually, though not always, read from an academic manuscript. Despite the fact that most academic conferences revolve around a formal presentation, most scholars know that the most important moments at conferences rarely occur during these official presentations. The best moments usually happen informally: in hallways; unintentional and serendipitous meetings with other colleagues; times spent over coffees, meals, or drinks. Ironically, perhaps, the informal space of conversation and interaction usually provides the most meaningful and sometimes life-affirming times at conferences. An unconference attempts to create space in which more of those informal exchanges can take place. While there might be a few keynote addresses, unconference organizers collaborate with attendees to co-create a list of topics, questions, or areas of interest around which attendees can enter into conversation with each other. Once the list emerges, attendees volunteer for brief presentation slots, panel discussions, or conversations. Attendees can also make most, if not all, of their meals, coffees, and after-dinner plans together. In all, the unconference tries to distinguish itself from formal academic conferences through the strategies of cooperation, informality, and improvisation as a means to foster realities of creativity, connection, and growth. And it was in this format that we tried to think more deeply and more Christianly about what it might mean to engage in acts of civility, especially in a moment of such national incivility and unrest.

The question "What can we do to be more civil?", was often the

Introduction

question driving many of these discussions; however, Calvin L. Troup's presentation aimed to change the conversation we were having and, we argue, change the Christian conversation on civility more broadly. He suggested that we need to turn away from what we could "do to be more civil" to something else, something deeper. For those in attendance, Troup's talk not only sparked lively conversation, but it also touched nearly every interaction we had over the next few days. Not everyone agreed with Troup, but he certainly changed the conversations we were having. Those discussions are the impetus for this volume. And just as Troup changed our unconference conversations, we believe this volume might do the same for your own conversations.

To understand how Troup changed the conversation for us, we want to offer a bit of ground clearing on two matters. First, we provide a brief overview of the recent conversation Christians are having on civility. Then we turn to an explanation of Troup's central, conceptual move, the move we think changes things. But first, the conversation.

The Recent Christian Conversation on Civility

Recently, three Christian authors have offered important books that form, for us, the current Christian discussion of civility in the public square. First, and perhaps most notably, is the recent work of theologian and former president of Fuller Theological Seminary Richard Mouw. In his book *Uncommon Decency: Christian Civility in an Uncivil World*, Mouw grapples with the problem of how Christians can be civil in a world that is falling apart. He opens his book with a metaphor describing our lack of civility; it is like two people are driving cars at each other on a one-way road. Both refuse to stop. Both are gaining speed. Public life is like a destructive game of "chicken." Who will back down first? Beyond the metaphor, Mouw thinks that pluralism is the issue that is at the heart of incivility. For example, he notes the anxiety Christians feel when mosques appear "in our neighborhoods," or New Age people show up in our schools or business.[1] In this context, Mouw calls Christians to be quieter, gentler, more polite people who possess a "convicted civility,"[2] or an ability to hold two things together: civility and truth.[3] In the rest of the book, Mouw offers a mix of theological convictions, heart attitudes, and intellectual arguments that he thinks are necessary for convicted civility. He offers them as ways of navigating hot button issues like sexuality, other religions, or hell. In his follow up book *Adventures in Evangelical Civility: A Lifelong Quest for Common Ground*, Mouw emphasizes the deep Calvinist theological sources from which he draws to engage the world as a public intellectual. He discusses authors like Cornelius Van Til, the doctrine of the *imago Dei*, interfaith dialogue, and the proliferation of "identity" theologies.[4] In all, Mouw offers his readers more theological nuance on how to remain convinced about the truth of Reformed, evangelical Christianity. Taken together, Mouw's work suggests that Christians can be civil if they think the right thoughts and behave in ways that display their convictions, but they do so with a deep sense of politeness and respect for others.

Second, communication scholar Tim Muehlhoff offers several books related to civility. In his book *I Beg to Differ: Navigating Difficult Conversations with Truth and Love*, Muehlhoff, like Mouw, opens this book with a metaphor that captures for him our current lack of civility. Muehlhoff describes a married couple who is "experiencing conflict" and who meets with him as a mediator.[5] To his surprise, the man and woman each bring a manila folder. "Each of them had over the years separately compiled evidence to prove the other wrong."[6] This is what our current state of civility is like, which makes difficult conversations all the more challenging. What Muehlhoff offers is a "four-part communication strategy" that equips Christians to have these difficult conversations.[7] He offers a chapter on each strategy, which can be summarized in the following questions: What does this person believe? Why does this person hold this belief? Where do we agree? How should I proceed? The author also offers a series of case studies, exploring practical conversations around topics like finances, religious difference, or excessive media use.

His next book, co-authored with theologian Richard Langer, *Winsome Persuasion: Christian Influence in a Post-Christian World*, draws on slightly different theoretical ground to offer similarly practical advice. Early in the book, the authors argue that Christians are a "counterpublic," or counter-cultural group of people who live outside of the norms of American culture.[8] However, as a counterpublic, Christians can still make persuasive arguments to wider culture on a host of important topics. Rooted in Christianity as a counterpublic, Muehlhoff and Langer offer Christians advice on how to craft persuasive appeals to a secular world and how to engage in appropriate community building. Finally, the authors offer several chapters applying all these concepts to the issue of same-sex marriage.

Introduction

Muehlhoff and Langer's next book, *Winsome Conviction: Disagreeing without Dividing the Church*, returns to the central concerns of *Winsome Persuasion*, but this time focuses on how Christians disagree with other Christians. The authors admit that Christian convictions differ wildly. They offer a taxonomy that describes the structure of Christian conviction, from timeless and eternal truths to contextually bound policies. Christians certainly have non-negotiable convictions or "confessional beliefs," like the Apostles' Creed or the Nicene Creed, which Christians ought to treat as "timeless truths."[9] When Christians put those truths or beliefs into practice, they become more "moral mandates" that address spiritual or ethical concerns, not unlike the mandates Jesus gives to love God and neighbor.[10] Moral mandates are like the "North Star."[11] They provide "what direction to go but don't provide" specific "instructions" for living. Moving toward even more specificity, "core values" provide "desired ends" to which Christians ought to live (like fairness, loyalty, or liberty), although Christians disagree as to what values to prioritize over others.[12] Finally, "guidelines for conduct" are policy decisions people make, although they are far from universal.[13] Policies are always, the authors insist, bound by time, place, and context. The taxonomy is practical. It provides language to understand our convictions more deeply, understand them in historical and social contexts, and, perhaps most importantly, understand how other Christians come to their own convictions. With the language of confessional beliefs, moral mandates, values, and guidelines for conduct, Muehlhoff and Langer are convinced that Christians can learn to keep fewer universal disagreements from dividing the church. Taken together, all three books assume that practical communicative interventions—either engaging in successful conversations or rhetorical messages—are the main effort that will bring about more civil Christian communication.

Third, author and social critic Os Guinness offers a slightly different approach to the need for civility. Like Mouw, Guinness sees pluralism and diversity as a problem facing our world. However, he focuses on the concept that widespread violence is the actual problem that must be addressed, be it violence in places like the Middle East, Bosnia, or at home. But his proposal for civility is counterintuitive. For violence to cease, we need a civil public square that is free from coercion. For Guinness, the framers of the American Constitution offer a "vision of a civil public square . . . in which everyone—people of all faiths, whether religious or naturalistic—are equally free to enter and engage public life on the basis of their faiths, as a matter of 'free exercise' and as dictated by their own reason and conscience."[14] The counterintuitive proposal, therefore, is this: the solution to violence is a public space that preserves maximal diversity for all. For diversity not to become problematic, there must be space for diverse peoples to enter the public square together and not coerce one another. Hence, if Christians want America to be a space free from coercion for them, then Christians have a responsibility to make America a space free of coercion for Buddhists, Muslim, Mormons, atheists, and the like.[15] The final chapter of the book offers practical advice on cultivating leadership for such a public square, which must start with self-critique. In his follow-up book, *The Global Public Square: Religious Freedom and the Making of a World Safe for Diversity*, Guinness intensifies his previous arguments. Rather than focus on the U.S., Guinness turn his gaze wider and asks, "How do we create a global public square and make the world safer for diversity?"[16] Because he is a conservative Anglican, he does not affirm diversity for diversity's sake. Rather, he desires that everyone experience the deepest freedom from violence he can imagine, what he calls "soul freedom."[17] Throughout the book, he offers a series of steps that he believes will preserve freedom and justice in an increasingly pluralistic world.[18]

These authors all share a few conceptual commitments in common, despite a few differences. Written by Christians, these titles work from the assumption that incivility is a matter about which Christians need to meditate. Regarding the source of incivility, all three implicitly or explicitly assume that differences, diversity, or pluralism are some, if not the main sources, of the problem that drives incivility, be it the symbolic violence of uncivil speech or physical violence. All authors want Christians not to violate their own consciences on the matters about which they are convicted. While we will return to the limitations of these approaches below, it is enough to say, at this point, that in each case, these works are centered on the recovery of civility as a technical, practical, or rhetorical practice. This means that all the authors think, like any of us at the unconference did, there are things "to do" right now that will solve the problem of incivility.

In response to the desire "to do" civility, Troup offers an alternative approach, or perhaps more accurately, an alternative logic to approach the question of civility. Instead of asking, "What can we do to be more civil?", Troup wants us to ask, "What are the conditions for the possibility of civility?" Because Troup's alternative was what animated much of our discussion, we want to describe, or maybe more honestly justify, his move in three different ways: first from philosophy, then from Scripture, and finally from practical experience.

"The Conditions for the Possibility of…"

While Enlightenment philosopher Immanuel Kant's massive and important philosophical project is outside of the scope of this book, we want to point to one passage as an illustration of how Troup uses the phrase in his own work. In Western philosophy, the statement "the conditions for the possibility of…" appears most famously in Kant.[19] In one brief and obscure passage in *Critique of Pure Reason*, Kant writes, "There are…three original sources (capacities or faculties of the soul) which contain the conditions for the possibility of all experience and cannot themselves be derived from any other faculty of the mind, namely sense, imagination and apprehension."[20] In this passage, Kant argues that what humans call "experience" cannot exist on its own. It is dependent on three capacities: sense, imagination, and apprehension. For our purposes, it is not important to know how Kant defines those capacities. Rather, he simply argues that there are things that make experience a possibility. Troup uses Kant's phrase in a very similar way. He keeps the structure of the phrase but completely replaces the content. Troup wants to get to the conditions that make civility a possibility. Civility cannot really exist on its own. It is dependent on certain capacities. Troup does not use the word "capacity"; rather, he uses "virtue." For Troup, humility and hospitality are the virtues that we need for civility to even be possible. But more on that later. We also think this same logic appears in Scripture.

Like Kant, the scope of the Gospel of Luke is outside the scope of this chapter, but we want to unpack a phrase that appears late in Luke's gospel, as Jesus enters Jerusalem. The author notes that as the Messiah entered the city triumphantly, he did not respond with joy. Only in Luke's gospel does he lament. Luke writes, "As he came near and saw the city, Jesus wept over it, saying, 'If you, even you, had only recognized on this day the things that make for peace! But now they are hidden from your eyes.'"[21] While not explicit in this text, commentators have offered their interpretations on the things that make for peace. New Testament scholar Leon Morris notes that what the Old Testament assumes about peace must apply to this passage. Peace can only take place when there is "right relationship between the creature and the Creator."²² Biblical scholar Charles L. Childers, using language similar to Kant, suggests that "the conditions upon which peace could be had" were the conditions of "repentance and acceptance of Jesus as Saviour and Lord."²³ Like Childers, New Testament scholar Fred B. Craddock suggests that "repentance and forgiveness of sins" are the things that make for peace.²⁴ Not dissimilar from Kant, Jesus's lament, and the reflections of modern interpreters, all seem to imply that peace needs certain conditions to bring it about. There are conditions for the possibility of peace.

However, commentators have also situated peace within larger biblical and theological contexts. As with nearly all laments, Jesus's tears reveal his "concern for the city."²⁵ This means that Jesus's prophetic critique is fundamentally about his longing for the good of those people whom he loves. Perhaps in the spirit of that love, New Testament scholar Joel Green gives a sophisticated addition to the insights above. Jerusalem's politico-religious system was embodied "in the temple's concern with . . . holiness . . . and the consequent segregation . . . of Gentile from Jew, male from female, and the like."²⁶ In addition to the things that make for peace, there are things that inhibit peace. As Green says, Jesus weeps over the temple's segregations, which make it closed off from the peace Jesus brings. Furthermore, Green notes that peace, in the Gospel of Luke, has holistic, salvific significance. By this, Luke links "peace and justice, the gift of God that embraces salvation for all in all of its social, material, and spiritual realities."²⁷ So, peace is not simply a reality that is created under certain conditions. Peace is itself a condition that brings about the possibilities of other realities, like God's social, material, and spiritual justice.

Finally, we would like to offer the practical example of fire. When I (Naaman) was about ten years-old, I joined a Boy-Scout-like group at my local Pentecostal church. There we learned basics of camping, hiking, and other related outdoor activities. As part of our training for an extended camping trip, I was taught how to build a fire. Before anything, I was taught that there were three things necessary to build a fire. I needed fuel, that is, wood of various sizes from very small pieces of tinder to larger logs. I needed heat, usually in the form of a match, which I used to start the fire. Finally, I needed oxygen. Because we camped outside, this last bit was only a problem if I built my fire without enough room for it to breathe, to intake air as the flames grew bigger. As a child, I was taught, without knowing it, this same logic. There are at least three conditions that must be in place if I had even the possibility of fire: fuel, heat, and oxygen.

Introduction

Changing the Conversation

We take such lengths here to illustrate and explain the logic at work in Troup's speech for two reasons. First, this logic is the main means Troup uses to change the Christian conversation on civility. As we understand the insightful work of Mouw, Muehlhoff, and Guinness, each of these fine authors think of the recovery of civility as a technical, practical, or rhetorical practice. Mouw offers theological and practical resources for the task of achieving politeness and conviction. Muehlhoff offers insights from communication studies for the acts of interpersonal conversation and rhetorical engagement. While Guinness is closer to Troup than the others,[28] he still grounds his affirmation in the idea that civil behavior can be a political reality if only we think about civility like the Founding Fathers thought about civility. In this sense, all their work offers some form of practical application, whether lessons learned, interpersonal advice, or a political program for the public square. There is nothing wrong with all these things in and of themselves. However, Troup's move is to ask a different question. He wants us to shift the discussion from "How can we be more civil?" to "What are the conditions for the possibility of civility?" Troup wants to go deeper than the technicalities of civility because he believes unless we get at the things that make for civility, we are doomed to fail.

In Chapter 1 ("Humility and Hospitality: Two Conditions Necessary for the Possibility of Civility"), Troup argues that we have lost civility because we have lost the conditions that make civility possible, namely, hospitality and humility. He opens first by naming several temptations that keep us from being civil people. As a means of engaging these temptations, Troup dialogues with the church father Saint Augustine of Hippo. As a way of resisting the temptation we all face to master or dominate others, what he names as the temptation toward "empire," Troup offers Augustinian antidotes: commonwealth, love, households, and localities. These concepts set the stage for his case for why humility and hospitality are the conditions that make civility possible and why without them, techniques and practical advice will not bring about civility. Hospitality is the practice of welcoming the neighbor as though they are ourselves, and humility is the virtue of not thinking of oneself at all. Not thinking of oneself is what we need in order to engage in meaningful hospitality.

Second, Troup's question about the condition for civility opened up an intense dialogue, because the very question he asked encouraged us not only to question his work but also to think more deeply about who we invited to write for this book. At the unconference, once Troup asked, "What are the conditions for the possibility of civility?", we could then ask, "Are there conditions to the possibility of humility and hospitality that Troup did not consider?" His own logic, therefore, animates each chapter of the book, interrogating the ideas that serve as Troup's foundation. Likewise, and in an effort to embody the hospitality and humility Troup discusses, we, the editors, thought it was an act of embodied hospitality to invite as a diverse group of authors as we could, authors both from within and outside of the Christian experience. These include people who identify as men, women, BIPOC (Black, Indigenous, and other people of color), and LGBTQ+. A broad spectrum of experience and expertise displays what Guinness suggests—a Christian public sphere free from coercion, and a (hopefully) hospitable space of humility. What these chapters offer is less of a destination, and more of a trajectory of insights, which we will gather together in the concluding chapter of the book. Many of these insights offer perspectives that are a product of faith-based communities and education. Others offer the perspective of groups that, at times, have suffered at the hands of those same communities. We are convinced that listening to all these voices will provide us a richer and more nuanced perspective on how we might best contend with the recent tumult in U.S. culture.

We offer these chapters to readers in Christian colleges and seminaries and to pastors and lay leaders. Because of the perspective of the authors, the chapters will be of special interest to students and scholars who want to commit to biblical frameworks, as well as those readers studying the intersection of religious and secular publics, discourses of civility, and persuasion, politics, and faithful cultural engagement. Although all our authors are scholars, we have made an effort to write in a conversational style.

Remaining Chapter Summaries

In the first part of this book, Chapters 2 and 3 offer two differing foundations from which to engage Troup's insights, from a philosophical perspective and from the lived experience of a community.

In "Substantive Discourse: Love, Justice, and Hierarchy as the Basis for Civility" Chapter 2), rhetorical scholar Mark A. E. Williams argues that if we are to recover civility in our present moment, we need to return to

Introduction

Saint Augustine's view of the world, because it provides the only foundation for civil discourse to take place. Saint Augustine thought reality (or ontology) was comprised of two things: substances and appearances. The rightly ordered, hierarchical relationship between substances and appearances is what enables us to love people and things justly. For Williams, we live in a world where virtually no one really believes in substances anymore, and, as a result, no one can agree on what love, justice, or civility is. Without that agreement, civility is impossible. Since agreements are only possible through an Augustinian view of reality, then we need his view for the possibility of civility. Because he takes ontology as his starting point, Williams is offering a bird's eye view from which to think about the relationship between hierarchy, social agreements, values, and civility.

Rooted partly in her experience working with vulnerable communities in an urban context, nonprofit organization (NPO) leadership and social work scholar Michelle Shockness recasts hospitality as a practice that is, fundamentally, an interaction. She begins "Hospitality as Interaction: Reflections on Everyday Enactments of Empire" (Chapter 3) by asking us to consider the ways empire can manifest in our hospitality. Would-be hosts can harm would-be guests in a variety of ways, especially when hosts do not seek a guest's consent (that is, their "acquiescence" or their "yes" to our hospitality) and overlook the labor guests perform. Both mistakes undercut the mutuality necessary for a truly hospitable encounter. As a way of disrupting these enactments of empire, Shockness encourages us to see that the identities and roles between hosts and guests are more fluid than we might imagine. She also draws from the anti-oppressive practices common to social work with vulnerable communities. From these insights, she reimagines humility as something we endeavor to do in three ways: (1) to see the people we assume to be guests doing the work of hosts, (2) to receive someone's "no," and (3) to engage in an interaction with others and with God. In short, Shockness interrogates Troup's insight from proximity to those Jesus might have described as "the least of these."[29]

Chapters 4, 5, and 6 follow in the spirit of Shockness's work, thinking of the issues Troup raises in light of various forms of suffering, injustice, or perhaps "inhospitality" that Christians have historically performed. In "Reverse and Covenantal Hospitality: Expanding the Paradigm of Giving and Receiving in Cross-cultural Mission" (Chapter 4), missiologist Susangeline Y. Patrick suggests that, rather than hospitality, American Christianity needs to embrace a reverse and covenantal hospitality. She describes not only the history of how American Christians unfortunately embraced colonialism, but she also notes that a minority of faithful missionaries who resisted such abuses. The colonial problems that plagued the past haunt contemporary Christians today in the form of neocolonialism. As a means of resisting this colonialism, Patrick points to the examples of the early church and Scripture, suggesting that Christians can re-imagine hospitality as having a reciprocal character and an inversion between host and guest—a reverse hospitality. She also describes a covenantal hospitality, in which Christians can embrace interactions between God the Creator, humans, and the land.

Rhetorical and media scholar Naaman Wood also investigates colonialism as a force that limits the embodiment of virtue in "On the Limits of Love: Entanglements with Colonialism in the Sixties Scoop and the Christian Reformed Church in North America (CRCNA)" (Chapter 5). Taking up Troup's emphasis on virtue, he claims that colonialism limits how we love each other, and Christians must understand those limitations if we desire to make civility possible. He discusses two colonial realities: the Sixties Scoop and the founding violence of North America. However, Christians can acknowledge and counter colonial limitations through an understanding of our mutually constituted identity and the skill of offering multiple meanings to Scripture that offer healing to those who suffer. As a case study on how one Christian community is dealing with their colonial entanglements, he explores the CRCNA's 2016 denunciation of the Doctrine of Discovery.

In "There Is No Civility without the Recognition of Power: How Perceived Persecution, Hostility, and Unilateral Conditions Impact Christian Calls for Civility" (Chapter 6), sociologist Jaime Harris explores the relationship between the church and the LGBTQ+ community. Drawing from his own experiences, Harris asks the question: "How does the church's hostility and rejection of others impact the potential for the church to practice hospitality and civility with those they rejected?" He starts with the church's misperception of itself as a persecuted minority. He describes both how useful incivility can be to the Christian community and how liberal and conservative conceptions of civility undermine honest dialogue. As a potential antidote, he concludes with Martin Luther King Jr.'s linking of love and justice.

While Williams and Shockness draw our attention to conceptual difficulties in thinking about civility, and while Patrick, Wood, and Harris suggest that the Church's own actions undermine the possibility of civility,

Introduction

the final chapters step back and consider what opportunities might present themselves and what challenges we must confront if we are to practice civility and hospitality in these challenging times.

In "On Regulating Civility: The Directing Meta-virtue of Integrity and the Barmen Declaration" (Chapter 7), rhetorical scholar Annalee R. Ward and literary scholar Mary K. Bryant use the Barmen Declaration to ask the question: "How does practicing integrity challenge the call to civility?" They examine the historical context of Germany from World War II through 1934 before defining what integrity looks like. They turn with a reading of the Barmen Declaration as an act of integrity and make some suggestions about what it might mean for us today. Just as Ward and Bryant call us to consider the role of integrity in practicing hospitality and civility, the following chapters point to other considerations that must be made if we are to effectively engage wider culture in any meaningful way.

In "Suffering and Civility: Rethinking the Role of American Evangelical Tradition in Public Discourse and Public Life" (Chapter 8), rhetorical scholar Mark Allan Steiner suggests that any meaningful public engagement on the part of American evangelicals must embrace not only humility but also suffering. He claims that the current notions of civility offered have not sufficiently dealt with two key problems within evangelicalism: first, a profound lack of trust present in our culture and in our polity, and second, our dysfunctional Constantinian expectations about our place in creating and sustaining political life. He submits that suffering is the means evangelicals can use to become more civil people. He describes suffering as a condition of our reality, as necessary to flourishing, and as a sign of faithful discipleship. He closes his chapter by illustrating what suffering might look like for evangelicals as they relate to racial justice and racial reconciliation.

Finally, in "Marginally Persuasive: Recovering the Cruciform Power of Prophetic Witness" (Chapter 9), rhetorical scholar John B. Hatch offers an extended meditation on what motived widespread evangelical support for President Donald Trump. He draws on the insights of biblical scholar Walter Brueggemann's prophetic imagination and literary critic René Girard's theory of the scapegoat to illustrate how biblical faith aims to delegitimize and disarm the power-grabbing spirit of the world. He uses their insights to analyze the history of conservative American evangelicalism, revealing that uncritical support for Trump constitutes a paradoxical capitulation to empire in the name of saving God's commonwealth. By way of correction,

Hatch insists that we recover prophetic witness through a recovery of lament and through an acceptance of persecution.

Conclusion

Although many of the chapters offer constructive suggestions toward a Christian recovery of civility, we are not entirely convinced this book is about answers. Indeed, as we will discuss in the book's concluding chapter, we are not entirely sure there is an answer to this problem. Rather, this book serves two purposes: first, we welcome you, the reader, to a profound and engaging conversation, one that has challenged many of our preconceived notions of what Western Christianity is and how we choose to talk about, much less imagine, hospitality, civility, and humility; second, and we will return to this question in the book's conclusion, we wonder: "Are hospitality, civility, and humility sufficient to deal with the moment in which we find ourselves?" For now, we welcome you to a vibrant and all too timely conversation and ask you to join us as we consider how humility and hospitality might change the way we imagine civility in what many of us see as deeply uncivil times.

PART I
CHANGING THE CONVERSATION ON CIVILITY

Chapter 1

Humility and Hospitality

Two Conditions Necessary for the Possibility of Civility

Calvin L. Troup

Introduction

What is a common way to incite personal conflict with someone who is upset? Assume a slightly patronizing, sober tone and tell them firmly, "Just calm down." Questions of civility and virtue easily take on a similar tone and posture—we assume that we are the ones who are civil and virtuous and then claim that the rest of society is falling apart around us. Others simply need to quit yelling at each other, stop hurling invectives, and speak more courteously. People need to "just calm down." Contrary to this impulse, I do not believe we can dispense with questions concerning civility and virtue so simply.

In practice, civility and virtue are important and difficult, and we can offer no easy fix. In a culture beholden to bombast and diatribe, some suggest that solutions lie in procedures and methods. If we can train people to employ the proper techniques, then *voila*, civility and virtue will flower. I think such a proposal is nonsense. We will not address the root problems of incivility until we acknowledge that we are personally and directly involved in the problem. Because we usually assume that our reasons and our rancor are virtuous, the questions of civility and virtue implicate people like us. So, we need to think together, first, about the temptations and conditions that keep us from being civil people and, second, about the conditions that contribute to virtues that promote civility. Along the way, the church father Saint Augustine of Hippo will guide our thinking on these matters.

The Temptations and Conditions That Inhibit Our Civility

Through the course of my three decades in academic life, civility and virtue have declined noticeably. Civility had been, for many years, a standard topic in rhetorical reflection, from Plato, Aristotle, and Isocrates to Cicero and Quintilian. These authors all assumed that civility was necessary to the flourishing of public life. Today, civility is absent from most, if not all, our everyday lives. Incivility cannot be attributed to "them" alone: "They are not being civil." Incivility implicates us as participants in a variety of contexts. Civility and virtue pertain to our practices, to our experience, and to common temptations people like us face today.

I want to name three temptations before turning to four conditions, all of which impede our ability to be civil. First, we might be tempted to start in the wrong place. We might ask, "How can we be culturally relevant about this?" Of course, cultural attentiveness is pertinent but not primary. Relevance is not our starting point. It is a question that comes much later. We need to think about starting questions. More on that below, especially with Saint Augustine.

The second temptation is to be blinded by our intellectual pride. "We are brilliant. We are well-schooled. We are credentialed." The French philosopher Jacques Ellul suggests that, to the contrary, we intellectuals and educated people are more susceptible to propaganda than the rank and file.[1] Ellul argues that, as a trained intellectual, I am more susceptible to propaganda than most of my neighbors in the Beaver Valley of Western Pennsylvania. So much for intellectual pride on matters of civility, since propaganda promotes the strong, unfounded opinions that drive activism, rather than deliberation.[2]

The third temptation is our sheer personal pretense. "I have a well-developed, personal capacity for self-righteousness. The vices of incivility do not touch me. And I am very concerned about how our crisis in civility affects other people." Media studies calls this phenomenon the "third-person effect."[3] Furthermore, I have been widely exposed to self-righteousness as a church member and in my academic communities. Even though my academic and church communities ordinarily reside on opposite ends of the ideological spectrum, in self-righteousness they appear as twins. The two main groups of people with whom I live and move compete neck-and-neck for the crown. So, both of my communities invite self-righteous pretense; nevertheless, I am responsible for all my own self-righteousness.

Now for a few conditions. My field of academic study, communication studies, has spent much time over the past 30 years talking about rhetorical training as the answer to the problem of incivility. But here is what I think is the foundational problem: we do not have the conditions necessary to implement the solution. Rhetorical scholar Jerry Hauser illustrates how conditions for rhetorical training have dissipated in his fine volume *Vernacular Voices: The Rhetoric of Publics and the Public Sphere*.[4] Although this is not the point of the book, he talks about growing up in a household where his extended family engaged in wonderful conversations, presumably around the dinner table. They talked about politics, and, perhaps most importantly, they disagreed. Later in his life, Hauser's formal rhetorical training proved effective, in part because of what happened in his household. That condition—learning to disagree with those you love around the dinner table—no longer exists in our society. Less than 20% of families have family meals together with any regularity.[5] If Hauser's example is illustrative of anything, it is this: formal rhetorical training will only make a difference if we practice disagreement within the context of the household and practice it early and often. Without that condition, I suggest that it is unlikely that rhetorical training or techniques alone will produce civil people.

Secondly, the media conditions in which we are working—particularly the news media and social media—preclude civility. Media tend to apply to politics the dynamics of sports and entertainment. Media favor competing ideologues of every sort, which it frames in venues that only admit polarity and conflict. Polarity and conflict preempt civility.

Thirdly, civility is not niceness. Civility is not: "We need to be nicer and not so mean." Instead, civility requires goodness; and goodness is a completely different thing than niceness.[6]

Fourth, I want to offer my own heritage as an example of a tradition within the larger scope of evangelicalism, which is itself given to separation and dissent. One grandfather, who died before I was born, William E. Troup, was a German Reformed pastor. Through the ecumenical movement of the early twentieth century, his congregation in the Kenmore neighborhood of Akron, Ohio became part of the Evangelical Reformed denomination. But when ecumenical momentum (supported by Reformed theologians and brothers Reinhold Niebuhr and H. Richard Niebuhr) led to union between the Evangelical Reformed and the Congregational Christian Churches to form the United Church of Christ, he and his congregation opted out of the union to become independent and fundamental. Their choice produced hardships for them. In the late 1950s, for example, the congregation had to go to court to retain their church building. That is one side of my family.

Paul D. McCracken was my wife's grandfather. He was a leader in the Christian Amendment Movement.[7] The Covenanter Church was instrumental in that movement. It is today the Reformed Presbyterian Church of North America, and it is the founding and controlling denomination of Geneva College, the school where I am president. That denomination has been a dissenting denomination. A recent book published by Oxford University Press, *Founding Sins: How a Group of Anti-Slavery Radicals Fought to Put Christ into the Constitution*, examines the role Covenanters played in early America. The opening line of the book goes like this, "The United States was not founded as a Christian nation, because slavery was in the Constitution and Jesus was not. The people who said this, rather loudly and for quite a long time, were called the Covenanters."[8] From its inception, the denomination has questioned whether we can see our country the way that Jesus Christ sees it—as a people first, not predicated by a human political arrangement, system, or structure—independent of how any temporal political party, group, or ideology might happen to see the country. In short, my Christian biases are not mainstream in any sense, and they have engaged public life not seeking to maintain the status quo.

Regardless of the temptations and conditions in which we find ourselves, we are all navigating difficult waters. Our present circumstances are not what most of us expected in this season of our life in North America. And so, what we want to think about together are a few coordinates to help us navigate these temptations and conditions. I would like for us to think together with Saint Augustine (354–430 AD), because I have no idea where to start on my own. I think he can help us dig a little deeper to find some roots that might contribute to civility and virtue.

HUMILITY AND HOSPITALITY: TWO CONDITIONS NECESSARY

Commonwealth, Love, Households, and Localities

Saint Augustine is trying to remind us about some places we might start to think about civility and virtue. In *City of God*, Book 19, Saint Augustine engages the things we have been struggling with in some very serious ways. I want to talk about four themes he develops. He talks about commonwealth, love, households, and localities. And if we can hear him, I think he can help us develop some of the conditions, or more specifically the virtues, necessary for the possibility of civility.

Saint Augustine says we long for commonwealth. Not only Christians, but all human beings—made in the image of God—long for commonwealth. He exemplifies this by using passages like Isaiah 66 that look toward the new heaven and the new earth, embodied in the city of Jerusalem. The prophet hears, "The sound of an uproar from the city! A sound from the temple!"[9] And later says, "Behold, I [the Lord] will extend peace to her [Jerusalem] like a river, and the glory of the nations like an overflowing stream."[10] Isaiah envisions the streets of Jerusalem, with the sounds of a dynamic but peaceful life in the city. The prophet Zechariah also talks about the city yet to come, but in a slightly different register: "Old men and old women shall again sit in the streets of Jerusalem, each with staff in hand because of great age. And the streets of the city shall be full of boys and girls playing in its streets."[11] Saint Augustine claims that scenes like this one reflect a longing in every culture, in every context—we can feel this longing that people have for the peace that we associate with commonwealth, for peace in the city. Consider the porch culture of a city like Baltimore, Maryland. In 2015, during a time of unrest, people simply longed to sit on their row house porches on summer evenings to discuss current events or watch a Baltimore Orioles baseball game on a portable television.[12] These are not romantic visions. These are lives people have led. These are moments we have had. Saint Augustine captures that longing with this term, commonwealth.

But he also talks about the antithesis of commonwealth—empire—which is at its heart the sin of mastery over others. The City of Man, says Saint Augustine, is founded on fratricide. Cain kills Abel. Same family. Romulus kills Remus. Same family. Rome, therefore, is founded on fratricide. There are problems between the races. There are problems within the families of every racial group. There are problems between ethnicities. There are problems within the families of every ethnic group. We cannot deny societal challenges. Yet there are also challenges in our homes. Empire is like domestic trouble—in-home violence—a sin through which we seek to control, to master other human beings. Therefore, the violence of brother against brother is the basis of empire. Mastery means that empire is structured by a deep hierarchy that produces evil. Commonwealth, on the other hand, employs a shallow hierarchy, not a deep one—and only enough hierarchy to stop evil. Saint Augustine says "no" to empire and "yes" to commonwealth.

Secondly, in Book 19, Saint Augustine talks about our need for ordered loves, not for justice. He quarrels with the Roman statesman and philosopher Cicero throughout *City of God*. Saint Augustine loves Cicero—Cicero is great, and the Roman statesman Cato is great. He holds Cicero's claim that a commonwealth must be established on justice in high regard. This is Cicero's position: to have a commonwealth you must have a high view of justice. But Saint Augustine replies that justice never works. Why? For the simple and universal reason that people can never agree about justice. Justice is always disputed. When did a major court case end with the losing side saying, "Wow, they got it right! We should have seen it sooner! Of course, we got what we deserved. What were we thinking? Why did we even contest the case?"

Even more pointedly, Saint Augustine says, the Scriptures teach that justice divides. The parable of the wheat and the tares, a favorite of Saint Augustine's, exemplifies justice. Justice will be served. Although the reckoning is delayed, finally there is separation of the wheat from the chaff.[13] There is separation of the good fish from the bad fish in the parable of the dragnet.[14] In the parable of the sheep and the goats, there is separation of the sheep from the goats.[15] Note that the goats contest their separation, "But didn't we…?" Saint Augustine observes that the appropriate work of justice—the very nature of justice—is to divide. Justice is divisive. Justice says: "You are right, and you are wrong. You are sent to prison. You are out. You are exiled. You are sentenced to death." When we ask for justice, we are asking for a division. You cannot build commonwealth from division, Saint Augustine says. Justice cannot deliver.

The only way you can build commonwealth is through shared loves—common, well-ordered loves. Saint Augustine grounds civility on the proper ordering of loves, which we can begin to understand through a simple example. I enjoy talking with my students about my dog, Watson. Watson is a rescue dog, a mixed-breed animal with the markings and height of a Bernese Mountain dog but not as much weight. He is a tall guy and can put his paws on my shoulders and look me in the eye. I love Watson and miss

Humility and Hospitality: Two Conditions Necessary

him a lot because he no longer lives with us. Now he lives in Manhattan, Kansas (home of Kansas State University), with one of my daughters and her family. But whether he is in Kansas or at home, if I ask any group of people, "Should I love my dog more than my wife?", they all know the right answer. If I love my dog more than my wife, there is something wrong in the household. If I love the Pittsburgh Steelers football team more than I love my daughters, people know there is something wrong in the household. Loves can become disordered. Practical virtue is simply putting loves in their proper order.

Where does the order of loves as a virtue come from? The starting point for Saint Augustine's ordering of loves is not some philosophical issue he ran across in Plotinus or Cicero or Plato. The order of loves comes directly from the two great commandments: "You shall love the Lord your God with all your heart and with all your soul and with all your mind.... You shall love your neighbor as yourself."[16] These are love commandments. Love God. Love your neighbor. And what this means is that we are to practice faith—not some nominal, undefined faith, but faith in Christ. If we want to be civil and virtuous, we need to be worshipping Christ publicly, observing what He has commanded all the time, day to day, moment by moment.

The third thing Saint Augustine talks about in Book 19 is the importance of households for building commonwealth. As philosopher Jean Bethke Elshtain explains in a wonderful book, *Augustine and the End of Politics*, for Saint Augustine, the smallest social unit is the household.[17] All of us are in households. Notice that the term is not *marriage*; the term is not *family*. *Household* is a much more flexible and expansive term, and it is a term important in the Scriptures. The woman Lydia, a widow, is head of household. She is a householder. Among all the issues that emerge concerning households, Saint Augustine says that households built on humility—not mastery—are essential to the commonwealth. He insists that in the Christian household, everyone serves, especially the head of house. Heads of house must make themselves low out of love for the others.[18] They are not to think poorly of themselves, but they must take the role and use the role in humble service toward everyone else in the household.

In the ancient world, humility was countercultural. As philosopher Alasdair MacIntyre discusses in *After Virtue*, there is no category for humility in the Greco-Roman world. Greeks and Romans expected leaders of cities and commonwealths to seek glory and honor.[19] Humility was associated with the humiliation of slaves. It only was tied to slavery. Everything that was good was associated with glory and with honor. Therefore, even the household becomes a place of political hierarchy, a site of power relations. Yet in *City of God*, Book 19, Saint Augustine speaks about a household order rooted in Divine Law, an eternal law manifested in God's creation of the first house. He pays homage to natural law, saying that even people who are not Christians understand this law as an eternal law through natural means.[20] Like Christ, we are to embrace humility and refuse glory and honor.

Fourth, the localities of civic laws and culture emerge and vary, but they are important and valuable to the commonwealth. This is a theme Saint Augustine develops in many places, including *Confessions* and *On Christian Doctrine*.[21] Saint Augustine notes that real differences take place in civic law from time to time, place to place, and from one local custom to another. Because household order depends to some degree on these local realities, households will differ from time to time and place to place according to the customs, cultures, and laws of the locality in which they are found. But the divine grounding and the natural law never change; therefore, the household order for the Christian family is the deliberate subversion of the mastery of politics and hierarchy, because the leader of the Christian household is to follow Christ. Jesus said that he "did not come to be served, but to serve," and we know service can be played out in different ways and places.[22] Saint Augustine urges us to think of a commonwealth as a city in which the households are held together by temporal agreement about local customs and local laws.[23] The dynamics of common loves fashioned in local customs is part of what holds cities together. And then cities, or commonwealths, can align with one another and that is it. There is no super-commonwealth, no empire. There are just alliances between commonwealths.

This means that culture is a wonderful thing, but it is a humble thing. There is no high culture in Saint Augustine. Culture is low. Culture is local. It is where we live. It is honorable, and it is hospitable to others from other localities. And this honorable culture, which is low in one sense, needs to be held in high regard. Augustine came to this conclusion in a letter on fasting. After a long exploration of what Scripture and the Church Fathers say on the proper means of fasting, he cites a conversation he once had with Ambrose, the Bishop of Milan. As a catechist of Ambrose, Augustine once asked him about what to do when you are in another town and their way of fasting is different from your own. Ambrose responded, "When I am here [in Milan], I do not fast on Saturday; when I am at Rome, I do fast on Saturday. To whatever church you come, keep its custom, if you do not

Humility and Hospitality: Two Conditions Necessary

wish either to receive or to give scandal."[24] In other words, both Augustine and Ambrose want us to honor local culture if we want to live at peace with each other and worship God truly.

Similar to the plurality of worship customs, Saint Augustine expects a pluralistic civic sphere until the end of time. He expects temporal commonwealths that are multicultural, multiethnic, and multiracial. Remember, for Saint Augustine there is no mere City of God and City of Man, because nobody lives in either city. We live in the earthly city. And the earthly city is always a mixed multitude.[25] It is mixed culturally. It is mixed spiritually. It is mixed ethnically. It is mixed in every conceivable way, and we can have commerce with one another because of temporal loves that we share with everyone. We can live in a commonwealth that works together for everyone.

Two Conditions (or Virtues) for the Possibility of Civility: Humility and Hospitality

So, when we talk about civility, here are some of Saint Augustine's basic coordinates or conditions, or more rightly, virtues. Civility for Saint Augustine needs at least two things to become a reality. First, civility depends upon the virtue of humility. A good entry point into Saint Augustine's view of humility appears in *The Screwtape Letters* by C. S. Lewis. In letter 14, Lewis explains that humility does not mean thinking poorly of oneself. It means not thinking of oneself at all.[26] The focus of attention is directed toward the neighbor, toward the sojourner or stranger, toward the brother, and toward the enemy. Humility does not deny one's own gifts, abilities, and accomplishments; it says, "I am not here for myself. I am here to serve others." This notion of humility is stated plainly about Jesus in places like Philippians 2. Jesus Christ never says in Scripture, "I never created anything." Jesus never said, "I am not wise." He simply does not pay any attention to himself. His focus of attention is entirely on his Father in heaven, on obeying God's will, and on the people in his presence, who he was teaching, healing, training, and helping.

Second, civility calls for hospitality—welcoming neighbors in and going out of our way for our neighbors. In our civic life, we need to love our neighbors as ourselves. And Saint Augustine says, to the greatest degree possible, we need to follow and have high regard for the customs of the city and for the laws of the city. We need to extend ourselves by opening our own households and living in our communities, not to the boundary of our personal preferences or comforts, but to the boundaries of God's law.

But what does Saint Augustine suggest that we should do when the civic law and local custom conflict with faith in Christ and God's law? He says always obey Divine Law. Was Daniel civil? Listen to the conversations that Daniel has with people who are about to put him to death. I take Daniel to be civil in tone, in carriage.[27] The apostle Paul apologizes when he says something bad about the high priest, not knowing he was the high priest.[28] Person after person in the Scriptures engage in dialogue with people who are intensely opposed to them, yet they stand unmoved. They remain in obedience to God's law. They are civil and obedient. They are practicing civic virtue in Christ. We are to profess the truth amid conflict between civic law and Divine Law. Shadrach, Meshach, and Abednego confessed that their God might save them or not. It did not matter.[29] And then, like Shadrach, Meshach, and Abednego, we are to expect persecution. We are to expect that if we are being challenged because of God's law, then we are not going to be exempted any more than the Lord Jesus Christ was exempted.

But then there is something in Saint Augustine that I never expected. It is something we need to hear. He urges us, when we must obey God and cannot obey local customs and civic law, to acknowledge that we are a pain to the people who are in leadership in those local areas and in those government positions. I did not expect Saint Augustine to say that. But Daniel does this, as do the apostles in the fifth chapter of Acts. They recognize the burden they place on civil authorities. They are not movement people or political activists. They are not carrying banners and saying, "You are all messed up, and you do not know what is going on." Instead, they plainly say, "Here we stand. We know our stance is not a comfortable thing for you, and we cannot do anything else but stand here. We cannot accommodate this." We must follow Christ.

And what does Christ do? He does not count equality with God as something to be grasped.[30] In our household of faith, Jesus, our head of household, has not grasped equality, an equality that is in fact his right, but instead he took on the form of a servant. And not only is he humble, but he is also hospitable. He says to us, "Come unto me all you who labor and are heavy laden, and I will give you rest. Take my yoke upon you and learn from me, for I am gentle and humble in heart."[31] And he says to us, "Come, everyone who thirsts, come to the waters; and he who has no money, come, buy and eat! . . . without money and without price."[32]

We must cultivate these conditions, these virtues, so that civility might flourish. Civility and virtue are not techniques. They are not methods. We cannot figure out the right persuasive method to become civil. Virtues must be practiced, and we must practice them in the hardest place to practice them, in the household. And when we do that, we will be ready to face persecution with civility and virtue. Such practices must be grounded in Christ and his two-fold law of love in Luke 10:27.

PART II
FOUNDATIONS FOR CIVILITY

Chapter 2

Substantive Discourse

Love, Justice, and Hierarchy as the Basis for Civility

Mark A. E. Williams

Introduction

"Why do I have to wear my seatbelt?" My five-year-old tossed this challenge at me from the back seat of the car in years long past, and it still rattles around my mind occasionally. In the end, it is a surprisingly tricky inquiry, one with a tension that is at the heart of every civic decision we are asked to make as free citizens in a free state, ideally removed from tyranny or even government interference in our private affairs. And that sounds very appealing, being free from interference. But it proves very difficult to accomplish, and it is unclear whether and to what degree anyone actually wants to be free from government interference. I assume the government is not interfering in my life by repairing the roads and sewers in my neighborhood; those are public affairs. But then what are private affairs?

Some things are (clearly?) private: my own body, my own family, my own faith. So surely my decision to wear or not wear a seatbelt is none of the government's business. My body, my choice. Surely my family's decision to get the fifteen-year-old a construction job rather than send him to school is none of the government's business. My family, my choice. Surely, if I have decided to trust in prayer rather than material physicians to heal my child's appendicitis, that is none of the government's business. My faith, my choice. Of course (not?). Does freedom simply mean that everyone is in charge of their own boundaries and their own identity and their own self, and that whatever I want to do must be placed outside the reach of everyone else, as far as possible? Is that liberty? If not, who gets to draw the lines that restrict my choices about my body, my family, or my faith? And on what authority are those lines drawn?

So, "Why do I have to wear my seatbelt?" The question is, as they say, complicated. And the answer stands or falls on issues of who and what has authority in our common lives together. And that question of authority is what I wish to explore and challenge in response to Calvin L. Troup's inspiring and demanding essay (see Chapter 1). By my lights, Troup rightly notes that the rules for civil discourse will only operate within specific conditions of civility, and he summons us to reflect on those foundational conditions. That call is welcome. I want to think (civilly, I hope) with Troup about the foundational conditions for civility. I wish to suggest that authority and hierarchy are both essential and complementary tools not only in government systems but also in human love, and that justice and charity are equally complementary perspectives in the writings of Saint Augustine of Hippo.

In this chapter, I argue that if we are to recover civility in our present moment, we need to return to Saint Augustine's view of the world, because it provides the only foundation for civil discourse to take place. To make this argument, my chapter unfolds in three parts. First, I unpack Saint Augustine's views of both justice and reality, views in which the world is comprised of both substances and appearances. Through this distinction, I suggest, we can see the world properly. Second, I elaborate further on how appearances and substances allow us to see the relationship between love and justice. Namely, they help us see that hierarchy is at play in how we love what we love, and that people and things can be justly or unjustly loved. Finally, I describe how words work in both Saint Augustine's world and an alternative universe much like our own, one where virtually no one really believes in substances. This account of language helps describe how our world has become uncivil and offers a potential, if unlikely, way to return to civility.

Substantive Discourse

The Substance of Justice

I begin this section with a brief review of Troup's account of justice from his reading of Saint Augustine. Drawing on other parts of *City of God*, I offer an amended account of justice with the term "right," which I also place against the backdrop of Saint Augustine's view of reality. Reality, for the Bishop, is comprised of material appearances here on earth and substances within the mind of God, much the same way shadows point to a fuller reality. This reading of justice and reality helps us define justice more clearly and reveals that what is in dispute in *City of God* is much more about what we should look at and how to see things rightly.

Troup argues that justice cannot provide the necessary gravity for creating community because people can never agree about justice. Justice is always disputed.[1] That justice is disputed, I do not dispute. But Troup presents Saint Augustine's view of justice as necessarily dividing one person from the other. Justice is a force of division in human society that needs a remedy, and charitable hospitality is that remedy. But this transfer from justice to love as the foundation for that which creates community seems to me to solve no problems at all, at least as it is presently framed in Troup's essay. Why are we to assume that love is any less disputed than justice? There is little about the world today that suggests people agree on the definition of love, much less the True Scotsman qualification of well-ordered love. Love, it seems, can be disputed, too. So, if this is Saint Augustine's view—that justice is disputed and therefore love must be made the foundation of the commonwealth—then I do not think his view actually moves us toward a solution. But I do not believe that Saint Augustine emphasizes a cleavage between earthly justice (the problem) and divine hospitality (the solution). Rather, Saint Augustine sees a division that cuts through both, one that divides earthly justice from heavenly justice and earthly hospitality from heavenly hospitality.

Let us begin by placing Saint Augustine's view of justice within some cultural context that most of us in the contemporary world have lost. Saint Augustine uses a dizzying array of cognates for notions of justice, righteousness, and right. One symptomatic line can be worked out as a revelatory example. Saint Augustine says, "*ubi ergo iustitia vera non est, nec ius potest esse* (thus, where there is no true justice, there can be no right)."[2]

The wording hangs on a pleasant stylistic entanglement between *iustitia* and *ius*. *Iustitia* is righteousness or justice, often in the legal sense. *Ius*, on the other hand, refers to what is proper, or a legal right, or the right thing as duty. Saint Augustine's sentence, then, means something like, "Where there is no true justice, no right is possible." True justice empowers what is right. Without true justice, there is nothing that is more right than anything else, no legitimate claims that can be made upon another. Take true justice out of our conversation, and there is no answer to someone who plans to do whatever they want by violence, intimidation, or manipulation. This is why Saint Augustine next observes that it is deeply flawed to define right (*ius*) as the interest of the stronger—a common, cynical definition of right—since it reduces right to questions of power and politics. Right, Saint Augustine counters, "flows from the spring of justice."[3]

True justice, then, is the substance of virtue. This certainly differs from the somewhat negative light in which Troup presents Saint Augustine's views of justice: as something that divides rather than unites. But here we have a clearer idea of how Saint Augustine understands justice, and what he is doing with it in his *Civitate Dei*. It is imperative to remember that Saint Augustine's idea of justice, though intimately linked with his idea of love, is in fact foreign to the frames of equality and pluralism that are championed today.[4] Saint Augustine complicates justice in a way that (as Troup astutely suggests) will not easily align with anyone's contemporary politics.

Saint Augustine is heir to a classical vision that sees a tension between, on the one hand, the shadow realities that appear to the senses within the (material) world of time and space, and, on the other hand, the Truly Real, the essence of the thing, which lies hidden in the (spiritual) realm of substance.[5] Everyone has some intuition of this tension between what a thing really is and what it looks like. As an analogy, we all know that a mama tiger with her cubs appears cute, maybe even cuddly. But regardless of how apparently cuddly she might be, we also know the reality of that mother tiger is quite different, and you are likely to pay a very high price if you mistake this simple appearance for the powerful truth. What we know about that tiger, the ancients believed about most things, from straight lines to circles, to pleasure, to beauty, to justice. Each of these things might have an appearance in the world, but those appearances are only partial hints and shadows of a True Line, a Perfect Circle, an Eternal Pleasure, an Infinite Beauty, a Genuine Justice that sits—powerful, complete, sublime, and unchanging—in the Unending, Supernatural Realm where substances exist.

Of course, all appearances in the world around us are directly connected to some sublime Reality they are reflecting, just as the flat monochrome shadows we cast on the sidewalk are directly connected to our much noisier, more dimensional, textured, colorful bodies and clothing. Shadow appearances are directly connected to the substances they reflect, and those appearances are, thus, "rumors of glory" that we can glimpse here and now.[6] But at the same time, think of how limited and incomplete our knowledge of the human body—or a violin or a book or anything else—would be if everything we knew about these objects had been gleaned only from looking at their shadows on the sidewalk. While shadows can teach us a lot, shadows are never the final word because they are always an incomplete portrayal of substantive realities, realities which, for Saint Augustine and the Christians, dwelt in the heart and mind of God. What presents itself to our senses in this world is a mere shadow of a far more dimensional and substantive reality hidden in the spiritual realm.

Under this view, one that reaches back to Plato, justice can be defined as *treating things in accordance with their substance, not their appearance.* "Justice is the virtue that gives to each his due," is how Saint Augustine says it.[7] But this means, as he immediately points out, that the possibilities for love are expanded, deepened, and strengthened when we are just.[8] When we see the substance of matters, we can make choices that are in agreement with what is real rather than what appears real to us or (far worse) what we want to be real. Make no mistake: justice in the earthly city is a blurry, out-of-focus snapshot of True Justice in the heart of God. But the way we move closer to justice as it should be—true, substantive justice—is to strive to see beyond the appearances and into the substances of everything around us. And now we are getting somewhere.

The tension between the *Civitate Dei* and the earthly city is not a dispute between justice and love, but a dispute about what to look at and how to see. The earthly city is mostly content with appearances. For Saint Augustine, behaving justly and lovingly is a matter of seeing the relevant substances that dwell as unchanging truths in the heart of God. Justice sees that crime is intolerable; justice sees that the criminal is inescapably noble, bearing the very image of God as part of their substance. Seeing both perspectives is the only path to wise judgments. Of course, since appearances are blurry and substances are beyond the full reach of our fallen intellects, we will disagree about those substances. However, it is enough to suggest that we can disagree about substances in a substantive way, and such a disagreement will very likely (at a minimum) be civil. But if, by contrast, we either neglect substances or remove them from the center of our discussion, the chances to engage in civil discourse are at best greatly diminished; perhaps they are made impossible. Discourse that is not about substances inevitably goes from seeking shared understanding to seeking dominance over the other so that my will can be accomplished. Saint Augustine certainly believes this; where language will not allow us to tap into "true justice, no right is possible ... and it is a wrong idea of right to believe it means the interest of the strongest."[9]

Hierarchy, Justice, and Love

In response to Saint Augustine's view of reality and justice, I now turn to the difference between apparent and substantive justice as well as justice's relationship to love. I suggest that we do well to understand that we can choose to love justly or unjustly. As a result, loves must be arranged hierarchically, and I will offer several examples to illustrate the point. Therefore, as this section will explain, I argue a hierarchy of love creates the conditions for civil discourse.

While I have challenged an aspect of Troup's claim that justice cannot serve as the condition for community, on one level I agree with him. Our worldly attempts to create justice always result in apparent justice, not substantive justice. In the *Civitate Dei*, the substance of justice is, simply, to give pure worship to God. The appearance of justice in the earthly city is preparatory for this higher call, and it is focused on creating holiness by discerning and appropriately correcting evil. Earthly justice, however, must focus on correction, retribution, and punishment. This must be its central focus because of the pervasive and corrupting presence of sin in the present world. Thus, since justice in the earthly city is especially entangled with our crimes and sins, it is especially problematic in the building of community; but it is also particularly partial in giving insights into eternity, as Saint Augustine laments.[10]

While this makes justice different from love in the present world, it does not sever the two, as Saint Augustine's analysis of Rome's love suggests.[11] I suspect that is what Troup is emphasizing in his discussion of the inadequacy of justice and the adequacy of love as the foundation of community. This is why—and again, I agree with Troup here—Saint Augustine turns from justice to love, apparent and substantive, as the defining quality of a country. "A multitude of rational beings joined together by common agreement on the objects of their love" is, for Saint Augustine, the definition of a community, a nation.[12] Rome cannot be adequately judged by its laws, but it can be adequately judged by its loves. The flaw of Rome is its love of glory. For this and this alone, Romans developed their famous discipline, their courage, and their skills in every other arena. And this recognition that love is the defining quality of a people is what allows Saint Augustine to examine and critique his own culture, for he can assess what Romans love most since he is Roman. He can assess the propriety of that love because he understands something substantial about love.

The partnership between justice and love nevertheless remains, and this means the objects of our love can be judged as *justly* loved or *unjustly* loved. What we love can thus be critiqued as worthy or unworthy of that love. Where we fail to love justly—fail to love what is properly loveable with the proper love—we fail to love at all. Where we withhold love unjustly, we are like a farmer in a drought who refuses to irrigate his fields. Where we lavish love unjustly, we are like a confused soul pouring bottled water into the Pacific Ocean in hopes of making the sea drinkable. Glory cannot be justly loved in the way Romans love it. That is why Rome is wrong and can be criticized as wrong; it lavishes its supreme love on an object unworthy of that type of love. Rome loves amiss, and no citizen of the *Civitate Dei* can, therefore, be a full Roman citizen because the loves that define the *Civitate Dei* are higher, better, and more proper than the love of glory that defines Rome's highest ideals. Thus, the citizens of God's kingdom must reject Rome's loves; they must not choose the earthly city's brass above the heavenly city's gold.[13]

Saint Augustine's distinction between just and unjust love makes hierarchy a necessary component of both justice and love. Love, like justice, can be misapplied. Not all love is proper and right. Some loves are higher, better, more right. Some loves are lesser, worse, or even wrong. The difference is in whether we are giving to the object of our love the type of love proper to its substance. Here there is neither equality nor individual rights. Rather, the substance of the thing we love—money, spouse, prestige, a friend, success—simply merits some types of love but not others, and we can get it right or wrong. What we desire is simply irrelevant; the eternal, unchanging substance of the thing loved is the only relevant issue. Note that *all things made by God* are declared good, and all things made by God are, therefore, properly lovable. But not all objects of love are equal. The important question is this: What sort of love is appropriate for this or that object of my affection? And here the answers will vary according to the substance of what we want to love and the quality of love we wish to offer.

Take Troup's simple but insightful example of the pet compared to the child. How much should Troup love his dog? Well, infinitely, if he is loving the dog *as a dog*. But how much should he love his dog as one loves a child? Not at all. If I am loving ice cream as one should love nourishing food, then no amount of that quality of love is appropriate. None. Loves, of course, may overlap in their actions and attitudes. One should feed both one's dog and daughter. As well, one should allow neither to climb onto the dining room table with muddy feet. But more than quantity of affection separates the two. The dog is properly loved as a fellow mortal who bears the gift of life with all its mortal pains and mortal pleasures. The daughter is properly loved as a fellow immortal who brandishes the inescapable image of God through the world and thus lives a different quality of life and so requires a different kind of love.

When one tries to love a perfectly fine thing (ice cream, a dog) in the wrong way (as nourishment, as a daughter), we love unjustly; we fail to treat the object according to its substance. Treat ice cream as one should treat fruits and vegetables, and the body falls ill, however pleasant the taste. Love a dog as one should love a daughter, and the soul falls ill, however indulgent the sentiment. Lest anyone accuse me of simple cold-heartedness and an inability to understand, let me be clear that I have owned dogs my whole life. I have loved them profoundly. I have wept bitterly at their deaths, and the absent companionship of those fellow mortals still pains me. I am also absolutely aware of the difference between the type of love I have rightly given to those delightful creatures and the type of love I have rightly given to my son, my daughter, and my wife.

It is these conditions—an acceptance of hierarchy in loves and a willingness to critique loves as qualitatively proper or improper—that create the possibility of civil discourse. Saint Augustine observes that, according to his definition of a community, "it is clear that the better the objects of its love, the better the people, and the worse the objects of its love, the worse the people."[14] Romans loved glory as if it were the ultimate purpose of human life. They were wrong to do this because when the substance of glory is considered, it is found to be unworthy of serving as the ultimate object of one's love since better substances can be identified and justified as the target of ultimate love. We now turn to consider how hierarchy in love, propriety in love, and substantive purpose may serve, pragmatically, as coordinates for triangulating civility in discourse.

Love and Substantive Discourse

I have said that disagreement about the substance of a matter is exactly the sort (and perhaps the only sort) of disagreement that can be approached civilly, and I have hinted at why I believe this to be so. In this closing section, I wish to consider more carefully the practical understanding of such a claim. Why are substances necessary for civil discourse? The answer is best understood by comparing the job communication would have to do in two different worlds: Saint Augustine's world, where substances are accepted as more real than material stuff, and an alternative universe (somewhat like our own), where virtually no one really believes in substances. This understanding of how words work goes a long way in explaining how communities can destroy civil discourse in at least two terrifying ways. And while I think chances are slim that we can regain Saint Augustine's sense of civility, I close this chapter with a constructive way forward.

In Saint Augustine's world, words are themselves appearances—stimuli presented to our senses. But like all appearances, they are attached to and represent a substantive reality not of our own making, but something existing entirely apart from our words about it.[15] Our words may represent this reality more accurately or they may represent it less accurately. The accuracy depends on our understanding of the substances we are discussing and our individual integrity; I can be right, or I can be wrong, or I can lie. Let us consider an example.

If I tell you that grophs are terrible beasts that frequently attack and often kill people who enter a room with them, and that, furthermore, there are a couple of grophs in the room next to us, then we are facing a few possibilities. Either I am correct and the word groph references a real beast that is a real threat to you if you enter the next room, or I am mistaken. I can be mistaken in two ways. My word groph might represent a real beast, but not one that is a serious threat to you. Alternatively, I can make the mistake of believing that grophs are real when they are not. I can be right, or I can be mistaken. But there is still another possibility: I might be lying.

The first two possibilities open an option for you and me to engage in genuine discourse about grophs. You might express confusion and ask what

I mean by a groph. In our discussion, you discover that I am describing a reality that you represent by the phrase hungry tiger. Or perhaps we find out that I am using the word groph to represent that thing you call a mosquito, and now we must explore why I think these creatures are deadly when you think of them merely as annoying. Or, maybe, by the word groph I mean a species of winged, fanged, kangaroo-vampire gnomes. But even here we have a basis for discourse. We can try to figure out why I believe such creatures really do exist (while you do not) and why I think there are some of these gnomes in the next room. One of us has an inaccurate understanding of the world's realities. Though we might both be profoundly sincere in our beliefs, we cannot both be right. But discourse and clarification in all these situations remains possible precisely because we both believe we are talking about something substantive, something independent of our own making, something whose existence (or lack of existence!) does not depend on our words about it.

And that brings us to that third option. Perhaps the word groph reflects nothing real at all and I knew it was without connection to any independent reality. I knew it was just a word for a fictional creature that I and some of my friends made up. If so, what possible reason could I have for telling you about the terrifying grophs in the next room? In this third situation, I am afraid the most plausible explanation for my statement about the grophs is that I was making a power play; I was attempting to manipulate you. I was using words with no reality behind them to try and get you to behave in a way that would benefit me and my group, though all along I knew my words referred to fictions made up by my group, my tribe, my party. My words did not refer to anything real, and I knew it. The word was merely a power tool to carve what I wanted out of the raw material of your psyche. But, of course, we cannot do that with the word tiger, because the word tiger refers to a real creature. Our description of a tiger can be more accurate or less accurate, but only because the tiger is a fixed reality and real tigers do not change regardless of what we say about them.

What is true of grophs and of tigers is much truer of good and of wrong. When we describe donating blood as a good act, we might mean that the word good references a substantive quality (Goodness itself, as it is known to God), and this act of donating blood imitates that quality in some partial but recognizable way. My description of your donation as good is accurate, because good is a real thing, and what you are doing really does reflect its substance. Of course, this also means that my description can be inaccurate. If I say, "Donating blood is the highest good that any human being can do!" then that description is, almost certainly, less accurate than simply calling your donation a good act. But the accuracy of my description hinges on there being a substance for the word good, just as the accuracy of our descriptions of a tiger hinge on the fact that tigers are real.

But if the word good is like the word groph, if it is a word that refers to nothing substantive, then you and I can decide it means whatever we like. Now in this situation, if I describe your donating blood as a good thing, I simply mean that me and folks like me have decided that we like it when you do that. And, of course, that means when we describe something as good, we can never be inaccurate, even when my group and I apply that description to apartheid or lynching.

Severed from substance, words do not mean anything substantive. They do not hold meaning at all. They can, of course, be used to try and put my tribe or group in power so that we can make the world more like what we want. Severed from substance, words inevitably become tools of power. They are used to signal identity ("Ah! You Are One of Us") and to disempower those who are not in our group. Our words are either a reflection of the Real or they are a lie; they are substantive revelation of what is outside of us and over us, or they are insubstantial revelry in our private feelings and our collaborative desires for power. To reiterate (because the point is so crucial): if the word good is not a description of an act that imitates a substance, then it must be a game of word play about how I want you to feel, so that my agenda is advanced. And here there is no discourse; there are only power games maneuvering to create power bases which can impose one's view on others. Saint Augustine describes such speech as a "lust for power" (*dominandi cupiditate*) that rules "with a most oppressive domination" (*cum saevissimo dominatu*).[16]

In a world of these power games, there are two equally horrifying ways to destroy civil community. One is to assume that I know the Substantive Truth. The other is to assume that there is no Substantive Truth to be known. The first way deceives me into believing that I am qualified to rule over you. The second way deceives me into believing that nothing rules over me. Both errors end in a suffocating, crushing culture of oppression and injustice. Raw power is the currency of both views, the second no less than the first. Neither can encourage hospitable discourse. Both necessitate a self-centeredness that renders self-interested transactions and temporary alliances between factions possible but community unthinkable. Such views may use the word community to talk about their transactional and power-based interactions. But that is, Saint Augustine would note, because they do not understand the substance of community, of love.

Civil discourse about justice, even in disagreement, is possible, but it is possible exactly because, and only when, both speakers recognize that they are talking about a reality that is independent of and larger than their words about it. They are not free to make whatever they wish out of the word "justice." They speak while understanding that their speech is chained to a thing indifferent to their words and sitting in judgment on them. And their words are, ironically, empowered by this servitude, for surely the power of words is in their limitation to the real, not their liberation from it. Anchored to the Real, it is possible to build community, even when we disagree; severed from the Real, we must compete for the victory of our own pointlessly arbitrary power base.

Thus, civil discourse begins by admitting that things are not meaningless but meaningful reflections of meaningful substances. This is the first point on which to fix the bearings of civil discourse. If we wish to have a hospitable discourse that rises above our power tribes and constituencies, we must reach for a substance that underlies those mere appearances and that swaps manufactured identity for human substance. And we would probably be wise to seek the deepest, most precise understanding of that human substance, of that actual purpose that comes from our being persons.

If one accepts meaningful substances as an actual aspect of life, then proper or improper responses to them are a logical extension. Groph as hungry tiger suggests a different response than groph as mosquito. So, the first point in triangulating an area of civility in our discourse is to recognize that discourse is tied to substance. The second step is to seek an understanding of the substances and their qualities. The last step in hospitable discourse is to critique our own (and others') responses to those substances, recognizing that some ways of honoring certain substances—of loving—are more appropriate than others. Disagreement is possible, but such disagreements only return one to a reconsideration of the substances. When words are connected to substantive reality independent of their own making, they can be tools for crafting hospitable civility among us. When words are understood, instead, as tools for crafting a world of our own making, they can only serve as weapons for our tribe. This is the dark underbelly of one present set of assumptions making up the Euromerican culture, and these assumptions must be abandoned if we hope to return to civility.

Substantive Discourse

The chance is slim. Perhaps there is a real Just Way, independent of our understanding, unresponsive to our expressions, and indifferent to our opinions of it. Perhaps we both would like to remake our present world in a way that more accurately reflects that Just Way. If so, and if it is also true that neither of us (though acquainted with this Way) know it fully, then it is possible—just barely possible—that we might come to live together in a begrudging tolerance because we recognize a sliver of similarity in our views about that Real Justice that we each seem to care about. That begrudging tolerance eventually, under just the right conditions, might become overgrown with a quiet respect. And that quiet respect could eventually, if everything went just right, blossom into a timorous love. All this would happen through discourse, and through the imitation of the Word appearing within our words. The chance is slim, but it is the only chance we have of growing into our humanity while bearing within us the Word of God. Expect disappointment along the way.

The substantial view is essential to civic discourse that can meaningfully call out corruption, abuse of power, oppression, and all other forms of injustice, all of which are failures of love. But the very idea of substance is virtually unknown at present, and its perspective and assumptions are almost completely absent in today's educational system. Indeed, one seeks in vain for advanced or introductory texts in my own discipline, communication studies, that do not assume spin and power and partisan activism are the point of discourse. But there are other views, even if we have only met them in the most cursory way in this chapter. And that introduction leaves us with a host of questions. How does one induce substance from appearance? How does one discover the hierarchy of substantial loves? How does one argue about things that cannot be perceived?

All these questions have meticulous and well-conceived answers, of course. Saint Augustine was not unacquainted with them, but they are certainly beyond the scope of a single chapter, or perhaps even of a single book. It is to be hoped, if the idea and power of substantive discourse has proved intriguing, we will in the future dig those answers out again and become more acquainted with substances. But for now, perhaps, it is enough simply to introduce the thought that such things might be. The communication corollary is this: if substances are real, then and only then can there remain that slim hope that civil discourse is possible.

Conclusion

Saint Augustine saw clearly that the urban civilization he had known was failing and that only those things we managed to internalize would survive the collapse. Saint Augustine was echoing Plato, who had watched the Athenian empire implode during the Peloponnesian War. Plato, too, noted that only what was inside the soul endured.

What we love shapes our souls. Discourse is the result of understanding that our loves are more real and more powerful than the moon or physics. Discourse is the result of understanding that our loves are directed toward substances, also more real and more powerful than matter. Discourse is the result of understanding that those real loves can be aligned more or less appropriately with those real substances.

When disagreement emerges in such settings, it is anchored, even at its most heated, to a search for a common bond, a shared understanding of something independent of my view or your view, a Real that is bigger than either of us. We may argue about the nature of the Real, but that is because we each want the other to understand more deeply a truth larger than either of us. We argue as lovers—lovers, at least, of the substance (*justice, beauty, goodness*) that we each see differently and only partially. In discourse, we must first be tied not to a common understanding, but to a common reality that we both seek to understand. That reality must not be a thing we are making, but a substance impervious to our opinions of it. If it is a thing we make, our words will inevitably be tools of dominance. If it is a thing making us, we are members of the same household, serving under the same lord.

Discourse becomes uncivil to the exact degree it rejects its role as a shadow of substance. Discourse becomes more civil to the exact degree that it abandons the lust for power and chooses to represent substances. This, I suggest, is one secret for beginning to understand Saint Augustine's hospitality more deeply.

Chapter 3

Endeavoring Hospitality as Interaction

Reflections on Subtle Enactments of Empire

Michelle Shockness

Introduction

Some years ago, a woman came to my parents' home seeking assistance with her vehicle. My mother, on hearing the doorbell, came to receive her guest. The guest asked to speak to the lady of the house. My mother, unfettered, responded, "Yes," another indication of her identity as host, and waited, but the stranger seemed to be waiting for someone else. They stood together on the doorstep of our family home in awkward silence for some time: the guest waiting for the lady of the house; my mother waiting for the reality of their situation to dawn on her guest. Finally, my mother broke the silence of their interaction by softly closing the door. After waiting a few seconds, she reopened the door and again attempted to receive her guest. However, her identity as black host went unrecognized as the white stranger waited for the physical presence of a host commensurate with her expectation.

In sharing my mother's story with friends and colleagues, I have been met with incensed reactions toward the comportment of the would-be guest. However, for those who share in an identity of other, stranger, alien, or unrecognized host, the experience is often met with knowing nods and little surprise. As my mother's story illustrates, the enactment of hospitality is not immune from the impact of empire. By empire, I refer to a hegemonic system which parcels out identities of winners and losers based on prescribed groupings, a transactional system which celebrates privilege and hubris on the one hand and reproduces inequality and injustice on the other. Rather than a system in service to all, empire supports a system in service to a few and prescribes disadvantaged encounters for the rest.

As a way of resisting these kinds of everyday enactments of empire, I offer an interactional account of hospitality, one that unfolds in three ways. First, I explore three overlooked matters that can often lead to enactments of empire: the overlooked acquiescence, or "yes," from guests; the overlooked labor required of guests; and the overlooked mutuality that is essential for healthy hospitality to take place.[1] Next, resisting imperial impulses related to hospitality involves, I suggest, recognizing and embracing the implications of two insights: the host and guest as fluid identities, and the sociopolitical reality of interaction as explored through the lens of Anti-Oppressive Practice (AOP), an approach with roots in social work. Finally, endeavoring hospitality as interaction involves striving to recognize the unrecognized hosts, finding meaning in another's "no," and living out civility as a spaciousness for others. I offer that these considerations are important for Christians who, as participants in a corporate vision of civility, can endeavor everyday enactments of hospitality.

Acquiescence, Labor, and Mutuality

Drawing on concepts and insights from social work, I suggest that hospitality can become an enactment of empire when certain conditions are overlooked: acquiescence, labor, and mutuality.

In my work as an instructor and across my practice within the nonprofit sector, I have noted that a lack of *acquiescence* is often one of the first areas of great transgression in working within marginalized communities. By acquiescence, I refer to the "yes," the free will choice of every human being to accept or deny that which another offers. This ability to acquiesce, to say "yes," is foundational to our humanity and something we can exercise and honor in relationship to others: the ability to ask and to accept and extend permission to other human beings. Sadly, it is this foundation of our humanity that other human beings, who are also fashioned in God's image, can transgress. Well-intentioned outsiders with great visions of transforming communities can fail to ask, consult, or invite the participation of communities and their stakeholders. When a community's members are perceived to be "just that poor," they can be cast in the role of "guests" in their own community and homes. The well-intentioned "host" offering "anything we can give" breeds the implicit belief that "they will take anything we offer." It is through this flawed lens that communities can then be perceived and engaged, or commandeered, as charity projects through caring presumption.

The "yes" of acquiescence is also enshrined within the field of social work through concepts like self-determination. Among the primary values of Canadian social workers is the "respect for the inherent dignity and worth of persons."[2] Out of dignity and worth follows a commitment to "uphold each person's right to self-determination, consistent with that person's capacity and with the rights of others."[3] Self-determination has also been described as the "highest" of social work values[4] and as the "natural right" of clients.[5] Periodically, the concept of self-determination has been connected to moral and emancipatory aims, and more recently it has been conceptualized as empowerment, where the awareness and challenge of oppressive societal structures and conditions are understood as necessary.[6] Self-determination has been depicted as providing a balance to power and a form of moral restraint upon the social worker. But self-determination is not without critique,[7] especially since tensions can exist among the rights of the individual, the family, and greater community or society.[8] While a full conversation on the right to self-determination is beyond the scope of this chapter, I suggest that all persons, including those who are often on the margins of society, have the right to self-determination, to human agency, and to the choice to say "yes," whether others in society equally uphold this right or not. For persons who are often on the margins, it is this right to choose that can be quite easily missed, circumvented, or dismissed.

Second, overlooked acquiescence is often accompanied by the overlooked labor that hospitality demands of guests. My mother's ability to offer hospitality to her guest was in direct proportion to the labor of her guest in identifying our household, in identifying my mother's identity as a household head, and in receiving that which was offered as a hospitable invitation. There are implicit expectations of the hospitality interaction that can be assumed as given. A host's desire to act hospitably requires a guest's labor to recognize and receive that hospitality. It requires the guest to engage in interaction, whether invited or imposed. It requires effort on the part of the guest. Where invited, where the "yes" is given, guests participate in the give and take of an interaction. Where hosts do not extend hospitality to engender an invited interaction (that is, where acquiescence is overlooked), hospitality becomes the imposition of resources—a "care" whose means of delivery runs antithetically to its purported aim. Yet, even with this imposition, labor is required of the guest, even if this labor is the action needed to survive the interaction. I refer here to the challenge and pain of those upon whom this type of compassion has been foisted at the expense of their autonomy, ingenuity, self-sufficiency, and self-respect.

Both overlooked acquiescence and overlooked labor can transform hospitality into a subtle enactment of empire, an economy of the privileged actor and the underprivileged acted upon. A generous offer I fielded when I was working with a nonprofit organization some years ago illustrates this point. A group had approached my organization with new school supplies that I assumed were for use within our program. They asked, and I enthusiastically accepted, "Yes, we can use the supplies." But the group had conditions. The group leader wanted the group members to have the personal experience of placing the donated school supplies directly in the hands of the children who attended the program. She shared their vision of setting up a table in the community on Saturday, the day that worked best for their members, and envisioned the children and their families lining up at the table so that each member of their group could have the experience of giving.

In the discussion that followed, I tried to navigate, though perhaps not clearly enough to be received, the need for a "yes" from the community. As a nonprofit, we had labored many years for our "yes" and so, respectfully, I could only answer "yes" for the nonprofit. I explained that we could use the donation to add to the resources we offer, and we could also ask, within our relationship with the children's families, if one or more of the supplies were wanted or needed. I attempted to reason with this well-meaning group leader and explain that it would be an imposition on the community to set up a table among homes, within the community's space, to hand out that which was neither invited nor requested. Against this proposed imposition, I attempted to speak to what can occur when well-meaning intentions lead to helpers remaining so transfixed on their need to give as to miss the "yes" of the targeted recipients of this help. The group's plan would have overlooked the labor of these targeted community members unwillingly cast in the role of guests of a "hospitality" staged in their own community. Our interaction did not end favorably as the group leader chose not to proceed with the donation. I ended the call with the weight of having said "no" on behalf of the community, even if inadvertently. The group leader further communicated that they intended to take their donation to an organization more amenable to their plan.

There could have been great need for this donation within the community, and my unwillingness to carry out the plan of this group blocked receipt of it. But had I supported this plan for strangers to "host" our community partners in their own homes, I risked imposing undue labor on the community, and such an imposition of labor is a subtle, pernicious form of empire. Had I carried out the plan, I would have likely risked the relationship that existed between my organization and the community.

Finally, overlooked mutuality can also function as a form of empire. Mutuality can be defined as the combined, agreed-upon labor over time that guests and hosts invest to create and sustain hospitality. The term "mutuality" describes the open give and take that comes with sustained trust. It is a practice that is nurtured over time and with ever-deepening mutual care. For hosts, it requires the unmaking of aspiring martyrs with romantic notions of self-sacrifice for the poor and a remaking of purpose to exclude the notion of faceless others to be saved. Within the field of social work, mutuality has been described as the give and take relationship adopted between client and worker rather than a relationship built on one-sided giving.[9] It invites consideration of the interdependence that exists between client and worker[10] and includes a sense of reciprocity and mutual responsibility for the work ahead.[11]

Where there is no consent, no giving and receiving of permission for the interaction, then no mutuality can begin to exist. In hospitality as interaction, mutuality can be offered by the host, but where it is declined by the guest, it is no longer mutuality. As such, acquiescence is embedded as a precursor. Where the host continues to pursue mutuality, the risk is in the foisting of hospitality on those who do not have capacity or inclination to say "yes." This is a mimicry of mutuality, a one-sided offering which attempts to span the relational gap between host and guest; it usurps not only the choice of the targeted recipient, but also the interdependence, reciprocity, joint responsibility, and joint learning that define such mutuality. With reference to communities at the margins, the result can be a patronizing, orchestrated, and managed engagement with already marginalized communities in which hosts address their own needs for interaction as synonymous with the guests' needs. When hosts fulfill their own needs, they can deceive themselves into thinking that, by their effort, they have offered hospitality. For guests, receipt of this managed offering limits the potential for mutuality, as the host unwittingly redirects and restricts the creativity, synergy, and discovery that make for a mutuality built over time. In effect, hosts risk treating guests as objects, as things to fix and as exoticized others, rather than as neighbors to grow to know. They risk subordinating guests to the perpetual role of manageable strangers and aliens. As has been my experience, it is rare to meet the guest willing to labor beyond such transgressions.

The overreliance of hosts on their own characteristics can also endanger mutuality. The belief that a host's characteristics, such as their authenticity, candor, or technique, can fix the relationship, establish mutuality, compensate for acquiescence, and remedy a lack of guest labor misrepresents hospitality as a solitary journey. This overreliance suggests that hospitality can be prescribed rather than discovered. I offer the following memory as illustrative of this point.

I was working as a youth worker while simultaneously completing my graduate degree in social work. I was onsite, meeting with one of my youths about a personal crisis, when I decided to practice a technique that I had learned in class. I still remember the slight turn of her countenance when I made my pronouncement and waited for the effect. The youth, who previously had helping professionals in her life, met my gaze mid-crisis and with a slight smile stated simply, "You just turned it on, didn't you?" What could I say? I admitted that she was right and assured her that this was the last of my techniques that would be rolled out. We could just talk.

Over the years, I have witnessed many aspiring hosts making the same mistake I made in this moment. They wrongly assumed that a technique, characteristic, or even their good intentions—"We mean well" or "We just want to help"—can create, control, or carry the hospitality interaction. Like the youth in my example, guests can also be quite adept at seeing through such efforts to usurp their labor. Had our relationship been less established, I wonder whether this youth would have undertaken the labor of teaching me. I still fondly recall her kind correction that communicated to me the power of acquiescence and the responsibility that a negotiated mutuality carries.

A host's labor and good intentions still require the need for the labor and acquiescence of the guest in the realizing of mutuality. "Yes" is not offered for all time. It is reaffirmed and nurtured, and as graciously, emphatically, subtly, and slowly as it may have been offered, it can be withdrawn. I appreciate this youth's gentle nudge from my well-intentioned navel-gazing to a wider view of interaction. I also appreciate the unrecognized labor that she and many others have undertaken to challenge my belief that attempts at authenticity, candidness, forgiveness, kindness, or technique could compensate for the acquiescence, mutuality, and labor that make hospitality possible. If overlooked acquiescence, mutuality, and labor function as everyday enactments of empire, then how might those of us interested in hospitality identify and resist these practices? The next section serves as a conceptual way to begin the process of identifying and resisting these practices.

Fluid Identities and Anti-Oppressive Practice

In the context in which hosts can unknowingly engage in subtle enactments of empire, I suggest that two postures can serve as a corrective: understanding host-guest identity as fluid and attending to the system elucidated through the lens of Anti-Oppressive Practice (AOP). In this section, I discuss how God's identity as stranger motivates a fluid understanding of host and guest, a fluidity explored in Christian and philosophical traditions. Additionally, AOP encourages a greater awareness of the sociopolitical context of hosts and guests, insight which may limit harm. I conclude this section with a reflection on how fluid identities and sociopolitical awareness can help Christians resist the enactments of empire related to acquiescence, labor, and mutuality.

In the biblical tradition, the value of the stranger is acknowledged in the stranger's identity as often being intertwined with God's divine presence. Christian ethicist Christine D. Pohl notes that the stranger can bring a message or blessing from God, or may also mediate God's presence, such that when followers of God respond "to vulnerable strangers" they do so in "anticipation of divine presence."[12] As the writer of Hebrews makes explicit, "Do not forget to show hospitality to strangers, for by so doing some people have shown hospitality to angels without knowing it."[13] Jesus makes explicit this tradition in presenting those who are marginalized—the least of these—as those who are sought after and welcomed precisely because God's identity is bound up with their experience.[14] As Jesus claims at the end of the parable, whatever happens to those experiencing marginalization in its many forms happens to God. Additionally, whatever we do to those who have been marginalized we do to God.

Humility and Hospitality

This fluidity between God's identity and the stranger offers a ready example for Christians to understand the reciprocal identity between host and guest. In her research exploring Christian hospitality, Pohl notes that in communities where the roles of guest and host are not "tightly defined" and where mutuality does not pervade, the myriad gifts of both host and guest are not recognized and experienced.[15] For "the deepest condescension may be expressed in a person's unwillingness to be a guest—reflecting an unwillingness to recognize another person's capacity to help us."[16] As Pohl further cautions, "there is a kind of hospitality that keeps people needy strangers while fostering an illusion of relationship and connection. It both disempowers and domesticates guests while it reinforces the hosts' power, control, and sense of generosity."[17]

Likewise, in their discussion of radical Christian hospitality with homeless populations, social workers Amanda Sackreiter and Tonya Armstrong observe the potential for a "blurring of boundaries between persons" engaged in hospitality.[18] "[W]hen a stranger enters the household of the host," they argue, "he is no longer a stranger, but part of the household" and, therefore, also a host.[19] Pohl also points to a fluidity of the guest-host role in the post-resurrection biblical story of the Road to Emmaus. "Jesus comes to them as a stranger (they do not recognize him), but they welcome him as a guest, and in the breaking of bread together, Jesus becomes their host."[20] Hospitality is truncated if it does not move beyond the meeting of physical needs to also include the "recognizing and valuing" of the guest.[21]

The fluidity between host and guest is also present in philosopher Jacques Derrida's reflections on hospitality. Theologian Andrew Shepherd offers this reading:

> Derrida notes the inherent tensions and paradoxes within the word "hospitality," which, derived from the Latin word *hospes*, combines the words of *hostis*— which originally meant stranger, but came to take on the meaning of "enemy" or "hostile" stranger—with *potis*, to have mastery or power. The multiple meanings of the Latin word *hostis* is paralleled by the polysemous nature of the French word *hôte* which means both the one who gives (donne) and the one who receives (reçoit). Through a simple etymological analysis, therefore, Derrida raises a number of intriguing, and potentially unsettling questions: In the act of hospitality, who is the "host" and who is the "guest"? Who is

assisting who?—That is, who gives and who receives? And, is it the "host" or the "guest" who poses a potential threat?[22]

Derrida invites consideration of the other, the guest, and their contribution to hospitality, not as given, but as question. In troubling identities, intentions, and roles, Derrida invites a new vantage from which to engage assumed meanings and to consider anew the nature of hospitality.

In addition to the fluidity of identity, AOP advocates awareness of sociopolitical context to limit the harm hosts might perform. AOP examines and addresses inequalities in social relationships and in the ways larger systems privilege some while also creating challenges for others.[23] Such practices require of the social worker both acknowledgement of the sociopolitical context which contributes to the experienced oppression of clients and action towards societal transformation.[24] The worker's own privilege is implicated in this acknowledgment of sociopolitical context, because the worker cannot live outside or beyond these systems. The worker's multiple and intersecting social locations and intersecting privileges and oppressions can become places of critical self-reflection, where workers can expose the assumptive thinking that impacts interactions with those with whom they work.[25] Through AOP, workers use the lenses of inequality and privilege to understand their clients' experiences and choice of actions, as well as their own. Understanding another's experience relies on recognition of one's own privilege and the space between worker and client as ground that must be traversed. Though the worker may see and attempt to traverse this ground in a way that encourages the client to say "yes," AOP encourages a worker to understand and empathize with another's possible "no," and perhaps to also understand the potential sociopolitical roots for this decision. The Canadian Association of Social Workers' *Code of Ethics* asserts that it is "the client's right to make choices based on voluntary, informed consent," and which includes consideration of the risks that may arise from involvement with the worker.[26] Thus, workers, sensitive to dynamics of privilege and oppression, must choose not to exert their power to circumvent or unduly pressure others or to insist beyond clients' consent.

An acknowledgement of the fluidity of identity and recognition of the dynamics of privilege and oppression can offer a further reorientation to acquiescence, labor, and mutuality.

A realized fluidity of identity between host and guest ensures that participation in each role is not so entrenched as to allow perennial ascriptions of these identities; guests are not always relegated to being guests, nor hosts to always being hosts. This fluidity of identity also acts as a litmus test to the quality of acquiescence, mutuality, and labor that characterize the hospitality interaction. Likewise, recognition of sociopolitical location and awareness of systems of inequality as elucidated through AOP also expose the limits of empire and the practices that propagate its health. With greater awareness also comes recognition of those who often go unrecognized in the hospitality interaction. There is also hope for greater acknowledgment of "yes," "no," and the sociopolitical realities within which each is offered. Taking into account fluidity of identity and AOP, Christians might be able to endeavor hospitality in practical ways that avoid empire and embrace hospitality as an interaction.

Endeavoring Hospitality as Interaction

Recognition of host-guest identity as fluid and embracing of AOP's awareness of systemic inequality can aid those Christians endeavoring hospitality. I offer, practically, that endeavoring hospitality can take the form of three actions: recognizing the unrecognized host, finding meaning in another's "no," and practicing spaciousness.

First, I live in a city of many households. In endeavoring hospitality, some will be among the recognized, while others will be among the unrecognized. Among unrecognized hosts that I have met, some are individuals living on (or near) the street. In attempting hospitality, some of these unrecognized hosts often encounter unaware guests. I was inspired by the resolve of one man in stating to me that his work in the world was to greet everyone who passed him where he stood on the street corner, his doorstep. Another woman shared her frustration, stating to me that her offering of greeting and conversation from where she sat on the street, her doorstep, was often ignored. Others I have met also discussed feeling the need to qualify their attempt at interaction. Unrecognized hosts must negotiate the assumed "no" of unacknowledged interaction and the added labor this entails, including challenging this lack of recognition. Unrecognized hosts are also challenged by the image of the host that "does not look or sound like me" and by interactions with unknown others who may subscribe, even without awareness, to a prescribed image of the host. Equal ability to navigate a lack of recognition does not exist for all unrecognized hosts, nor are there equal risks in challenging this lack of recognition. Ultimately, challenging from a disempowered position can risk further marginalization. Included among unrecognized hosts are also those whose multiple identities include Christian, and which expose them to sisterly and brotherly injury by virtue of belonging to God's family and believing the promise of equal membership and participation. Their complex negotiations of hospitality, the act of when to "close the door" and whether to reopen it again, are a risky, unrecognized labor often overlooked. Unconscious agreements with systems of inequality serve as blinders to hospitality as interaction. Recognizing these blinders and challenging their prescribed responses can invite the negotiation of roles as equal participants. For the relatively privileged Christian, endeavoring hospitality must, therefore, include a willingness to accept hospitality from those who might not conform to their image of a host, both inside and outside of the church. Recognizing others is not an act to be rolled out on special occasions, but a practice that spans all social relations. It is a practice that indicts and challenges the understanding of one's position as it relates to others and the surrounding system. This practice demands transformation of the self as a step in the work of recognizing those previously unrecognized. It demands endeavoring to explore and own one's identity as guest.

Second, endeavoring hospitality also includes finding meaning in another's "no" and in avoiding the imposition on others of one's own need to host. Over the years, I have had many wonderful encounters with others, including opportunities also to receive both "yes" and "no." My invitations to others may not have been as formal as asking, "Would you like to receive hospitality from me?" But "noes" were also, at times, communicated with subtlety, with a figurative sliding back away from the table, or a getting up, or a leaving. "Noes" are uncomfortable and at times painful because they set limitations on the offering of relationship. "Noes" challenge the belief that just the right approach, technique, or character trait is responsible for another's saying "yes." I do not want to discount the dynamics of oppression and inequality that may greatly impact the capacity for relationship, places where increasing self- and sociopolitical-awareness would benefit. I do want to highlight that "no" is another's choosing for themselves the labor, relational risk, and vulnerability they are willing to undertake in relationship.

Accepting a "no" can also be consecrated ground. Another's "no" can be honored and in the same way that God honors our "noes." God is one who stands at the door and knocks; God does not force open the door.[27] God is the host who accepts our "yes" and "no" with equanimity. Finding meaning in another's "no" is consecrated ground, because we follow God into the very act of asking and receiving. We are invited to meet with the God who is the stranger, alien, and host—the God we do not fully understand. Hospitality is a space to understand the experience of another person alongside one's own.

Even if a hospitality interaction ends with "no," we are still invited to consider the impression and significance of this interaction. We are given opportunity to grow to appreciate the "noes" where the labor is deemed just too great. We can learn about capacity, both ours and others, and about the relational limits and conditions of both "yes" and "no." We can be encouraged to creatively consider the many ways that care can be communicated after a "no" to hospitality is given.

Here, I explore Calvin L. Troup's ideas on the path to civility. Troup implies that incivility is a problem we need to personally resist. I draw from his work that when we resist incivility in personal ways, we acknowledge fault and participation in dynamics that promote incivility, namely the vying for self-righteousness at the cost of vilifying others. Further, when we set aside our defensiveness and grudges to take up the mantle of joint fault and responsibility, we then can embrace a joint hope for renewed civility, but that hope can come at personal and household cost. Troup also maintains that well-ordered love is exemplified in love of God and love of others, the two greatest commandments. Thus, he concludes that civility requires hospitality—welcoming in and going out to neighbors.

For the Christian household, I concur that these are beneficial guides in recovering civility. But in recovering civility across our earthly city, Christian practice invites participation. It cannot demand it from our neighbors and community. Love, even love well-offered, can remain a love unrequited, a hospitality unrequited. There is a necessary labor for our neighbors and strangers in our host practice, including the labor of saying "no." In crossing the threshold into our homes and spaces, we can acknowledge that our invitation implicitly requests guest participation and labor. In recovering civility across our community, there is a requisite community acquiescence, a labor, in realizing our hope of commonwealth.

Finally, endeavoring hospitality also includes practicing spaciousness. Opening our homes and entering our community as sites for interaction, we travel as with Christ to the unexpected encounter, with the unexpected other, and for the unexpected response. The call to spaciousness speaks to the vulnerable ground that is within us all, that we carry into relationship, which is easily transformed into ground that is as hard as clay and brick. Part of the host's ongoing labor is tilling that hard ground as a space suitable for "yes" and "no," for now and in the future. Tilling our vulnerable ground as spaciousness for others is not a technique or a method but a practice. It includes eyes to see and ears to hear, room to receive and to respond, and vulnerability to enter into the many ways another's response allows relationship.

I admit that one of the most profound relationships in my life, my relationship with my best friend, began with a mimicked mutuality on my part. We were teenagers, and she was the new girl at the church. I was on the teen leadership team and was asked by our youth pastor to become her friend. Nearly 30 years later, my scripted hospitality still comes up in conversation, as does her grace and labor in accepting what was insincere regardless of my good intentions. Her grace and capacity for rich relationship allowed us to grow into a relationship together that now has a healthy foundation of trust, love, and mutuality. However, I recognize that the greatest labor for this came from her side of the relationship in overcoming the barriers that I unwittingly set. Many years later, I endeavor to reciprocate the spaciousness that has been extended to me, knowing that there will be barriers that I encounter and that I still unwittingly set, and that may require a labor beyond that which a potential guest may have capacity to offer.

For Christians endeavoring hospitality, there is requisite action in recognizing the unrecognized and their labor, in exploring the meaning in others' "noes," and in adopting a posture of spaciousness, tilled ground which allows for all these practices to grow and thrive.

Conclusion

In attending to labor, acquiescence, and mutuality, we acknowledge the work of others in realizing our hope for hospitality and, ultimately, in realizing civility and commonwealth. The path to civility is not the solitary journey of one person or household, but a corporate sojourn of mutual labor. Our mutual labor and our interactions with others are how we make a civil commonwealth. Every household is implicated in this labor for commonwealth. As such, our households are not so separate as to preclude impacting others, where our everyday enactments of empire can unwittingly impose labor on others.

Therefore, a hospitality that co-creates commonwealth is a hospitality that is as much an action of the empowered and privileged as it is of the disempowered and marginalized, and where guest and host roles are fluid. It is a hospitality that acknowledges and confronts sociopolitical oppressions, and which acknowledges the roots and understands the reasons for "no" and "yes." Finally, it is a hospitality which requires spaciousness, a vulnerable nurturing of transformative practices with potential to heal, and to challenge our incivility.

As I conclude these reflections, my great-great-grandfather is close in thought. I was told that my grandmother, as a little girl at family gatherings, would watch her grandfather slip away from the crowd. Alone, he would crouch down and rock himself, and cry for a time. It was understood that this was something he did. I was told that he was taken from West Africa, that my great-great-grandfather was a great chief, and that, as a survivor of a slave ship, he carried the trauma and experience of his whole history in his body. As I reflect on civility, I wonder at the nature of hospitality that could have been extended to include him, his trauma, and his resilience. However, close in thought is also my great-great-grandfather's great-granddaughter, my mother, who softly closes the door on a stranger, but she opens it and tries again. In the everyday, we see the hope for commonwealth.

PART III
LIVED CHALLENGES OF CIVILITY

Chapter 4

Reverse and Covenantal Hospitality

Expanding the Paradigm of Giving and Receiving in Cross-cultural Christian Mission

Susangeline Y. Patrick

Introduction

A KENYAN FRIEND OF MINE arrived in the U.S. to further her education in a doctoral program. In one of the social events she attended, a graduate student asked her if she had ever worn clothes before she landed in the U.S. Stunned by such unusual rudeness, my friend deliberately answered, "No, someone gave me clothes and shoes. It was the first time I have ever worn shoes. Wow! It felt so different." More shockingly, the person who asked her the question sincerely believed what she said. The graduate student might have suffered from ignorance about present-day Kenya or a general lack of cultural competencies. However, this kind of arrogance and sense of superiority often occurs in cross-cultural encounters, including ones that are supposed to be hospitable.

Christian church groups and mission organizations, for example, frequently overuse images of extreme poverty of the Majority World (or those nations in Asia, Africa, and Latin America) and frequently depict Majority World peoples as the voiceless recipients of American Christian assistance.[1] As a result, many Christian churches and mission organizations tend to perceive the Majority World as impoverished. For example, many

Americans have difficulty accepting the realities of China's ultramodern infrastructure or Nigeria's wealth. Because of such arrogance and sense of superiority, many Christians imagine themselves as givers in relation to these recipients who are less privileged. This chapter challenges these stereotypes and their harmful effects. I argue for the theories and practices of hospitality, especially as they apply to Christian missions—practices that acknowledge how marginalized peoples are also contributors and givers.

American Christianity needs to embrace a reverse and covenantal hospitality. My chapter unfolds in three sections. First, I tell the story of how the majority of American Christian missions embraced colonialism, how some resisted, and how the colonial problems that plagued the past haunt Christians today. Second, drawing on the examples of the early church and Scripture, I show how Christians can reimagine hospitality as having a reciprocal character and a fluidity between host and guest—a reverse hospitality. Third, I expand on the Scriptural and early Christian paradigms of hospitality to suggest a covenantal hospitality in which Christians can embrace interactions among God the Creator, humans, and the land. A paradigm of hospitality that gives specific considerations of the Creator God and the land can lead to mutual transformation, not only to human relationships but also to how Christians can live in *shalom* with creation.

Hospitality in Christian Mission

Hospitality in Christian mission must reject the attitude of condescending pity and embrace solidarity and partnership. I begin this section describing the formation of the attitude of condescending pity in the history of European missionaries' engagements with Native American tribes. Next, the response of Indigenous people's resistance, hospitality, and missionary work offers an alternative to oppression, as does the faithful examples of European solidarity with Indigenous peoples. Finally, this history remains with twenty-first century Christians in the form of neocolonialism and American cultural and economic dominance.

First, a lack of mutuality in mission emerges from a way of practicing hospitality in which the roles of host and guest are fixed and giving only is perceived to be moving in one direction. In North America, a lack of mutuality begins with the Spanish Catholic mission in the context of competing powers of Spain and Portugal in the late fifteenth century.

Spanish Catholic missionary work in America during the sixteenth and seventeenth centuries operated from the firm belief that God had granted them permission and providence to convert and subjugate Indigenous peoples. The 1513 document *Requerimiento* charted the method of such exploitation.[2] When Spanish conquistadors arrived on Indigenous lands, they would read the *Requerimiento* to Indigenous peoples. It demanded that Indigenous peoples recognize Spanish authority and willingly serve Spain. If the Indigenous peoples refused, the conquistadors could enslave them. Church historian Mark Noll remarks that, in the eighteenth century, early Franciscan missionary Junípero Serra in California held a common attitude among missionaries and treated Indigenous Christian converts "like small children."[3] These exploitative and paternalistic postures further aided Spanish missionaries' harsh treatments and strict disciplinary methods such as public flogging of Indigenous Christians in the American southwest. Spanish Catholics also portrayed the Indigenous people as lapsed Christians, possibly the lost tribe of Israel, and as converts who needed to adjust and assimilate to the European way of life, including its patriarchal family structures.[4] Matrilineal groups, such as the Puebloans, struggled under an enforced patrilineal system.

The stereotypical image of a male European missionary as the giver of hospitality also has historical roots in the Puritan settlers at the Massachusetts Bay Colony in the early seventeenth century. These early settlers in North America produced and circulated images of Indigenous peoples as helpless. In 1629, for example, the seal of the Massachusetts Bay Colony depicted a Native American "calling for missionaries with the words of Acts 16:9, 'Come over and help us.'"[5] The irony, of course, is the Puritans were refugees, escaping from governmental persecutions in Europe. Yet, they perceived themselves as superior and demonstrated a condescending pity toward Indigenous peoples. The Puritans' belief in divine providence did not aid them in taking up a posture of humility. Put differently, their missiological inclinations did not acknowledge the Indigenous people as the host of the land upon which the Puritans were guests.

Additionally, American foreign mission efforts in the nineteenth century and the first half of twentieth century revealed an attitude of cultural superiority that resembled the Massachusetts Bay Colony's. The memories of Native American, African American, and Asian American mission endeavors are often left out in mission histories. Furthermore, late nineteenth and early twentieth century mission tracts, reports, letters, and magic lantern slide shows depicted the perceived need for missionaries to save peoples in Africa, Asia, and the Americas from their physical and spiritual miseries. While these reports coupled real and imagined realities of the Majority World, they were "often sensationalized in an imbalanced or dehumanizing manner."[6] Mission historian Dana Robert explains the larger context in which such communication took place. "The spread of Christianity to Africa, Asia, and the Americas occurred within the colonial framework in which European peoples poured into other parts of the world."[7] Because colonial empires sought to civilize and subdue Indigenous peoples and their lands, governments and Christians worked together to make them more European and "civilized" through education, such as founding boarding schools for Indigenous children in the U.S., Canada, South Africa, and Australia. For example, the American government attempted to eradicate Indigenous cultures and languages through educational programs that forcibly removed Native American children from their homes and placed them in Christian and secular residential schools.[8] One of the many ill-effects was severe cultural loss for later generations of Indigenous tribes.

Second, despite these examples of missions that lacked mutuality and respect for Indigenous peoples, Indigenous Christians resisted cultural domination and discovered ways to survive. During the eighteenth century in California, the Chumash people embraced the Christianity of the Spanish Franciscans, but they also participated in acts of retribution, resisting hard treatment and sexual assaults from colonizers. For instance, in 1775 an alliance of Indigenous Chumash Christians and non-Christian Kumeyaays attempted to destroy the San Diego Mission. Later injustices further provoked the Chumash Christians to lead a resistance at mission Santa Inés and at missions at La Purísima and Santa Bárbara in 1824.[9] Their reaction to persecution reflects these Indigenous people's autonomy independent from the Spanish perception of them. The Indigenous revolutionaries were not the "small children" many Europeans imagined them to be. And missionaries were not capable hosts; rather, they were poor guests of the Indigenous people and their lands.

In addition to resisting domination, Indigenous Christians extended hospitality to European missionaries and worked to spread the Gospel in North America. But European settlers, such as the Puritans, received and sometimes abused Indigenous hospitality. Not only would the European settlers not have survived without the Indigenous people's provision, but

Indigenous Christians often took leadership positions. The Presbyterian Mohegan pastor Samson Occom, for example, co-founded significant Native American Christian settlements later known as "Brothertown Indians." Fluent in English, Latin, Greek, and Hebrew, Occom traveled to England to raise funds for the education of Indigenous youth, and he also wrote a collection of hymns and spiritual songs.[10] Moses Tunda Tatamy and many other Congregationalist Indigenous Christians acted as the backbone of the Indigenous church in New England. Indigenous communities sometimes bestowed generosity on missionaries through their linguistic capabilities to communicate in both English and Indigenous languages. One such example is Cockenoe, from the Massachusetts tribe, who became a teacher and translator to the famous Puritan missionary John Eliot. Cockenoe helped Eliot translate the Ten Commandments and the Lord's Prayer.[11] Contrary to the image of Europeans helping Native Americans, the Indigenous people often led their own initiatives and hosted settler Christians.

Indigenous Christians also made significant mission efforts outside of New England. In the early nineteenth century, Iroquois Catholic Ignace La Mousee spread Christianity to the Blackfeet tribe in Montana. As social ethicist and sociologist Howard Harrod documents, "Between 1812 and 1820 a band of Christian Iroquois under the leadership of La Mousse left Mission of Caughnawaga on the St. Lawrence River and migrated toward the Northwest" in hopes of spreading the Gospel.[12] In the early twentieth century, an Alaskan-born Christian named Tillie Paul created an alphabet for writing in the Tlinglit language, compiled a Tlinglit dictionary, and translated many hymns and prayers Tlinglit Christians still use today. Historian Edward E. Andrews documents how some Native Americans such as Good Peter, Deacon Thomas, and Black evangelists such as Philip Quaque, performed important pastoral work in their communities.[13] The resistance, hospitality, and agency of these Indigenous Christians demonstrate that the condescending pity many European Christians bestowed on them was, in fact, an unwarranted act of violence. However, not all European Christians acted this way.

Some missions and missionaries from Europe fought against imperialism, acted in solidarity with Indigenous peoples, and shared the Gospel in respectful ways. In the early sixteenth century, Dominican priests Bartolomé de Las Casas and Francisco de Vitoria advocated for Indigenous human rights.[14] Others followed Las Casas and de Vitoria's example. "In 1537," as Noll points out, "protests by two other Dominicans, Bernardino de Minaya and Julian Garces, led Pope Paul III to condemn atrocities perpetrated by Spanish conquistadors on the Indians and to declare that Native Americans were entitled to full respect as human beings."[15] The French Jesuit missions in North America during the sixteenth and seventeenth centuries established parishes that were free from government funding and military assistance. They lived among Indigenous communities and immersed themselves in Indigenous cultures. Jesuit missionary Jean de Brébeuf contextualized the Christian message into the Huron culture. The Ursulines and the Recollects were also active Catholic groups that immersed themselves in Indigenous languages and culture in seventeenth century North America. In the context of forced removal of Native Americans in the 1830s and 1840s, missionaries such as Samuel and Ann Worcester relocated with the Cherokees to the Dwight Presbyterian Mission in the "Indian Territory" in Oklahoma.[16] In the late nineteenth century, the Women's Indian Rights Association and Bishop Henry Benjamin Whipple's Indian Rights Association also sided with the Indigenous people and fervently fought against the colonial framework. These anecdotal examples reveal that Christian hospitality does not have to take the form of violence. It can and should take the form of solidarity and friendship with Indigenous peoples.

Recognizing Indigenous hospitality also meant the respectful engagement with Indigenous people's languages and cultures. In 1721, Hans and Gertrude Egede sailed from Norway to Greenland, and in 1723 Hans translated the Apostles' Creed, the Ten Commandments, and some short prayers into the Inuit language, "illustrating them by similes and parables, a mode of instruction which he [Hans] perceived to be particularly acceptable to the natives."[17] The contextualization of the Gospel into Indigenous cultures validates Indigenous cultures as legitimate, not as something evil to be eliminated or to be converted into European cultural forms.

Finally, while colonial exploitation is no longer the norm in the twenty-first century, vestiges of it remain in what missiologists Craig Ott, Stephen J. Strauss, and Timothy C. Tennent describe as "neocolonialism in the form of cultural and/or economic dominance."[18] In his seminal book, *Neo-Colonialism: The Last Stage of Imperialism*, former Ghanaian Prime Minister Kwame Nkrumah argues that "neocolonialism" occurs when large nation states, like the U.S., enact policies and practices in which "smaller states" become "incapable of independent development and must rely" upon the West.[19] Western modes of economic "development" in this context are, simply put, forms of "exploitation."[20] Additionally, philosopher Tsenay

Serequeberhan notes that many peoples of European descent perceive places like Africa as lacking cultural "maturity."[21] Such perceptions motivate the West to place many Majority World countries in a subordinate status.[22] In this neocolonial context, industrialized and modernized nation states use modernization and capitalism as a mode of dominance, expanding their economic and cultural influences throughout the rest of the world. While Christian confidence and influence should not be tied with economic and cultural dominance, many American Christians view and use economic and cultural dominance as their entry point to carry out missionary efforts.

Neocolonialism is evident in the many contemporary missionary efforts, which engage in unidirectional hospitality. Neocolonialism manifests in short-term missions when, for example, missionaries alone determine what programs they perform instead of what the local community needs or wants. Likewise, mission organizations often use stereotypical representations of the Majority World. For instance, teary-eyed African children are frequently the only faces of the poor used for fundraising. Other popular types of imagery feature a "selfie" of a short-term mission volunteer with a group of children, or a family receiving gifts from missionaries. Such images present the Majority World as having less dignity, ingenuity, or substantive role to play in Western missionary efforts. Hospitality is portrayed as a mode that only runs in one direction—from American Christians to people in the Majority World. While it does not look like the violent oppression of our colonial past, it still bears with it the same condescending pity that was present in some early missionary efforts to North America.

Only a few organizations highlight the idea of building community together. In the twenty-first century, some mission organizations rightly work to alleviate poverty, global hunger, diseases, human trafficking, and other pressing issues, but such work does not assume that the American Christian is the unidirectional distributer of hospitality. Calvin L. Troup states that Christians in the U.S. need to be more hospitable, and his impulse to make room for others is good and biblical. However, this understanding must work against a history and context in which Christians have imaginatively placed themselves in a fixed and unidirectional position of power and authority. It may unintentionally perpetuate the neocolonial idea that the social or religious "other" is in need of charity. Christians, therefore, need to reimagine their roles as host and guest as interchangeable depending on the context.

Humility and Hospitality

The Early Church and Scripture as Resources for Reverse Hospitality

To describe reverse hospitality, this section begins with the way the early Church thought about poverty. In the Greco-Roman world, the poor were not deserving of charity because high class peoples did not consider them as having humanity. Early Christians who lived under the Roman Empire reimagined the poor as being made in *imago Dei* (the image of God). Based on this early Christian perspective, contemporary Christians can reimagine poverty not as a mere deprivation of material resources but as a violation of one's humanity. Furthermore, the life and ministry of Jesus shows that he accepted hospitality from others and made a strong identification with those who are poor. Taken together, Christians today can embrace a reverse hospitality, a hospitality of mutuality, reciprocity, and fluidity.

Countercultural to the Greco-Roman notion of hospitality, early followers of the Jesus Way imagined that people who lived on the margins of society were both capable of giving and receiving charity. As historian Gary B. Ferngren explains, charity to those who were poor in the ancient world was largely unthinkable. In the Greco-Roman world, the upper-class and educated were the only people who possessed *humanitas* (humanity). Hospitality, therefore, was largely practiced among people of the same class and only as a means of securing future charity for themselves.[23] The only people elites gave charity to were rich people who lost their fortune. As such, charity was a safety net and always conditional, a way of securing others' charity if a disaster or misfortune struck the giver. Furthermore, the Romans perceived inequality to be natural, so the poor were not considered as important or deserving of access to resources. There was no reason to be good to those who were poor or to assume that the poor were *humanitas* in the way the elite were. Against this social background and grounded in the imago Dei, the early church offered an alternative image of those who are poor.[24] Ferngren states that the Cappadocian Fathers used the *imago Dei* to redefine the poor as people who bore the face of Christ, thus challenging the idea that only the rich and the powerful would share special relations with the Divine in the Roman world.[25] Likewise, Amma Sarah, the fifth-century Desert Mother in Egypt, taught that one could only begin to please God through giving alms to people who need healing and hospitality.[26] Thus, the loving nature of God compels a Christian to honor the poor, the socially oppressed, and the physically impaired. The elevated status of the poor is not theoretically seen as a lack to be filled by material goods. Rather, acts of dignity and honor uncover and reveal their hidden humanity.

This ancient Christian reimagining of poverty should shift our current understanding of poverty as a mere lack of materials to a violation of humanity, particularly connectedness, personhood, and *shalom*. Economists Steve Corbett and Brian Fikkert point out the differing perceptions between the poor and non-poor regarding the significance of poverty. Poor people typically discuss poverty "in terms of shame, inferiority, powerlessness, humiliation, fear, hopelessness, depression, social isolation, and voicelessness."[27] While poverty certainly includes material lack, Corbett and Fikkert encourage an enriched understanding of hospitality as the offer of honor, worth, hope, safety, and social and spiritual connectedness. As the reflections on neocolonialism above suggests, hospitality that centers solely on material distribution may not empower people. It often only serves to exacerbate the damaging effects of shame, inferiority, and powerlessness. As a result, hospitality should serve to invest those who are poor with social belonging. Urban Studies scholar Janice Perlman identifies such belonging with the term *gente*, or being somebody. In her ethnographic research in the *favelas* (slums) of Rio de Janeiro, Perlman discovered that not being *gente* was a major contributing factor in keeping people stuck in the vicious cycle of marginality.[28] Reimagining poverty should foreground the power of those who are poor to survive in unjust circumstances. Missiologist Bryant Myers suggests that poverty grows out of "relationships that lack shalom, that work against well-being, against life and life abundant."[29] In societies that lack God's *shalom*—or God's peace and justice—systemic injustice keeps those who are poor from living their fullest existence. Reimagining poverty can present those living in poverty not as victims but as survivors who display their agency in their continued fight against systemic limitations and obstacles.

In addition to reimagining poverty, Christians can reimagine hospitality through the life and ministry of Jesus, who demonstrated an ability to receive hospitality. The Incarnation took place in the Virgin Mary's womb. Mary, a young and ordinary woman, provided her own body as a hospitable space for God's body. When Herod murdered children under the age of two, Egypt proved to be a place of shelter and safety for the holy family. At the time of Jesus's three years of ministry, women provided Jesus financial support. These examples lead theologian Amos Yong to characterize Jesus as "the exemplary recipient of hospitality" as well as a proclaimer of the hospitality of God.[30] Yong argues that "the Christian condition of being aliens and strangers in this world means both that we are perpetually guests, first of God and then of others."[31] Yong implies that when Christians are involved in alleviating poverty, our hospitality must take on the fundamental understanding that we also rely on the hospitality of the poor.

If Christians can emulate Jesus's example and receive hospitality from the poor and the outcast, then those gifts might help us see more clearly both God's strong identification with the poor and their generosity. Matthew 25:45 states that whatever was done to the "least of these" was done to God. In this passage, Jesus claims that whatever happens to the marginalized happens to God personally. If American Christians understand that whatever happens to people on the margins happens to Jesus, it would be difficult to treat the marginalized as helpless. The strong identification of God with the marginalized encourages us to see the marginalized as people who possess life and eternity, who are generous and have many resources to offer.

Taking these reimaginings together, reverse hospitality embodies a two-fold dynamic of giving and receiving. Christian hospitality certainly encourages the virtue of becoming more welcoming, at least in the biblical idea of welcoming strangers as receiving angels or even God Himself.[32] At the same time, Christians need to cultivate the ability to be better guests when receiving hospitality from people in poverty. People who are perceived as the poor often are givers. They often host and accommodate long-term and short-term mission volunteers, sometimes to the point of great sacrifice. Missiologist Stanley Skreslet affirms such reversal: "By ceding control and sometimes relying on others to take the initiative, missionaries are enabled to receive hospitality as well as extend it in Christ's name."[33] New Testament scholar Andrew Arterbury also points out Luke's narration of the Gentile Cornelius offering hospitality to Peter. When Peter, a Jew, becomes a guest of the Gentile Cornelius, Luke communicated to his audience the need "both to extend and to receive hospitality as a means of spreading the gospel."[34] In embodying a two-fold dynamic to hospitality, Christian missions can leave behind images of poor people needing our help. Instead, they might produce images of volunteers receiving hospitality from their local hosts as gracious guests. Such images would also encourage Christians to learn valuable wisdom from those they meet as well as cultivate a true ability to be adaptable.

Through reverse hospitality, Christians can also embrace hospitality as having a reciprocal fluidity for host and guest. If God in Christ is a recipient of human hospitality, then all forms of hospitality likely demand interchangeability of both guest and host. As such, hospitality often requires reciprocal relations, not as mutual indebtedness that requires or expects the poor to give, but to empower through recognizing what the marginalized can and do contribute. Christian hospitality can perceive the poor as both host and the giver, and the rich as both guest and recipient. Reverse hospitality can then challenge and overturn the stigma of the poor's fixed status and shame. Church historian Amy Oden argues that "early Christians teach us that hospitality is more akin to compassion, to suffer with. The sense of solidarity with the stranger, the widow, the sick, in early Christian texts is palpable."[35] In such a reciprocal and fluid engagement between the giver and recipient, new opportunities can transform personal and social relations, which I will touch on more below.

Reverse hospitality does have limitations in terms of how hospitality is practiced in context. For example, a tourist passing a homeless person on the side of the street would differ from people who are trying to establish a long-term friendship with a relatively poor neighbor in the same community. To think of hospitality in a reversed way, the social context may not allow a homeless person to express hospitality to a passerby, or a poor neighbor to show generosity without being misinterpreted or being suspected as a stranger with hidden motives. Another challenge is that reverse hospitality requires vulnerability and risk on the parts of both host and guest. Navigating political obstacles, cultural barriers, and complex expectations is hard work. Reverse hospitality may not be able to address all the social, emotional, and spiritual sufferings of the poor. Despite these limitations, reverse hospitality calls us to see that we might receive just as much as we think we give. *Shalom*, the well-being of individuals and communities, might be just that—the recognition that we are both guest and host.

A Covenantal Hospitality

In this final section, I describe a hospitality beyond mutual giving and receiving between humans. A multidirectional paradigm of covenantal hospitality should include the land as God's gift to both guest and host, a gift which serves as the condition of all our giving and receiving. Such a model presses Christians to rethink the source of hospitality. Hospitality belongs to God the Creator, both in the eschatological sense of the Kingdom of Heaven and our more immediate present and future. Human interactions centered on giving and receiving are dependent on God's provision mediated through the land. Much of American Christianity encourages a disconnection with the land, as if human society could live without it. To the contrary, human existence relies on the environment, plants, and animals. Therefore, Christians receive the land as an ongoing gift from God the Creator. A hospitality of mutuality is not only dependent on this gift, but it also strives to contribute to the well-being of the land.[36]

Within the practice of giving and receiving upon the land God has given, hospitality invites both host and guest into a relational transformation, in the form of trust, friendship, and partnerships. If the errors of our past and neocolonial present have brought about wrong relations between many Indigenous peoples and settlers, mutual hospitality can build trust and foster healthy relationships between the givers and recipients. Minister Robert Lupton proposes, "If trust is essential for building relationships and making enterprises run effectively, then we have to find a way for outsiders (recipients) to become insiders (givers). Recipients must become dispensers, authors of the rules, builders of community."[37] Mutual friendship can also build up harmonious family structures, communities, and societies. Political scientist Robert Putnam notes that reciprocal society "is more efficient than a distrustful society.... Trustworthiness lubricates social life."[38] Mutual trust can be invaluable in the relationships between missionaries and a local community. Dana Robert uses Jesus and the woman at the well as an example of such transformation. Jesus's request for help from the Samaritan woman resulted in dialogue, and as a result, "The good news spread along a chain of relationships of knowing and being known."[39] Social scientists Deepa Narayan and Patti Petesch recommend local partnerships that can "build on the strength of local cultures to foster more inclusive development processes."[40] With the land being the gift from the ultimate Giver, both giver and recipient can find mutuality in being recipients and partners of the land. The thriving of the land thus provides the foundational gift for relational transformation and balances the unequal power dynamics between the giver and the recipient.

Covenantal hospitality also extends beyond anthropocentric limitations, such as human relations to the animal world. The creation stories in the Book of Genesis demonstrate a picture of what many Western Christians have called stewardship of creation, meaning that God had mandated human beings to care for the natural world. However, Scripture also hints at a reverse role between the human beings as the care giver and the animals as the care recipient. Examples of how God provided for human beings through animals are in both the Old Testament and the New Testament. One of the most significant examples is in 1 Kings 17:2–16, in which the ravens brought food to feed the Prophet Elijah. In Matthew 21:1–11, a seemingly insignificant colt provided Jesus the ride into Jerusalem. Beyond the animal world, even plants sometimes provided hospitality for human beings, such as the plant that grew and shaded the Prophet Jonah in Nineveh in Jonah 4:6. Hospitality is given and received in the context of the entire creation.

Covenantal hospitality can open up a creative way of engaging in short term missions. Here, I offer two examples. About 15 years ago, a small group of Christians traveled to a then isolated village in a Muslim-majority area of Central Asia. The people in the village hosted the group, me included. Children followed us around and adults chatted with us in friendly manners. More than that, an elderly couple even allowed the group to spend the night in their home. The next day, another family invited us for lunch. The young mother prepared the best of their delicacies. When we realized the food she gave us was all she had, we were caught in a dilemma of whether we should eat the food. After a brief discussion, we thanked her and ate the food because our act would honor her. To return her hospitality, we also offered her gifts we had previously prepared. Her gift of hospitality was far more precious, though.

Another moving story exemplifies the importance of being a gracious Christian recipient in an inter-religious context. When I was finishing my PhD, my mentor's wife, Kimi Silo, shared a story with me. When she and her family lived in India, she frequently purchased rice from a Hindu woman from an outcast background. Over a long period of time, they both established a friendship. When Kimi's family was leaving the region, her friend knitted a sweater for Kimi's son. The yarn was very costly, far beyond what the friend could afford. Kimi was moved to tears and treasured such sacrificial giving. In both examples, these Muslim and Hindu women are givers who provided precious gifts of substance and friendship. They honored and partnered with the land and channeled peace and kindness toward strangers and friends of different religions. Christians can learn from their example that uplifts the community and brings healing and peace in a multi-religious context.

People who have faced the struggles of poverty have much to teach Christians. For Christians who enter into a cross-cultural or inter-religious context, it is important first to listen and learn from the local people. Christians must learn from others' wealth of wisdom, stories, and perspectives. Becoming a gracious guest, recipient, and learner can enable American Christians to be better witnesses in our own social, political, and religious contexts.

The examples of mission trips that engage in covenantal hospitality demonstrate that churches can rethink their relationship to those who are both marginalized and local. The poor are not only in distant geographical locations. Sociologist Alvaro L. Nieves suggests that Christians should grasp the global picture but act locally: "Church groups (youth and adult) with good intentions often want to help poor people. They work hard to mobilize financial resources and coordinate travel and activities to distant places inside and outside their own country. . . . The world is at our doorstep, but we sometimes fail to realize the opportunities 'to act locally.'"[41] Engaging local communities close at hand can raise awareness of how to give and receive hospitality from the ones around us.

Conclusion

My chapter advocates a reverse and covenantal hospitality that expands the paradigm of hospitality in Christian mission. In dealing with poverty, Christians should promote virtues such as dignity, goodness, kindness, and reconciliation. Reverse and covenantal hospitality imply that Christian mission needs to portray the marginalized as equals, givers, teachers, and friends. Such hospitality honors people on the margins with intrinsic value and dignity, unites people across boundaries, and heals the brokenness of creation. Mission volunteers and organizations may learn to be better guests, to encourage and to be encouraged, to nurture and to be nurtured, to give and to receive hospitality, thus fulfilling the goodness and *shalom* of the reality of God and creation.

Chapter 5

On the Limits of Love

Entanglements with Colonialism in the Sixties Scoop and the Christian Reformed Church in North America (CRCNA)

NAAMAN WOOD[1]

Introduction

IN 1960, JULIA ALVAREZ'S FAMILY left the Dominican Republic for New York City, fleeing from the dictator Rafael Trujillo. Decades later, Alvarez published her novel *How the Garcia Girls Lost Their Accents* (1991). The book narrates a coming-of-age story about four sisters of immigrant parents who navigate between their Dominican heritage and mainstream American culture. When the novel became a success, Alvarez thought that she had finally made her "*mami* and *papi* really proud."[2] Instead, she discovered "they were terrified."[3] When Alvarez reflects on their reaction, she notes, "My parents were the products of a dictatorship, where you didn't put stuff out there publicly. You can get killed for it."[4] Her parents were not terrified of her success. Rather, they were terrified of public attention. Under the dictatorship of Trujillo, such attention often meant death. The novelist concludes, "You know, you can get rid of the dictator, but the dictator that survives in your head is there."[5] For Alvarez's parents, the old traumas of dictatorship transformed what should have been an outpouring of love into an outpouring of fear.

Julia Alvarez's story expresses an identical point Saint Augustine of

Hippo makes about the forces that limit virtue. In discussing the virtue of courage or fortitude, Saint Augustine criticizes an ancient author, Varro, and his claim that suicide can be a courageous act. Varro notes that "Pains and anguish of the body...are evils," so intense as to justify suicide.[6] In those cases, the one who suffers these evils displays courage when taking their own life. Saint Augustine rejects Varro's interpretation, saying, "There is a mighty force in these evils [i.e., the pains and anguish of the body] which make fortitude into homicide."[7] Saint Augustine's insight mirrors Alvarez's. There are circumstances and experiences that limit or distort the manner in which individuals can live a life of virtue. For Saint Augustine, physical suffering can distort what we take to be courage. For Alvarez, the internalization of dictatorship can distort what we take to be love.

Extending Alvarez's and Saint Augustine's insights, I suggest that colonialism constitutes a "mighty force" that limits the embodiment of virtue, and Christians must understand those limitations if we desire to make civility possible. My argument unfolds in three sections. First, in illustrating how colonialism can limit love, I discuss two colonial realities, the Sixties Scoop and the founding violence of North America. Second, I suggest that Christians can acknowledge and counter colonial limitations through two means: an understanding of our mutually constituted identity and the skill of offering multiple healing meanings to those who suffer. Finally, mutually constituted identities and multiple healing meanings provide a way to evaluate how one Christian household, the Christian Reformed Church in North America (CRCNA), grappled with its colonial entanglements and the limits those entanglements placed on its love. The denomination's 2016 denunciation of the Doctrine of Discovery report and synod deliberations serve as a case study. I conclude with two implications for Christians interested in creating the conditions necessary for civility.

The Sixties Scoop and Founding Violence

Before turning to a description of the Sixties Scoop, a bit of context regarding Residential Schools in Canada, the precursor to the Sixties Scoop, is in order. I then turn to a brief description of the Sixties Scoop, its language of salvation, and its negative effects on Indigenous children. The Scoop illustrates how colonial conditions can entangle virtue with vice, in this case love with violence. By way of concluding the section, I argue the Sixties

Scoop suggests that contemporary Christians need to reflect on how the founding violence of North America limits the virtues we embody. First, a note on Residential Schools.

Residential schools were state-funded, Church-run institutions that engaged in dehumanizing violence against Indigenous children. For both the church and the state, education served as a means of converting Indigenous peoples to Christianity, civilizing them from their so-called heathen ways, and assimilating them into the body politic. The government forcibly removed Indigenous children from their homes and placed them sometimes thousands of miles away. While some Residential School survivors report positive experiences, many experienced their Christian education as a systematic assault on their bodies and culture. As conservative Canadian Prime Minister Stephen Harper confessed, the schools aimed "to kill the Indian within the child."[8] Christians cut students' hair, forbade traditional practices, and stripped Indigenous students of their names.[9] Many survivors report that Christians strapped, humiliated, handcuffed, manacled, beat, neglected, locked away, and sexually assaulted students.[10] Furthermore, Indigenous children "died in these schools in numbers that would not have been tolerated in any school system."[11] Residential Schools opened in the early 1800s, and the last school closed in 1996. Due to funding issues, the government began widespread school closures in the post–World War II period.

In the wake of Residential School closings, the government continued to remove Indigenous children from their households in a period known as the Sixties Scoop, and non-Indigenous participants often justified their actions with the language of salvation. The Sixties Scoop was a "wide-scale national apprehension of Aboriginal children by welfare agencies" that began in the 1950s and extended well into the mid-1980s.[12] Child welfare agents regularly deemed Indigenous parents unfit, removed children from their homes, and placed them in non-Indigenous adoptive or foster families. Child welfare workers and foster/adoptive parents often understood their work as salvific. They aimed to "save them [Indigenous children] from the effects of crushing poverty, unsanitary health conditions, poor housing and malnutrition, which were facts of life on many reserves."[13] Non-Indigenous households, therefore, functioned as the "solution to the lifelong dilemma faced by minority group children whose parents [had] been defeated by life's circumstances."[14]

However, Indigenous children suffered, even in so-called loving non-Indigenous households. Like Residential Schools, many Indigenous children experienced inferior care, which included spiritual, emotional, physical, and sexual abuse. Some provinces sold children to households in the U.S., and many American families used Indigenous children for labor. For children who were placed in communities that cared for them, their non-Indigenous families did not receive the resources necessary to preserve a child's Indigenous culture. Many Sixties Scoop survivors experienced long-term psychological distress and "intense struggles as they tr[ied] to come to terms with their Indigenous identities."[15] Struggles resulted not only because children were "separated from family and communities," but also because many non-Indigenous adoptive parents held implicit or explicit racial bias against Indigenous peoples.[16] Many non-Indigenous parents believed that Indigenous culture did not exist or that it was inferior to white culture. Indigenous children often did not learn anything affirming about their language, culture, or ways of life[17] and were cut off from their "worldviews, cultural and ceremonial practices, language, and community connections."[18] As one Sixties Scoop survivor reported, the message she received was, "You're a beautiful Indian princess and yet your people are dirt." Many also internalized racism and self-hatred. As another survivor remembers, "[As a child I] felt very ashamed of who I was, who I am. I didn't really want to be First Nations."[20] For such survivors, households of so-called love were also places that performed dehumanizing violence.

The Sixties Scoop illustrates that the colonial conditions in which households exist complicate commonsense conceptions of love and violence. Sixties Scoop households reproduced the abuses of Residential School, and racial bias against Indigenous culture created long-term harm, all under the justification of salvation. When understood within the historical horizon of Residential Schools, the households of the Scoop reinscribed older racialized oppressions into new social contexts. They made possible a violent existence that white Canadians perceived as loving. If Residential Schools facilitated colonial violence through Christian education, then the Sixties Scoop facilitated the violence of colonialism through familial love.[21] Love is not a virtue that keeps people from perpetuating acts of violence.

The Sixties Scoop also establishes the need to take seriously the founding colonial violence that continues to structure Christian love, though that violence ultimately failed to achieve its end. Scholarly reflection on the Sixties Scoop regularly situates the Scoop as a symptom of the foundational colonial violence performed upon Indigenous peoples when settlers arrived in the so-called New World. Many white Christians might bristle at the suggestion that the U.S. and Canada are founded on violence, yet this analysis simply emulates Saint Augustine's. When Saint Augustine saw the Roman Empire committing acts of injustice, he linked such violence to the violence that founded Rome: Romulus's murder of his brother Remus. Romulus's fratricide is Rome's archetype of original sin. His violence animated the entire history of the Roman Republic until the downfall of the Empire. In fact, Saint Augustine rightfully claimed that "Rome never was a republic" because its founding violence made Rome nothing less than a thief.[22] Following Saint Augustine, Christians should interpret the violence of the Sixties Scoop as a natural consequence of the violence that founded North America: the genocide of Indigenous peoples and the seizure of their lands. It is important to note that colonial violence against Indigenous peoples, while ongoing and damaging, did not achieve its end. Indigenous peoples were neither eradicated nor assimilated into the body politic. Indigenous peoples have preserved their culture, languages, ways of life, and sovereignty as nations. However, Christians need to give an account of how our founding violence constrains our current embodiment of virtue. While a full account is beyond the scope of this chapter, two insights—the concept of mutually constituted identities and the practice of multiple meanings—prove helpful in grappling with our colonial entanglements.

Mutually Constituted Identities and Multiple Biblical Meanings

In this section, I first argue that the ability to understand the colonial conditions of North America can be developed through an awareness of our mutually constituted identities. Historically, Western identities are rooted in dichotomies of difference like civilized/savage, colonizer/colonized, or White/Black, which colonizers used to justify violence. Those dichotomies, however, were often lived out at the points of contact between those differences, or in mutually constituted identities. As a result, mutually constituted identities exist as large cultural forces and within the intimacies of lived life. Second, I suggest that, out of an awareness of these identities, Christians should develop an interpretive skill: offering multiple, healing meanings to those who suffer.

Dichotomies of difference develop throughout Western history, and the gap or distance between those dichotomies functioned as the justification for the ways European colonizers often mistreated others. With reference to the earliest Western colonial projects, Indigenous legal scholar Robert A. Williams Jr. points out that Homer embraced the difference between the civilized and the savage as a justification for Greek identity.[23] In a similar register, German philosopher Georg Hegel argued that Western identity functions inside a double dichotomy. The individual Self comes to self-understanding only through violent contact with an Other. He went on to describe the Self as a Master to the Other's existence as a Slave.[24] Scholars from a wide variety of disciplines have noted how Europeans expended dichotomies and mapped themselves and Indigenous peoples on to them. Such dichotomies included but are not limited to the following: metropole/colony,[25] White/Black,[26] beautiful/ugly,[27] rational/savage,[28] civilized/uncivilized,[29] Christian/pagan,[30] and colonizer/colonized,[31] among others. European settlers justified colonizing behavior based on the gap or distance between the two elements of the dichotomy. To the extent white Europeans who settled North America understood themselves to be, for example, good, civilized Christians, they could justify the use of violence to civilize, Christianize, or save non-European peoples. And such dichotomies persist past the colonial moment. In Canada, it was, perhaps, the self-perception of white Canadians as "saviors" that blinded them to the violence they performed in Sixties Scoop households.

However powerful these dichotomies of difference were to the processes of colonialization, the identities of colonizer/colonized were often mutually constituted, albeit in asymmetrical or unequal power relationships. Throughout colonial history, Europeans often fretted over relations between colonizers and colonized peoples, between European settlers and Indigenous peoples, for example. Many such intimacies, however, took place in spaces like the household. In grappling with the children that resulted from the sexual intimacies of colonizer and colonized, settlers invented words like *Métis* (French and Indigenous), *mestizo* (Spanish and Indigenous), and *mulatto* (White and Black). Terms like *patois, pidgin, creole,* or *Black Vernacular English* marked the intimacy that emerged as colonizer and colonized encountered one another through language. Similarly, the colonial household was often a place where colonized peoples raised colonizer children. For example, in the Dutch colonies of Indonesia, Javanese women raised many Dutch children.[32] Similar arrangement occurred throughout French colonies in Africa and throughout the American

South. The households of the Sixties Scoops functioned as an inversion of these kinds of household arrangements. The reality of mixed identities, marriages, languages, or households did not eliminate the imbalances of power or diminish the injustices that colonized peoples experienced. However, mutually constituted identities complicate dichotomies of difference. A human and a household could be both colonizer and colonized, Black and White, Indigenous and settler, albeit in asymmetrical ways and asymmetrical power relationships.

Mutually constituted identities also occur as large-scale social forces such as nation building and impact everyday life. In reflecting on English colonizers and their colonized Jamaican counterparts, colonial historian Catharine Hall argues, "We can understand the nation," England, "by only defining what it is not," Jamaica. The "identity" of a nation state, she concludes, "depends on the outside," on an asymmetrical but mutually constitutive relationship with those Other peoples.[33] "Europe," she summarizes, "was only Europe because of that other world: Jamaica was one domain that constituted the outside of England."[34] Given these nation-to-nation relations, Hall also encourages historians to describe how these large social forces work within the everyday lives of ordinary peoples.[35] Black intellectual James Baldwin implicitly notes how such large social forces impacted his interpersonal interactions. Upon visiting a small Swiss village that had never seen a Black person before, Baldwin recounts how people responded to the existence of his hair and skin. Villagers suggested that if he grew his hair long, he might make himself a winter coat. If he sat in public for longer than five minutes, people would touch his hair or his hand expecting an electric shock or expecting his color to rub off. As Baldwin observes, "there was certainly no element of intentional unkindness" in these interpersonal interactions; however, there was "no suggestion that I was human."[36] From these interactions, Baldwin sees the large-scale dehumanization Europeans—imposed on Africans and African Americans—appearing in the innocent wonder of the Swiss villagers. "People are trapped in history," Baldwin concludes, "and history is trapped in them."[37] Within the households of the Sixties Scoop, similar events occurred. White parents incarnated the large-scale violence of colonization inside the love and safety they provided. The intimacies of everyday life inside a Sixties Scoop household reflected, embodied, and incarnated the global power imbalances that made the colonial project a reality. Large social forces manifest themselves within the intimacies of belonging, relationships, and virtue.

Within a shared colonial legacy, mutually constituted identities provide contemporary Christians a language to name the embodied conditions that entangle virtues with vices. The Sixties Scoop demonstrates that White Canadians failed to recognize the "mighty forces" of colonialism and racial bias. Those forces placed the vice of violence in a mutually constitutive relationship to the virtue of love. Simple awareness of colonialism or racial bias is not sufficient to disentangle contemporary Christians from our colonial legacies. Awareness is, however, an important and essential first step, a first step that can be coordinated with the practice of developing multiple interpretations from Scripture aimed to heal those who suffer.

In developing the skill of multiple interpretations, theologian Cynthia Crysdale focuses on the experience of those who suffer as they approach biblical stories, and she begins with her personal participation in group therapy. The group was made up of "highly talented, articulate, well-educated, middle- and upper-middle class women," who all faced serious life problems: "a handicapped child, a child who had died, a husband who turned out to be gay, childhood sexual abuse, the biochemistry of manic depression or clinical depression, an ex-husband who refused to let old battles die."[38] As many of the women came to terms with their suffering, they discovered that their healing demanded an embrace of a "good grief."[39] Such "good grief," they found, brought "relief rather than agony."[40] However, Crysdale notes how some well-meaning individuals outside the group had misused biblical stories, like Jesus's crucifixion, to harm these women. Many had been told implicitly and explicitly that just as Jesus suffered, they should live with their suffering, perhaps as a holy vocation. The women in Crysdale's group did not experience this version of the Gospel as good news. They experienced it as a "tool of infinite and indescribable pain."[41] For these women, the crucifixion must mean something else besides the misused meaning they encountered.

By way of example, Crysdale offers an additional interpretation of Jesus's story, which aims to heal those who suffer. Traditionally, Jesus's crucifixion and resurrection have been interpreted as having the primary meaning of forgiveness of sins. In the story of the crucifixion, we sinners enter the story as those who crucify or betray Jesus. Although contemporary Christians may not have been there at the crucifixion to nail Jesus to the cross (like the Roman soldiers) or deny him three times (like Peter), our sin enables us to take up their place metaphorically.[42] Crysdale wants to hold on to this reading of redemption, but she sees its pastoral limitations in the lives of those who suffer. "The wounded victims of the world," Crysdale argues, tend not to enter the story of Jesus's crucifixion as crucifiers or traitors; rather, they enter the story as "victims who have been slain."[43] For these victims, Jesus "becomes an ally and friend; God the Father becomes a grieving parent; and the Risen Lord signifies healing."[44] For the sinner who crucifies Jesus, God offers forgiveness. For the suffering victim, God is present to them, hears their voice, and enacts healing and justice.

Multiple meanings, however, need not stop at two; rather, the Christian tradition affirms with Crysdale that many meanings need to proliferate within a Christian community to meet various individuals in their various experiences. By way of example, the Lukan parable of the landowner has been read in various ways throughout church history.[45] In the parable, a landowner causes controversy when he pays each worker the same no matter how many hours the worker worked. Catholic theologian Saint Thomas Aquinas focuses on two different situations. First, when applied to an individual near death, Aquinas uses the parable to encourage conversion to Christianity.[46] Whether one serves God for years or a moment, the reward of salvation is the same. When applied to Jews and Gentiles, Aquinas argues that God shows no favoritism and offers salvation to both peoples.[47] In the fourteenth-century text *Pearl* the anonymous author uses the parable to comfort parents whose child has died at an early age. The child who has worked only one hour still receives God's full mercy.[48] The fifteenth-century Catholic theologian John of Goch interprets the parable to reject the idea that God rewards Christians according to their good works.[49] The same salvation is given to the Christian who does many or few good works. Finally, for Protestant theologian Martin Luther, the parable celebrates that God's goodness trumps our attempts to abide by the law.[50] Each of these examples illustrates and confirms Crysdale's insight. Multiple interpretive readings are necessary to speak words of healing to various people in their various circumstances.

An awareness of mutually constituted identities combined with the offering of multiple meanings can provide Christians with a means for self-criticism and cultural engagement necessary to reimagine the embodiment of virtues like love. The Christian Reformed Church in North America's (CRCNA) denunciation of the Doctrine of Discovery serves as a case study, illustrating how a household of faith can embody love both well and poorly.

The CRCNA's Denunciation of the Doctrine of Discovery

Before I turn to an evaluation of the denunciation, it is important to note that within Dutch Reformed discussion about colonialism and Christianity, the Doctrine of Discovery plays a large role in the Canadian context. Therefore, when the CRCNA denounced the Doctrine of Discovery, it did so in response to Canada's political context and within a legal understanding of the Doctrine's significance. The CRCNA's point of contact with the Doctrine is its Rehoboth Christian School, a Residential School that traumatized both White and Indigenous peoples. Within both Canada's history of colonization and the CRCNA's own Residential School, the substance of its denunciation of the Doctrine takes the form of two statements from the synod proceedings. I use the language of mutually constituted identities and multiple healing meanings to evaluate the strengths and shortcomings of the denunciation, particularly as it relates to the embodied love, spiritual common sense, trauma, and alternative meanings concerning the school.

The CRCNA's denunciation of the Doctrine of Discovery occurs in response to the legal manner through which Canada dealt with the legacy of Residential Schools. After the closure of the final Residential School, residential school survivors began to file lawsuits against the federal government. By 2005, there were over 18,000 cases, including several class-action lawsuits. While most lower courts rejected the rights of Residential School survivors to pursue their claims, in 2004 one Ontario Court of Appeals allowed one case, known as the "Cloud case," to proceed to the Supreme Court. The federal government settled the case out of court within a few short months. As part of the settlement agreement, the Canadian government had to provide funds for a Truth and Reconciliation Commission of Canada (TRC), and the government had to officially apologize to Residential School survivors. It is important to underscore that the formation of the TRC and the decision to apologize were not a result of Canadian goodwill. The Canadian government believed it was in their best interest to fund the TRC and apologize rather than have the realities of Residential Schools become publicized in a trial. The TRC began in 2008 and closed its work in 2015. The Commission published a multivolume report, which included 94 Calls-to-Action, all of which the federal government committed to implementing that same year. Relevant to the CRCNA's proceedings is Call-to-Action #49, which reads, "We call upon all religious denominations and faith groups who have not already done so to repudiate concepts used to justify European sovereignty over Indigenous lands and peoples, such as the Doctrine of Discovery."[51] The CRCNA formed a Doctrine of Discovery Task Force, which created a report titled "Creating a New Family: A Circle of Conversation on the Doctrine of Christian Discovery." The report and the denomination's deliberation constitute the CRCNA's response to Call-to-Action #49.

The report describes the Doctrine of Discovery as a series of three papal edicts issued in the late 1400s, which defined the relationship between European Empires and Indigenous peoples and continues to serve as contemporary legal precedent.[52] The CRCNA begins its description of the Doctrine of Discovery in 1452. That year, Pope Nicolas V issued a papal bull titled *Dum Diversas*. Addressed to King Alfonso V of Portugal, Pope Nicolas authorized Portugal "to invade, search out, capture, vanquish, and subdue all Saracens [or Muslims] and pagans."[53] Furthermore, Nicolas authorized Alfonso to take possession of "all movable and immovable goods whatsoever held and possessed by them and to reduce their persons to perpetual slavery."[54] In 1455, Pope Nicolas issued *Romanus Pontifex* as an affirmation of *Dum Diversas*, and it extended and specified King Alfonso's dominion. In 1493, Pope Alexander VI articulated how empires would negotiate with each other over lands they encountered through colonization. In *Inter Caetera*, Alexander claimed that one Christian nation could not take from another Christian nation lands the other had colonized. Taken together, the edicts provided a Doctrine of Discovery, whereby the Church sanctioned the founding violence that enabled colonizers to establish European sovereignty over Indigenous peoples and their lands. In isolated instances, some European Christians recognized the sovereignty and humanity of Indigenous peoples and lands. However, the spirit of the Doctrine of Discovery not only defined centuries of colonial expansion, it also became part of North American legal precedent. Between 1823 and 1832, Justice John Marshall's U.S. Supreme Court issued three decisions that used the Doctrine of Discovery as justification to dispossess Indigenous peoples of land.[55] As recently as 2005, Justice Ruth Bader Ginsburg echoed Marshall's language, refusing to recognize the Oneida Indian Nation's claims to land in New York State.[56]

For the CRCNA, its point of contact with the Doctrine of Discovery comes in its Residential School, the Rehoboth Christian School. The report notes that in most of North America, Residential Schools have closed or even been torn down. However, the CRCNA's Rehoboth Christian School is still open, still educating Indigenous children, "still financially and spiritually supported by many Christian Reformed churches."[57] Even though the school is still open and supported, it no longer boards children; it also no longer prohibits the speaking of Navajo or Zuni languages. The jail that once stood on the property has been torn down. And CRCNA leaders and school administrators have issued apologies. However, the report claims that "reconciliation must flow out of a sincere and rigorous search for truth," and the CRCNA has not performed a search for the truth.[58] "Hearings have not been conducted, and the search for truth has not been completed because not all people have felt safe to share their stories. The extent of the trespasses and their effects have not been fully revealed, acknowledged, or confessed."[59]

Given how the Doctrine of Discovery manifests itself at Rehoboth, the CRCNA denounced the Doctrine of Discovery as a heresy. Six separate recommendations comprise the denunciation, but the second and third recommendations comprise its most important content. The second statement reads, "That synod acknowledges that the existing Doctrine of Discovery is a false doctrine and we reject and condemn it. It helped shape Western culture and led to great injustices."[60] The third part reads, "That synod recognizes the gospel motivation in response to the Great Commission, as well as the love and grace extended over many years by the missionaries sent out by the CRCNA to the Indigenous peoples of Canada and the U.S. For this we give God thanks, and honor their dedication."[61] A year after the TRC issued Call-to-Action #49, these two recommendations represent the primary substance of the CRCNA's response. Mutually constituted identity offers a way to identify the strengths and the shortcomings of the CRCNA's response, most importantly how the Doctrine of Discovery limited the CRCNA's embodied love.

By way of strength, the report and deliberations imply at least two mutually constituted identities, the first of which is an orthodox/heretical identity. In connecting the Doctrine of Discovery to the CRCNA's Residential School, the denomination implies that, as an ecclesial organization, it bears a mutually constituted identity of an orthodox Christian community and that of a community that has been shaped and formed inside of heresy. The Doctrine of Discovery is a heresy for at least two reasons. First, the Doctrine produces injustice rather than *shalom*, or the wholeness and peace, that Reformed Christians claim that God intends for the world.[62] Second, while the report never uses the word "heresy," it implies that Rehoboth became a site for heretical work because it denied that authority of Scripture. As the apostle Paul says, the Church is a body "made up of many parts; and though all its parts are many, they form one body. . . . So it is with Christ."[63] In performing violence on Indigenous Christian bodies, it performed violence upon Jesus and upon itself. At Rehoboth, the CRCNA denied "Paul's imagery of the 'whole body, many parts' working in harmony and unity."[64] Rather, it engaged in a "power struggle of a dominant culture" which "lord[ed] it[self] over a perceived lesser/weaker, subhuman people."[65] In participating in the Doctrine of Discovery, the CRCNA refused biblical authority and participated in colonial injustices. As such, the CRCNA occupies an orthodox/heretical Christian identity.

The report claims that the effects of trauma remain visible in the lives of both Indigenous survivors and the Christians who perpetuated the trauma. Like the trauma of Canadian Residential Schools, Rehoboth denigrated Indigenous cultures and peoples. Survivors of the school share many of the same effects of trauma that are evident in the wider survivor community, including "deficiency in parenting skills," "depression and self-hatred," and the "lack of opportunity to contextualize worship."[66] But trauma also extends to those Christians who supported the work of Rehoboth. The insights of Indigenous pastor and activist Mark Charles—who has a Dutch mother, graduated from Rehoboth, participated in the deliberation, served on the task force, and helped craft the report—are crucial here. As far back as the ancient Greek philosopher Plato, the idea of perpetuator trauma describes the reality that when one group of people inflicts a trauma on another, the perpetuator is traumatized in the process. This is the source of a mixed traumatizer/traumatized identity, which Christians experienced at the site of their faith. The report rightfully claims that trauma occurred because "well-intentioned people . . . thought they were following God, but in fact . . . actively participat[ed] in an unjust and racist system" which "commit[ed] cultural genocide against a group of people believed to be inferior and even subhuman."[67] Because of Rehoboth, supporters of the school carry with them the identity of a traumatizer/traumatized Christian.

As a way of coping with the traumatizer/traumatized identity, traumatizers often deny the trauma they caused. For example, the report notes that CRCNA members often minimize the harm the school caused with the word *but*. "Yes, Rehoboth was a boarding school, *but*... Yes, students were punished for speaking their languages, *but*... Yes, children were taken from their homes, *but*..."[68] Charles also suggests the third part of the denunciation, which emphasized the "gospel motivation" and the "love" of those who worked at the school, is evidence of denial. He claims, "You can't reject and condemn the Doctrine of Discovery and label it as heresy and then deny that you were involved."[69] The third part of the denunciation overemphasizes the love embodied at the school and minimizes (or denies) the violence it performed. Such rhetoric, unfortunately, is an incredibly effective strategy because it supports the false common-sense belief that virtues like love can protect Christians from performing acts of violence.

Denial was also present in the comments of a synod delegate, who demonstrates what this false spiritual common sense looks like. During the deliberation, a gentleman identified as Tim resisted the implication that two people in his family who participated in the Rehoboth project could also be heretics and traumatizers. Tim names his great-uncle, who helped build the school, and his uncle, who spent nine years teaching there. Tim insisted that his uncle went to Rehoboth "because he heard God's call in his life. He didn't go there because of a Doctrine of Discovery or because he devalued some other people . . . he loved the Navajo people . . . and he cared deeply for those people he taught and served . . . and it can't just be ignored, because there were mistakes that were made."[70] Tim nullifies the possibility that everyday lived experiences—like love and God's call—could be formed inside larger historical and cultural forces that Tim's family experienced as spiritual common sense. The shift to the passive voice signals the content of spiritual common sense: the uncle's call and love mean that he was not one of the those who made mistakes. As Hall's work demonstrates, the large-scale social forces that make colonialism possible exist in the everyday life of people. Here, the entanglement of church and empire has defined Western civilization so profoundly that the heresy is not only treated as legal common sense but also Tim's spiritual common sense. What the report implies and what the Sixties Scoop demonstrates is that colonial conditions can entangle love (e.g., the loving, Gospel proclamation: "Jesus is Lord") with violence (e.g., "Stop speaking Navajo"). Similarly, the common sense that Tim's great-uncle likely experienced hid the reality that the love of construction work provided an infrastructure for violence. Buildings helped create the physical conditions upon which cultural violence could be performed upon Indigenous bodies, hearts, and minds. Nevertheless, these serve as evidence of a traumatizer/traumatized Christian identity.

Finally, the CRCNA also failed to fully listen to those who suffered and failed to provide multiple healing interpretations of the school's past and future. Charles recounts that the report originally included two stories of survivors, one from a Bureau of Indian Affairs boarding school and another from Rehoboth. "When our report got to the board of trustees [of the CRCNA], before it was released, they pulled the story of the Rehoboth boarding school survivor. It did not go forward with the full report."[71] He also notes that, during the deliberation, the synod spent a "twenty-minute sharing time about how great our boarding school was and the blessings that came out of it."[72] Taken together, the denial, the third part of the denunciation, and the sharing time refuse precisely what Crysdale claims is needed for those who suffer, for survivors of Rehoboth. True love for everyone within the denomination, especially those who suffered at the school, demands that the truth of violence be confessed and known. Tim's use of the passive voice—"mistakes were made"—could be reformed as "we were the ones who made mistakes." Because the CRCNA refuses to listen to the truth of its stories, the denomination cannot utter words of healing to survivors. In refusing to listen, the denomination cannot offer alternative interpretations about the significance of the school, an interpretation that a survivor might experience as a life-giving, Christian love.

Conclusion

As Alvarez, Augustine, the Sixties Scoop, and the CRCNA all demonstrate, the life of Christian households, be they families or institutions, exists within the conditions that limit our embodiments of love. Those conditions, as Augustine knew well, are a "mighty force" and have the power to entangle virtue with vice. I suggest that colonialism is one of those conditions our Christian households must grapple with more deeply if we desire anything like true civility in the public square, the true taking on of virtues like humility or love, or the true inhabitation of practices like hospitality. What that grappling means for households is an open question. However, Alvarez's parents, the Sixties Scoop, and the Rehoboth School all demand of us a willingness to rethink our history, a willingness to confess our identities as more complex and troubling than we might like to imagine, and a willingness to listen to those who suffer and offer new, fresh interpretations that aim to heal rather than harm. If these distorting colonial conditions traffic as common sense, then perhaps our current experience of common sense is part of that network of conditions that make civility so difficult to achieve. By way of conclusion, I offer two key implications for Christian civility.

First, White Christians need to understand our colonial history more deeply, especially as it impacts Black, Indigenous, and other people of color. On this topic, George Erasmus of the Indigenous Dene Nation urges us to take seriously the words of Reformed ethicist H. Richard Niebuhr: "Where common memory is lacking, where men [and women] do not share in the same past there can be no real community, and where community is to be formed common memory must be created."[73] For Niebuhr, Jesus's suffering and death is the center of all human history. He insists that the particularity of Jesus's experience offers the truest understanding of our current human history. "Jesus Christ is not only the Jew who suffered for the sins of Jews and so for our own sins; he is also the member of the Roman World-community through whom the Roman past is made our own. The history of empire through which his life and death must be understood is the history of our empire."[74] Here Niebuhr holds together what so many Christians pull apart: our individual sins are connected to the corporate sins of empire. In the same way that the Roman Empire destroyed Jesus's life, Erasmus wants us to see, as Niebuhr sees, that Jesus's death is at stake in all empires everywhere, including our American and Canadian Empires. If White Christians want to be in community with Christians of color, our memory and history can only be hospitable and loving if we take seriously the pain, hurt, and trauma settlers performed on bodies of color. That history, as Baldwin rightly claims, is not locked away in the past; rather that history is within us. White Christians can embrace the reality that God wants to forgive us of empire as much as any other sin we commit.

Second, a shared memory means that if White Christians want to be hospitable to those whom colonialism has wounded, we must engage in sustained, critical understanding of our mutual identities to utter multiple healing meanings. Colonial history demonstrates that neither virtue (like love or humility), spiritual practice (like hospitality), nor spiritual experience (like God's call) can save us from our sins any more than it did those who came before us. As the CRCNA implies, Christians have been historically shaped by both orthodoxy and heresy, both by traumatizing others and being traumatized. Christians should work to understand how colonial sins make ill use of our virtues and spiritual experiences. Such work is difficult and dangerous. But if we truly want to live in community with Christians of color, a critical understanding of our mutual identities is an integral portion of that hospitality. It is only with that recognition that we can offer readings of Scripture and history that include those whom colonialism has wounded.

The good news for all of us, as the prophet Isaiah reminds us, is that God's common sense is not our common sense any more than God's thoughts are our thoughts.[75] And perhaps more importantly, what seems impossible for us is possible with God.[76]

Chapter 6

There Is No Civility without the Recognition of Power

How Perceived Persecution, Hostility, and Unilateral Conditions Impact Christian Calls for Civility

JAIME HARRIS

Introduction

AS I CONSIDER THE IMPLICATIONS of Calvin L. Troup's call to civility and hospitality, I think back to one moment in 2001 when the Church displayed its incivility toward me. The large Southern Baptist Church of my hometown had a tradition of hosting its own high school baccalaureate ceremony. The ceremony included a sermon tailored specifically for soon-to-be graduates. The guest speaker that year was a visiting minister of a larger congregation elsewhere in the state. The speech carried on, like so many others, about God's loving plan for each of us, until this minister specifically addressed those of us going off to "those big colleges." He launched into a list of people with whom God did not want us to associate: atheists, Muslims, and homosexuals. We were told that we must avoid "those people." The Devil would use them to tempt us and lead us away from Christ. I found the speaker's warnings jarring, especially the very specific categories of these so-called doom-bringers. Sinners were never really enumerated in my church upbringing. I felt distressed by the nods and smiles of unambiguous agreement and applause from my friends, their friends and family, the local ministry—seemingly everyone in attendance. His words and the audience's reaction created a feeling of isolation that was overwhelming, and I felt immediately compelled to conceal my response. That sense of otherness and being unwelcome felt permanent and inevitable. It was also not entirely unexpected. The specificity of who those "others" were shed light on the reality that "us" is a carefully constructed and exclusive club. The membership requirements had been laid out, and in that moment, I realized how many people were categorically disqualified from a group that claims universal love as its central tenet.

I was, and still am, a Black man living in the Southern U.S. I did not live in a predominately Black city or neighborhood. I did not attend a predominately Black school. My hometown was mostly Latinx and White. In fact, there were very few Black people in my life, other than my family. I learned very early that I had to accomplish more than anyone else—mostly White and Latinx peers—to make people—mostly White and Latinx adults—get over their anti-Black prejudice towards me. The racial realities of life within the Christian and secular communities were always present but never discussed in polite (read: racially mixed) company. To overcome a lot of this, I did what many marginalized people do. I made a concerted effort to achieve beyond the obstacles and perceptions imposed upon me by my ascribed status. Sociologist and civil rights advocate W. E. B. Du Bois labels the phenomenon in which Black people must develop a self-identity while being aware of and contending with the hostile perceptions of a powerful outside (White) society as the "double consciousness."[1]

My attempt at building my Black self-identity was to rack up accomplishments and accolades, but those accomplishments were not considered that night at the baccalaureate service. I was a mostly "A" student, the drum major of the marching band, and a recipient of numerous academic awards. I volunteered at charity events and had just been voted "Best Personality" by my peers and "Favorite Senior Boy" by the teachers. While all of this was happening, I was also becoming aware of sex, sexuality, and my own sexual identity. I was not certain I was gay, but I knew I probably was. I also knew what being gay would mean to my hard-earned status as "one of the good ones." Therefore, defying these racial and sexual expectations was a major part of my identity formation. I did not see myself in any way as evil or even problematic. But that night, at that baccalaureate, my achievements did not and would not prevent me from being vilified as one of "those people" worthy of omission from their future—all in the name of God. Christians had just demonstrated a sentiment that inspired in me more dread and fear than any threat of eternal Hell ever had. And they did it with smiles on their faces.

In this chapter, I will discuss three problematic features of our social context, problems that have to be dealt with in order for civility to take place. First, while societal changes motivate many Christians to perceive themselves as being a persecuted minority, sociological evidence complicates these claims, claims that inhibit the possibility for Christians to behave in civil ways. Second, sociological studies of religion also demonstrate that Christian hostility (or incivility) with out-groups benefits Christian groups, primarily through group cohesion and participation. With such benefits, civility with outsiders proves detrimental to evangelical self-understanding. Third, both conservative and liberal accounts of civility impose unilateral conditions on civil dialogue. To the extent that Christians impose these unilateral conditions on LGBTQ+ individuals, they cause significant and ongoing harm. As an antidote to these problems, I conclude the chapter with a reflection on Martin Luther King Jr.'s conception of love and justice.

Christian Persecution Complex

Troup's call to hospitality, while profoundly laudable, takes place against an important and generally unacknowledged social context: White evangelical Christians perceive themselves to be a beleaguered minority when, in fact, they possess significant power, resources, and privilege. I begin this section identifying some reasons why Christians perceive themselves in this way. First, recent demographic changes confirm that the U.S. is becoming a less religious, and therefore, a less Christian society.[2] In addition, widespread secularization has increased throughout the West as well as violence against Christians worldwide. These realities have encouraged Christians to perceive themselves as a persecuted minority, as the example of the so-called War on Christmas illustrates. But sociological evidence complicates this perception. Research not only fails to register significant increases in antipathy toward Christians, but Christians also have access to considerable resources and representation. I conclude this section with three negative implications the Christian misperception of persecution has on the possibility of civility.

Feelings among Christians of isolation and waning power are, first, a result of demographic changes and the perceived significance of those changes in the religious landscape. For example, the growth of the segment of the population identifying as religiously unaffiliated—religious "nones"—has steadily increased to nearly one in five Americans.[3] Non-Christian faiths have also experienced an increase, now making up approximately 6 percent of the population.[4] Meanwhile, the Christian share of the population has declined from 91 percent in 1948 to 77 percent in 2009[5] to 65 percent in 2019.[6] As a result of the decline of Christians in the total population and the increase of other faith and non-religious peoples, it is not surprising that 51 percent of Americans perceive Christianity's influence on American life is decreasing.[7] That number is higher among evangelicals. For example, recent studies reveal that 67 percent of White evangelical Protestants believe Christianity's influence is waning.[8] Shifts regarding the perception religious people have of themselves reveal the impact of these changes. While 24 percent of all Americans understand themselves as a minority group because of their religious beliefs, 32 percent of White evangelical Protestants do.[9]

The decline of Christianity in the U.S. also coincides with shifts in authority, perceptions of secularization, and violence against some Christians, all of which yield for some Christians a feeling of a world that is hostile to them. For sociologists of religion, the data is well documented. "In most parts of the West," summarizes sociologist Philip S. Gorski, "Christian belief and practice have declined significantly, at least since World War Two, and probably for much longer."[10] Sociologist Mark Chaves has claimed this decline has less to do with "the decline of religion" and more to do with "the declining scope of religious authority."[11] As a result, many see social changes such as rulings allowing same-sex marriage, limiting prayer in public forums, and increased focus on multicultural sensitivity as evidence of secularization.[12] Furthermore, technological advancements and the rise of online religious expression, community, and resources have encouraged a renegotiation of religious authority more broadly.[13] And, in a global context, Christians have been harassed and persecuted in significant ways. In fact, cases of discrimination against Christian people and property have been documented and reported in more countries around the world than any other group.[14] It is not unreasonable or unexpected that Christians perceive these changes as indicative of hostility.

In partial response to these changes in society and instances of persecution worldwide, many American Christians exhibit a persecution complex, and the example of the War on Christmas serves as an important example. In recent years, one key author to name and describe this persecution complex is church historian Candida R. Moss.[15] She cites a plethora of examples, including David Limbaugh's book *Persecution: How Liberals Are Waging War against Christianity*;[16] a Democracy Corps focus group, which confirms that conservatives view themselves as a "maligned minority;"[17] and the words of former presidential candidate Newt Gingrich: "[T]here has been an increasingly aggressive war against religion and in particular against Christianity."[18] Studies on attitudes of Americans support the idea that powerful groups single out and target Christians unfavorably.[19] Much of the rhetoric of persecution circulates around culture war issues, like the so-called War on Christmas. Franklin Graham, the son of Billy Graham and current CEO of Billy Graham Evangelistic Association, wrote in *Decision* magazine, "[A]t its root and core, the war on Christmas is not really about Christmas—it's about the Son of God. The war on Christmas is a war on Christ and His followers. It's the hatred of our culture for the exclusive claims that Christ made."[20] Such rhetoric is one example that reflects this broader self-understanding, one that provides a clear and consistent message: the modern Christian is a hated minority as is evidenced by increased refusals to impose Christian practices, like Christmas, upon public spaces.

However, against these perceptions of persecution and minority status, longitudinal research on societal feelings towards fundamentalist and evangelical Christians finds that there has been no significant increase in antipathy.[21] Those with negative views towards conservative Christians are significantly more wealthy in the twenty-first century and are, therefore, able to mobilize that wealth.[22] Sociologist George Yancey demonstrates that highly-educated progressives harbored the most hostility towards conservative Christians, but they possessed little power to affect evangelicals' socioeconomic well-being.[23] What Christians may be facing, therefore, is not any substantial increase in hostility, but an increase in the sociocultural power of groups that may have previously held negative attitudes towards them. It is important to note that the groups that demonstrated the most antipathy were those most likely to have been marginalized by conservative Christian communities in the past.

Christian access to resources and representation also complicates the claim that Christians are a persecuted minority. Despite demographic decreases, Christians represent the largest religious population on the planet—approximately 2.3 billion people, or 31 percent of humanity—and are found in far more countries than any other group.[24] In the U.S., around 65 percent of the population identifies as Christian.[25] Furthermore, sociologists Brian J. Grim and legal expert Melissa E. Grim calculate the economic power of religious individuals and institutions is quite high. Conservatively, the total economic value of religion in U.S. society, the vast majority of which is allied with Christians and Christian organizations, is estimated at 50 billion dollars.[26] This is more than the revenue of Apple, Amazon, and Google combined. In addition, a recent survey sponsored by *Christianity Today* and the Evangelical Council for Financial Accountability reports that "tithers"—those who give at least 10 percent of their income—give more than 50 billion dollars to churches and religious charities annually.[27] This amount is slightly more than all the money donated to higher education in the U.S., including all the so-called liberal elite universities and colleges Christians tend to decry.[28] In addition, Christianity continues to hold a privileged place in American politics. Eighty-eight percent of the 116th U.S. Congress identifies as Christian.[29] Also, 81 percent of evangelicals voted for the 2016 presidential candidate Donald Trump, in large part because their support would provide unprecedented access to political power.[30] In relation to media, the Federal Communications Commission reports there are 2,400 Christian radio stations and 100 full-power Christian television stations, which provides tremendous cultural power to project Christian messaging.[31] Christians also effectively influence legislative agendas. In 2012, there were more than 200 religion-based lobbying groups in Washington, D.C. spending at least 350 million dollars annually to influence public policy; approximately 45 percent of them were Christian organizations.[32] Taken together, demographic, economic, media, and political evidence complicates the claim that Christians are minorities, let alone powerless.

The effect of the misperception of Christianity as a beleaguered minority has at least three implications for Christian civility. First, as Candida R. Moss claims, perceptions of persecution divide the world into "two parties, one backed by God and the other by Satan."[33] When implicitly or explicitly evoked, "the rhetoric of persecution suggests that the persecutors are irrational and immoral."[34] Furthermore, when persecuted, the proper response is neither understanding nor dialogue. "When modern political and religious debates morph into rhetorical holy war, the same thing happens: we have to fight those who disagree with us. There can be no compromise and no common ground."[35] Second, George Yancey rightfully argues that, while those with anti-Christian sentiments have gained economic and political power, such power is better understood as a lack of support,[36] or perhaps a lack of deference, rather than outright persecution. Finally, given the demographic, economic, media, and political resources to which Christians have access, allowing powerful institutions like the Church to perceive themselves as persecuted minorities is akin to giving a megaphone to the person who is already shouting loudly in the room. They were already being heard, but now few others can be.

To sincerely call for hospitality and civility, we must recognize that there is a majority group that believes itself to be a minority. And, out of that self-perception, Christians reject rational standing as dialogue partners to others, like members of the LGBTQ+ community. To paraphrase an often-used idea, when a person or community has been privileged for a long period of time, calls for equality by less privileged groups can feel like oppression. Out of that feeling of oppression, Christians, perhaps unintentionally, oppress others. It is this social context that must be addressed if Christian hospitality is to resist, as Troup puts it, the temptations of empire.

The Benefits of Christian Incivility

Like the social context of a Christian persecution complex, Christian communities have also used incivility or hostility with out-groups as a means for increasing group cohesion and participation. This insight requires a brief explanation of a theory from the sociology of religion known as the "supply-side," or Rational Choice Theory. Using that theory, sociologists have noted that high demands and tension with outsiders have historically contributed to increased participation and commitment. I offer an example of such hostility from my own personal experience with Black and White Christians, and I conclude this section with the implications of the benefits of incivility for Troup's call to civility.

In the sociology of religion, the "supply-side" or Rational Choice Theory of religion helps explain the persistence of religious activity in the U.S., which functions as a relatively free market in which congregants navigate costs and benefits. While there has been debate on how, why, or to what extent religion will decline in modern society, its demise has been, until fairly recently, assumed to be inevitable. Against these assumptions, some sociologists of religion note the diversity of religious organizations and institutions of the American religious landscape as a driving source for America's continued religiosity.[37] In that diverse religious context, sociologists liken religious organizations, like congregations and denominations, to any other business. Religious practices, beliefs, and values are considered products that religious leaders try to sell to a public. Religion may be focused on the otherworld, but there are still many real-world costs of operation. Partly because the U.S. has no State-sponsored religion and little government regulation over religious behavior, religious leaders need congregants to offer resources to sustain their organizations, things like time and finances. Religion, then, must be marketed to congregants. This is the "supply-side," or Rational Choice Theory of religion.[38] According to the theory, the religious marketplace operates like any other. The American religious market is also relatively free compared to many other countries, where the State may be actively endorsing or suppressing religion. A free market allows congregations to innovate and supply new religious products that rational, religious-minded people can and will consume. In other words, if there are more kinds of religious products to buy at different costs, increased numbers of people will find a product to their liking and use it to maintain a religious identity. Therefore, religious consumers "buy" religious products based on a rational cost/benefit analysis. Benefits may include things like salvation, community, identity, and contentment. The costs to such benefits may be religious strictness, tithing requirements, behavior restrictions, time consumption, or social tension and isolation.

Interestingly, strictness and conflict (or incivility) with out-groups can generate important forms of participation and commitment. Sociologists of religion Roger Finke and Rodney Stark suggest that strictness and high demands on adherents motivate increased religious participation.[39] For some, a strict adherence to religious tenets and an increased rejection of "worldly" values and beliefs are the price congregants pay for a more authentic and beneficial religious product. Sociologist of religion Laurence R. Iannaccone found that tension and conflict with the outside world benefits religious organizations because they provide symbolic boundaries for believers and strengthen ties to beliefs.[40] Heightened tension with broader society also compels members to commit more of their resources to religious organizations.[41] Indeed, throughout American history, the religious "sects" in the U.S that turned away from ecumenism and compromise, like Baptists and Methodists, grew the fastest with the most committed membership.[42] Low-commitment, mainline Protestant organizations, like Presbyterians and Episcopalians, suffered and continue to experience membership losses because of their lax requirements and ties to "worldly" institutions.[43] In short, religious conflict and tension are useful for maintaining and elevating commitment.

By way of example of the effect of incivility, I think of the differing metaphors that White and Black Christians in my own past have expressed. Before attending a Southern Baptist congregation, I attended an African Methodist Episcopal (AME) congregation with my family. Our AME ministers focused on forgiveness and loving our neighbors. We were constantly directed to stories of God saving the faithful from the oppression of the cruel and the tyrannical. Our ministers emphasized patience, perseverance, and turning the other cheek as we awaited the Kingdom Come. We did not spend a great deal of time discussing how Jesus overturned tables in the temple or Israel's wars waged in God's name. I do not think this is coincidental. The Christian lessons we were to enact were those that would promote our survival as a group—working-class, Black people in the hostile South. My White friends from the big Baptist church, on the other hand, were constantly speaking the language of Crusades—those past and those on college campuses. They knew their job was to build God's Kingdom on Earth at all costs. They routinely told me how they learned the U.S. is a Christian nation, and how they were to be a beacon to all others. They were taught that Americans had a God-given obligation to bring Christ and democracy to the rest of the world. These White and Black discourses could not have been more different in form and consequence. The Christianity I was taught spoke of survival and self-reflection, while theirs emphasized righteous dominance and expansion. We had the same Bible. We occupied the same town. We lived in the same year. We were only different in terms of our social, political, and economic positions. Christian identity was the key to my survival, whereas Christianity was the reason for their fight. I could also note that my church was shuttered due to a lack of membership, while the big Baptist church is still going strong.

If uncivil conflict with an out-group is an effective means of securing social participation and commitment in churches, then Christians might find it difficult to engage with Troup's call for civility. Troup builds a great deal of his argument for hospitality around the idea that people should be brought into one another's spaces. In contrast, hostility to outsiders encourages Christians to provide material benefits, resources, and power to their own churches, not others, and it discourages loving those perceived as enemies. Given how incivility can be beneficial to religious organizations in the religious marketplace, Troup's theory of hospitality needs to deal more intimately with this uncivil orientation. Giving up hostility and incivility for hospitality, humility, and civility is no easy feat. Like the Christian persecution complex, Troup's account does not offer adequate ways of overcoming benefits of incivility with out-groups.

Unilateral Conditions of Civility and the Harm to LGBTQ+ Individuals

In addition to the Christian persecution complex and the benefits Christians experience from incivility, the final contextual problem I want to address is the harm certain understandings of civility pose to marginalized groups, like the LGBTQ+ community. As a way of framing this harm, I begin this section with a description of both liberal and conservative notions of civility. Both accounts of civility assume the unilateral imposition of conditions. Such conditions can be very harmful, as illustrated by Christian conditions on LGBTQ+ individuals, for example. Such harm not only complicates LGBTQ+ participation in civil discourse with Christians, but it also calls on the need for Christians to acknowledge this harm and foreground the need for justice.

In an analysis of multiple works on civility, sociologist Melanie White highlights the logic of "acting as if," relating to both conservative and liberal accounts of civility.[44] In both strains, civility is the outcome of intergroup dynamics, and it is necessary for differing groups to coexist. The appearance of respect and recognition is afforded to parties engaged in dialogue. The more conservative view prioritizes the common good for all, which deemphasizes individual and group desires.[45] The more liberal approach understands civility as a political act that permits debate around the governing moral principles of a diverse society.[46] To this end, individuals must act as if others are worthy of respect and see beyond their own views to consider those of others. Civility is recognized by the ability to exercise restraint and tact. Neither liberal nor conservative interpretations of civility demand or even expect the sincere belief in the humanity and legitimacy of another. The key is the ability to pretend, to act "as if" one believes the point of view of the other party is worthy of honor or recognition. Rather than a deep sense of authentic respect for others, what White points out is the best pretenders are those that are often recognized as civil. Civility is a game to play.

Within the context of "acting as if," those who are perceived as more civil often impose unilateral civic codes that can cause harm to others. The example of conservative Christian conditions on LGBTQ+ Christians illustrates this point. Sociologist Todd Stillman defines civic codes as "boundary-maintaining discourses that establish and reproduce hierarchical social relationships both within and between cultures."[47] Moreover, "[c]odes of civility can also be used chauvinistically as evidence of the superiority of one culture over another."[48] Members and allies of the LGBTQ+ population are well-acquainted with the unilateral conditionality of certain brands of Christian hospitality. Congregations may tolerate LGBTQ+ individuals in church spaces. However, they can only be acceptable to the congregation and God under certain conditions, like the requirement of celibacy, as is the case in the Catholic church.[49] Others demand that homosexuals and transgender members undergo conversion therapy or ex-gay ministries—for which there is no clinical evidence of complete reorientation, while there is clinical evidence such therapies cause trauma—in order to become religiously and socially acceptable.[50] Religious tenets have also led pious parents to throw their LGBTQ+ children out of their homes.[51] This is to say nothing of the stream of "religious freedom" cases moving through the courts, in which some affirm the LGBTQ+ community as worthy recipients of discriminatory behavior in employment, public services, marriage, adoption, and access to healthcare. While the need to condemn sin can be attributed to Christian obligation, the fact that not all sin is so doggedly pursued as the sin Christians associate with non-traditional sexual and gender identity suggests the perceived expressions of incivility are not products of obligation but of preference. When applying civility to dialogue with the LGBTQ+ community, the differences in moral and political stance that most discussions of civility assume, and the resulting mistreatments, are often not small or negotiable.

For members of the LGBTQ+ community, it makes sense to wonder if it might be too much to "act as if" the belief in our categorical unworthiness and our active exclusion from society is a reasonable position. It is not unreasonable to assume that it would be difficult to refrain from stating that LGBTQ+ people are entitled to the same rights as any other person in the name of political tact. Put differently, who in the LGBTQ+ community possesses enough civility and concern for the common good to rhetorically erase their own existence? Who in the community is going to reduce themselves to a thought experiment? This is particularly important if one party has demonstrated a propensity to treat disagreement and lack of deference to their power as a sign of persecution and incivility, especially when such significant harm comes to LGBTQ+ members.

As a result, any discussion of civility should acknowledge the real consequences for LGBTQ+ safety, equality, and representation, including a commitment not to ignore the need for social justice. Troup's call to pay less attention to the laws of this world and emphasize the cosmic truths of Christian belief runs the risk of ignoring the effects that lack of attention has on the LGBTQ+ community. To marginalized communities, like the LGBTQ+ population or people of color, existence is political. Their safety in society is debated publicly, often without any requested or desired input from the very people being talked about. To be truly hospitable and civil, Christians must not retreat from justice when so many still utilize the name of Christ to legitimize the societal discord Troup laments. While Troup deemphasizes social justice, justice is the major mechanism of hope for the socially marginalized. When Christians desire to reduce the centrality of justice, such desire reveals the privilege and power that comes with dominant group status. The foundation for hospitality need not lay the foundation for unjust interactions and continued subjugation. I think a more thoughtful approach to hospitality and civility begins with the recognition of the inherent power to construct the unacceptability of the LGBTQ+ community.

Despite the limitations of liberal and conservative notions of civility, civility is still a vital and important starting point. It is noble to wish to achieve a state in societal affairs where denigration and hostile attacks are not the status quo, but I do not believe it should be understood as the concluding state of affairs. At least, it should not be for those who wish to claim a Christian identity—to follow the way of the Prince of Peace. Civility is, as White's work implies, a fragile masquerade. Hospitality can be similarly specious. The need for the appearance of virtuous civility rises and falls with changing social patterns. What is needed now is a virtue that is more than just utilitarian. I suggest that love and justice for all humankind are needed. Of course, love of God and neighbor is the highest commandment and deepest practice of Christian identity, and Troup centers love in his own work. Minority Christians, like Martin Luther King Jr., however, have always held love together with justice, and it is to love and justice that I now turn.

Love and Justice

Troup argues against the conflation of love and social justice, but this assertion problematizes hospitality and civility. He argues that love for others should not be influenced by precepts of lawful justice. To allow or deny the application of lawful justice should not be, for Troup, a measure of love. In other words, not only should the concepts not be combined, but one also should not be understood as an indicator of the other. Intellectually, the separation makes sense, and his examples support his assertion; however, I think, practically, it reduces hospitality and civility to nothing more than hollow, voluntary gestures that affirm an individual's moral identity and minimize the suffering and injustice others experience. This may not be the intent, but I do believe it is an outcome that we have already seen in abundance. But perhaps more importantly, Troup's assertion runs against the biblical wisdom of Christians of color, like Rev. Dr. Martin Luther King Jr.

In the foreword to *The Radical King*, Cornel West describes King's work as the embodiment of "radical love" that "flows from an imitation of Christ, a response to an invitation of self-surrender in order to emerge fully equipped to fight for justice in a cold and cruel world of domination and exploitation."[52] This application of radical love obviously addresses the oppression of African Americans in a White supremacist America. Writing from a jail cell, King calls for us to love our enemies, including our oppressors, and centers love in the pursuit of justice.[53] King is writing from a place of powerlessness and persecution, yet he demands love for the powerful and the persecutors "not because their ways appeal to us, nor even because they possess some type of divine spark; we love every man because God loves him."[54] I have argued how the Christian community is not operating from a place of powerlessness or persecution in America; however, I think King's lesson applies to all regardless of status.

Moreover, King argues that love compels the call for social justice. Social justice is not separate from love; rather, justice is the social embodiment of love. King writes, "What is needed is a realization that power without love is reckless and abusive and that love without power is sentimental and anemic. Power at its best is love implementing the demands of justice.

Justice at its best is love correcting everything that stands against love."[55] To love others so genuinely that one wishes to free the oppressed and oppressors from systems that perpetuate inequality, animosity, and hatred is central to the conception of radical love. This application can and should find purchase in the interactions between Christian and LGBTQ+ communities. Here, using the concepts of many evangelical Christians, one does not have to love the sin to recognize the oppression of and discrimination against the sinner or a community defined by one particular sin. Radical love requires more than the polite charade of hospitality and civility. It requires a genuine regard for all and assumes justice is the common good. All benefit from it, not just those who are capable of maintaining a temporary, fabricated civil peace.

For those who believe God hates entire groups of people and punishes nations with increasingly destructive hurricanes and war casualties for acceptance of the LGBTQ+ community, I suspect calls for radical love and social justice are ridiculous. For them, social injustice and personal hatred are signs of Divine justice and love. But for those who claim to believe in the boundless, unconditional love of God for all people, I ask you to reflect upon yourself and your community. Do your beliefs and actions reflect love or a hospitable proxy? Be honest.

Conclusion

I often wonder what my baccalaureate experience would have been like had the speaker treated the world as a place for faith to grow and deepen. What would have happened if college had not been described as a place of danger and hostility from innumerable "others"? What if diversity was described as evidence of God's creation and not the Devil's playground? I suspect the crowd would have smiled and nodded all the same, and the speaker likely would have gotten the same amount of applause. I cannot say this would have kept me in the faith. Indeed, I cannot say this is the experience that turned me away; however, it would have been interesting to have a story, a memory of Christian love and humanity that was different from the countless experiences of hostility and rejection that I and so many others continue to experience.

PART IV
OPPORTUNITIES FOR CIVILITY

Chapter 7

On Regulating Civility

The Directing Meta-virtue of Integrity and the Barmen Declaration

Annalee R. Ward and Mary K. Bryant

Introduction

ONE HUNDRED AND THIRTY-NINE REPRESENTATIVES AGREED. During the long days of May 24–31, 1934, German church delegates, soon to be known as the Confessing Church, prayed, talked, worshipped, and voted. They came from different regions, different backgrounds, different professions, and different denominations—Reformed, Lutheran, and United—representing eighteen different churches. Their meeting was the result of a cascade of events over the course of 1933. The Nazi party, through nationalist-leaning church members known as German Christians, had taken over the German Evangelical Church (*Deutsche Evangelische Kirche*), the federation of Germany's twenty-eight provincial Protestant churches. The German Christian movement equated patriotism with the Gospel, believed in a principle of racial superiority, and legitimized its beliefs with Scriptural support for the ruling government.[1] Resisting the conflation of Christianity with Nazi ideology, the delegates who came to the meeting in Barmen understood themselves as "acting out of the deepest concern for the integrity and authenticity of the Church's witness and message."[2] At the conclusion of their proceedings, the delegates unanimously approved Karl Barth's draft of the six-point Barmen Declaration.[3] It marked the inception of the Confessing Church of Germany, a loose collection of those united by these six Scriptural principles, and it stood in opposition to the German Evangelical Church, the newly appointed National Church (*Reichskirche*).

Through the Barmen Declaration, the Confessing Church spoke truth to power; however, the declaration was not received as a humble, hospitable, civil act. In Chapter 1, Calvin L. Troup argues that we need the right conditions for civility, and he turns to Augustine to argue that the conditions we need are rightly ordered loves characterized by humility and hospitality. As virtues, they are not easily achieved and require practice. Certainly, they contribute to civility, but the example of the Barmen Declaration urges us to consider the possibility that civility might not always be a sufficient goal. The desire to practice civility without first embracing integrity can contribute to an avoidance of conflict and difficult conversations. But to live a life of wholeness, of integration and integrity, one must gather the courage to first listen to what might be perceived as uncivil voices. That listening, along with love of God and neighbor, contributes to rightly practiced integrity, which, depending on the contextual need, guides the expression and emphasis of various virtues. The relationship between civility and integrity, while interwoven, must exist with integrity serving as the directing meta-virtue. Living our commitment to love rightly may then mean accepting incivility because integrity is acting as a meta-virtue, directing the practice of other virtues, including not only humility, hospitality, and civility, but also justice, compassion, and steadfastness.

Examining the historic example of the German Christians at the rise of the Nazi regime and the work of dissenting Christians through the Barmen Declaration, we argue that those who pursued civility first ended up compromising their integrity. Those who pursued integrity risked much but held fast to the principles that defined Christianity, although theirs was certainly an imperfect expression of integrity, as they, too, carried their culture's antisemitism.[4] We begin with a look at the historical context of Germany post WWI through 1934, then move to defining integrity through the work of Stephen Carter, and conclude with a reading of the Barmen Declaration, applying its implications to the seemingly uncivil calls for justice today.

The Historical Context of the Barmen Declaration

Life had been difficult for the Germans after their defeat in WWI, and those difficulties created the conditions in which many Christians found themselves supporting Adolf Hitler's regime. The terms of WWI peace had a "disastrous effect on Germany."[5] Huge payment demands caused inflation, job losses, "moral and cultural disorientation,"[6] and a "cult of violence."[7] As a result, the political landscape shifted in favor of the authoritarian state government. The conditions of a financial depression and the perception that Hitler wanted a Christian Germany proved ripe for political revolution with the support of Christians.[8] Initially, Hitler's rhetoric seemed supportive of the church, and church members and leaders tried to find common ground with the new government. The government's "crackdown on prostitution, pornography and abortion and its professed encouragement of the traditional family" reassured the leaders of Protestant churches.[9] They took these early commitments as a hopeful sign that the church could work with the state toward "the ethical and religious renewal of the *Volk*."[10] Furthermore, Hitler wrote in his autobiography, *Mein Kampf*, that "the Party would be neutral with respect to the confessional or denominational differences." He spoke about the valuable contributions to the nation of both Protestantism and Catholicism, and "he maintained that Church and State should be strictly separated."[11] He offered a way for the Church to be hospitable to the State. Both could coexist, each operating in their own sphere.

As Hitler rose to political power, Christians did little to resist. Hitler's appointment as Chancellor on January 30, 1933, served as a call to national pride for a despairing German country.[12] Nevertheless, Hitler indicated the direction he was headed, declaring, "All life may be summed up in three propositions: conflict is the father of all things, virtue is a matter of blood, and leadership is primary and decisive,"[13] or, as religious studies scholar Robert T. Osborn summarizes, "might is right."[14] Historically, the Church had long been deeply embedded in a German identity, as the State sanctioned and funded it with tax money. German pride ran deep, and people wanted desperately to believe Hitler could both restore Germany to glory, while at the same time valuing the church. Shortly after his appointment as Chancellor, Hitler consolidated his power. By March of 1933, with the passing of the National Emergency Termination Bill, commonly known as the "Enabling Act," he gained complete control of the country and became the supreme leader of Germany. In an early February speech to military commanders, he declared his intentions. Hitler would not tolerate "the expression of any principles that stand opposed to . . . the Nazi worldview," and "[w]hoever doesn't convert must be subdued."[15] He and his supporters put in place *Gleichschaltung*—total coordination, complete synchronization—a systematic reshaping of the German way of life. Nazism would touch every level and every organization of society and demand an oath of loyalty to Hitler from every person. Initially, few Christians challenged these realities.[16] Early on the Nazis employed terror, but "the central authorities of the Protestant church . . . did not want to have any information [about it]."[17] The church "wanted to be Christian and yet national. . . . [T]o celebrate Christ and Hitler, too."[18]

In the spring of 1933, Hitler moved to gain control of both Catholic and Protestant churches in Germany. He convinced the Catholic Church to sign a concordat on July 30, 1933. The churches assumed it allowed them to operate in the religious sphere and Hitler in the political, but it effectively signaled an endorsement of Hitler and his policies. The churches gave up the ability to appoint its own leadership or engage in social issues.[19] Taking over Protestant churches, because of their differing governance and diverse denominations, required more involvement on Hitler's part, as well as more support from Christians. In 1932, the Nazi Party facilitated the birth of a movement of "German Christians" within the German Evangelical Church.[20] These German Christians, easily subsumed into the Nazi worldview, collaborated with the Nazi government in a takeover of the German Evangelical Church. As beneficiaries of Constitutional protections and recipients of tax monies, the German Christians took a "union of Christianity, nationalism, and militarism . . . for granted."[21] Theologian Arthur C. Cochrane points out that the messages of this movement began in people's post-War needs. Those experiences of cultural disorientation and a desire for a return to glory became an easy justification for nationalism.[22] German Christians campaigned on the "belief that 'race, nationality, and the nation [are] orders of life granted and entrusted to us by God, for whose preservation God's law requires us to strive.'"[23] They gained control of church leadership and helped develop a unified German Evangelical Church constitution, which became State law on July 14, 1933.[24] Having theoretically completed Hitler's goal of settling the conflict among the Protestant churches, German Christians fulfilled their desire for a State Church.[25] This new German Evangelical Church was to be "a Reich Church which in faith acknowledges the sovereignty of the National Socialist State." It would be the National Church for "Christians, of the Aryan race."[26]

In the midst of the Nazi takeover of both Catholic and Protestant churches, those who objected looked for ways to accommodate the changes while still raising objections, but they soon found a need to voice more explicit resistance.[27] Leading up to this time, primarily Methodist and Baptist "free" churches received no state funding and were not as easily cowed by the National Party.[28] There were also various university professors and individual pastors expressing dissent and calling for a more nuanced understanding of war, pacifism, and the church's role.[29] Already in 1925, theologian Karl Barth delivered a speech arguing for a Reformed Confession of Faith to counter the liberalism of the current German Church. He called for a return to the preeminence of Christ and the authority of Scripture and for Christians to unite under a Confession committed to and beginning in Scripture rather than in ideology or denomination.[30] Another significant voice of dissent belonged to Pastor Hans Asmussen. With a group of twenty-one other pastors, he released "A Word and Confession to the Need and Confusion in Public Life" on January 11, 1933. Its five key points highlighted the centrality of Christ and the role of the Church as apolitical.[31] When Hitler's choice of Church leader, Ludwig Müller, along with Nazi troops, took over the Church's administration buildings and released a proclamation announcing himself as head of the Church, a group of fifty pastors and leaders signed the Bielefeld Confession. This document, however, "did not go beyond the question of Church organization" to the "real issue" as identified by Barth of the authority of Christ and his Scriptures.[32] These examples demonstrate that not everyone submitted to Hitler's control.[33]

While the Christians debated, nationwide laws institutionalized discrimination policies.[34] In March of 1933, distressed by the increasing violent attacks on Jews, the dissenters' frustrations with the National Socialists' demands grew. Their breaking point came when the "Aryan principle" was included as policy within the German Evangelical Church. First applied to civil service and then to education, the policy considered anyone with a Jewish parent or grandparent to be "non-Aryan." The policy also extended to anyone married to a non-Aryan, whether or not they were professing Christians.[35] This meant that many current pastors could no longer lead a church, and many converts were considered illegitimate Christians because of their Jewish ancestry. In response to Müller's takeover and alignment with the National Socialists, Lutheran pastor Martin Niemöller formed the Pastors' Emergency League. The League proclaimed its members to be bound to Scripture and the Reformed Confessions and opposed to the Aryan paragraph as it applied to the Church. It was well-received as thousands of pastors joined in support. Their objections were presented to the National Synod of the German Evangelical Church, making Niemöller the face of the movement opposing the German Church.[36] But the Synod never considered it and instead moved to elect Müller as Reich bishop.[37]

During this time, many within the church felt obliged to civility, but their civility only produced compromise. A majority of the country's Protestant churches signed on with the German Evangelical Church, now considered to be the National Church. Many of the members of the National Church found themselves trying to reconcile both State and Church through affirming Jesus Christ as Lord and the Word as authoritative while also expressing nationalistic support of Hitler, the State, and the German race. And they wanted to do it civilly. They longed to see a strong Germany along with a functioning church, yet they found their mixed motivations required concessions in their faith practices. German propaganda scholar Randall Bytwerk tells of a pastor who reflected on what it was like working with Hitler's officials: "[O]ne would be pushed further, step by step, until he had crossed over the line, without noticing that millimeter by millimeter one's spine was being bent."[38] By the time they realized where Hitler had pushed them, there was little integrity or conviction left within the German Evangelical Church.

By the end of 1933, the divisions within the Protestant church produced chaos, and chaos would not do for Hitler, who wanted unanimity. The National Socialists began to crack down on dissenters even as Niemöller's Pastors' Emergency League became more determined to unite Christians around a confessional stance. Meanwhile, those aligning with the Pastors' League and the Confessing Church movement tried to hospitably engage their counterparts in civil dialogue and debate, but they reached a point where conscience demanded a hard stance. Through the Barmen Declaration, the Pastors' Emergency League exercised the integrity to stand their ground. It was the integrity of pursuing their love of God before their love of country, leadership positions, and tax breaks that propelled them. This integrity took priority to humility, hospitality, and, for some like Niemöller, even civility.[39]

While Troup longs for a reinvigoration of civility, this history illustrates there are times in which civility is simply insufficient for a robust moral life while living faithfully as Christ's followers. Troup's call for civility, much like Richard Mouw's call for "convicted civility,"[40] can soon find itself as a call for compromise of convictions.[41] Compromise might be avoided if integrity acts as the director, or meta-virtue, to civility, humility, and hospitality.

Integrity as a Directing Meta-virtue

The virtue of integrity, when understood as a director of all one's virtues, functions as a "cluster concept" that spans and organizes a wide range of aspects of one's character rather than "one that is reducible to the workings of a single moral capacity."[42] Similarly, clinical psychologist Barbara Killinger identifies a number of character virtues—honesty, sympathy, empathy, compassion, fairness, self-control, duty—as traits that integrity requires us to incorporate to be people of good character.[43] In detailing how integrity is lived out, legal scholar Stephen Carter elaborates on a host of the other virtues that are involved, including, for example, commitment, forthrightness, steadfastness (which enables one to "stick to the course in the face of criticism and difficulty"), and compassion.[44] Implicit in many definitions of integrity is a commitment to truthfulness and honesty, but as Carter points out, it is honesty that is informed by the discernment of right and wrong.[45] This honesty is illustrated by St. Paul's call to speak "the truth in love" (Ephesians 4:15, NIV), which rarely is a brutal, bare honesty (Ephesians 4:15, NIV), but rather is one faithful to truth. This kind of truth-loving is at the heart of integrity and makes someone's integrity trustworthy and reliable. Based on these accounts, we suggest the virtue of integrity should be understood as a meta-virtue that directs which virtues should come to the forefront in particular practices, all of which contributes to a person's unified and teleologically directed integrity.

By way of illustration, consider the director of a musical ensemble who seeks to help the group produce one beautiful piece of music. This leader directs the voices or instruments to sing or play together in such a way as to achieve the musicality of the piece. One section needs to bring in the melody stronger while one section might be told to slow down. The director keeps the ensemble working together to achieve their goals with this piece of music. Similarly, integrity draws on civility, humility, honesty, and other virtues, but it discerns when some virtues need to take a backseat or "sing softly." Integrity thus directs or regulates the various virtues. One who has *integrity* is whole; our virtues are inextricably linked—they are *integrated*, acting in concert within us.

Stephen L. Carter not only discusses how various virtues contribute to integrity, he also provides a definition of integrity that involves three movements: "1) *Discerning* what is right and what is wrong; 2) *Acting* on what you have discerned, even at personal cost; and 3) *Saying openly* that you are acting on your understanding of right from wrong."[46] As philosophers J. L. Austin and later John R. Searle affirm, the distinction between action and speech is not always clear.[47] For our discussion of the Barmen Declaration, we understand speech to be action because the Declaration defends itself as an action that requires great discernment even as it is speech that explains its action.

Discernment, the distinguishing between right and wrong/good and bad, illuminates the virtues and their boundaries for Christian identity. Holding up to the light our professed values alongside our actions and decisions will show us whether we have said "yes" or "no" to Scriptural authority and reveals the virtues and values we should be pursuing. Having a *telos*, an end toward which one aims, provides boundaries within which to operate, and such boundaries allow the Church to be faithful to its calling.[48] As Mark Galli, former editor of *Christianity Today*, reminds evangelicals in his courageous 2019 editorial calling for Trump's removal from office, "Remember who you are and whom you serve."[49] For the Christian, loving God and loving neighbor as one's self provides such a *telos* and counters the narrow focus on virtue as an end to itself. Pursuing civility, humility, and hospitality are genuine goods when they are framed by the love of God—something for which Troup argues in Chapter 1.

Furthermore, discerning wisdom is connected to relationality, love, and life. The writer of Proverbs describes wisdom in relational terms. "The fear of the Lord is the beginning of wisdom"—acknowledgement, awe, love, and worship are due to God.[50] It is beginning with, as Troup argues, the rightly ordered loves of putting God first in one's life and loving neighbor as self. From this starting place, wisdom grows. As wisdom grows, so does the discernment that lies at the foundation of integrity. As Paul prays for the Philippians, "And this is my prayer: that your love may abound more and more in knowledge and depth of insight, so that you may be able to discern what is best."[51] Communication scholar Greg Spencer helpfully claims that discernment must include "the wisdom to recognize the difference between life and death—with the motivation to choose life."[52]

Carter also invokes conscience as a communal and practiced element of discernment. Conscience in children as well as adults is developed within communities such as family, church, and school. Societal norms add to the development of conscience as well; much of what society has deemed "right" makes up the foundation of a developing conscience. Although the conscience may always be active, one must make the willful choice to attend to the judgments of one's conscience in consultation with formative communities.[53] Discernment also takes ongoing attention and hard work. "[W]ithout use, discernment atrophies."[54] Discernment, therefore, is not easy. It takes work and thought and constant renewal, just as navigation requires repeated consultation with a compass to ensure one has not strayed from the right path. Accordingly, Carter's definition is best applied if considered as a circular process, moving through the action/speech, and then returning to discernment. For example, when the Aryan paragraph, which forbade Jews from participation in public life, was enacted in early 1933, eighteen pastors were dismissed and church organization itself became altered. Church leaders began to recognize that a tipping point had been reached.[55] It was not enough to discern whether the Church's direction and its role in Hitler's regime was acceptable. With each new development that revealed more of Hitler's real objectives and ambitions, the Church should have been reconsidering and reweighing its relationship to the State.

Integrity not only involves discernment but must move us forward into action. For the Confessing Church, that action meant taking the risk of speaking out. Political theorist Ruth W. Grant writes, "The person of integrity is one who can be trusted to do the right thing even at some cost to himself."[56] Actions in deed and word served as the logical outcome of discernment and were a source of growing fear for Christians in Germany. Ideas have consequences, but those ideas are expressed in language, in words. The overriding desire for unification within German churches, coupled with German pride, led many to surmise that unity should be their goal. Many Christians tried to speak civilly against Nazi ideology and its entanglements with the Church. However, as Hitler's demands grew increasingly strident, the time for professing true allegiances arrived as an either/or choice: either your allegiance put Hitler and the State first, or it put Jesus Christ and his Word first. For the men assembled at Barmen, action meant speaking out to affirm the supremacy of Jesus.

The Barmen Declaration marks a point in time when church leaders could no longer go forward as they had previously—as a group quietly accepting the changes Hitler and the Nazi Regime were making in the Church. Civility was no longer one of the Confessing Church's aims. Integrity demanded words and actions as followers of Christ. There would be no more compromising its values, including its commitment to God and Scripture. It was an act of integrity to come forward and publicly define the Church's source for discerning right from wrong, rejecting any role for the State in church leadership or direction, and asserting theological authority. Consequences ensued. Karl Barth was eventually fired from his position as a professor when he unapologetically refused to take an oath of allegiance to Hitler in 1935.[57] Martin Niemöller was arrested. Integrity calls for great courage in both action and speech.

We agree with Troup in his call for civility, hospitality, and humility, but we are convinced that without integrity these goals can be pushed past the limits of virtue and into vice: insincerity, pandering, and self-derogation. What is the use of civility if it fails to prevent inhumane activities? What of hospitality if it leads to sacrificing one's principles? What of humility if it leads to being bulldozed and to one's convictions being ignored? The limits that moral integrity places on the virtues we associate with civility ensure that calls for civility do not end up trumping what is truly good and right.

The Barmen Declaration and Its Implications Today

The Barmen Declaration is a theological and political act of integrity that models and helps us recognize similar acts of theological integrity today,[58] as the examples of theologian James Cone and historian Jemar Tisby demonstrate. Their insights suggest that Christians can avoid compromising their convictions by engaging in self-examination, submitting to the whole of Scripture's call to love God and neighbor in pursuit of justice, listening even to uncivil voices, and standing against their own communities when necessary.[59] Now we turn first to the Barmen Declaration.

The relatively short document opens with an introduction and moves through six sections. Each section begins with a statement from Scripture, followed by an affirmative declaration of its meaning and a negative statement against a false doctrine. The biblical "yes" and "no" served as a critique to the German Christians who had listened to other voices of authority.[60]

The first two sections speak against any political authority as a source of God's revelation and the State's attempt to make claims on certain areas of life. From the uniqueness of Christ as the Word of God revealed in Scripture to his claims on every area of life, these points affirm Jesus as the revelation of God, who alone is Lord. Against this Christian claim, Bytwerk notes the Nazis "were building not merely a political system but a worldview that claimed authority over every area of life."[61] For Barth, the Nazi worldview that German Christians affirmed committed a crucial theological problem. It placed Adolf Hitler as a source of authority, or revelation, alongside Scripture and Jesus. Barth rightly claimed:

> This man [Adolf Hitler] understood how to put the German people, and with it also the German church, in a dreamy state. And in this dream, the German people and the German Christians of the Evangelical and the Catholic Church dreamt that something like *a revelation of God had taken place in what this man thought, said, wanted, and did.* And the so-called Confessing Church was about a decisive "No" to this dream [emphasis added].[62]

The Confessing Church uttered that "no" with these first two points, insisting Jesus Christ is the true revelation of God and the authority, not Hitler or his thoughts, words, desires, or actions. If Jesus is Lord over every area of life, then Hitler cannot be.

The remaining points of the Declaration describe the Church's right response to Jesus Christ's lordship. The third point calls for the Church to testify to the truth of Christ's forgiving work, the hope of his return, and that forgiveness and hope are "solely his [Christ's] property."[63] This testimony rejects any suggestion that the Church could adapt its message to the Nazi worldview. Because Christ alone is the Church's message and source of comfort, it could not make "the cultivation of its convictions" the State authority's "business."[64] The fourth point notes that church leadership is for the ministry of the whole Church and not for giving special roles or powers to any rulers. While acknowledging the State has a role to play in justice and peace, the fifth point stands decidedly against any idea that the State could preside over all of life, either subsuming or replacing the role of the Church. The final point declares the work of the Church to be a ministry in service of God and not for any other purpose, such as the political purposes for which German Christians had committed themselves. Jesus's lordship stands above all ideologies and "worldly claims."[65]

In the context of broad acceptance of Nazi rule in the Church and the growing terror campaign, this was a courageous, uncivil, uncompromising Declaration. It originated with individuals practicing deep discernment, who formed a community that led the Confessing Church movement. It was a testimony of the truth of Scripture made to the broader Church that required the action of passing the Declaration unanimously—truly an action directed by integrity. Historian Shelley Baranowski describes the Declaration as an assertion of the right relationship of the Church to the State, and an appropriate description of Christian commitments made "with a force rarely heard in previous German Protestant history."[66]

However vital the Declaration was, the document begs critical questions: Was it sufficient? Did those involved with the Confessing Church do enough? And what might the Declaration mean for us today? Hindsight tells us the Confessing Church should have stood up sooner. They also should have definitively spoken against antisemitism. Barth himself later expressed regret that this version of the Declaration had removed any references to antisemitism.[67] But even if today we are able to identify its moral failures, the Declaration stands as a directive for future generations and today's Church to practice "extremely self-critical examination," as German theologian Eberhard Jüngel suggested, to ensure that its message and practices are free of outside influences.[68] Self-critical examination enables the Church to commit to God and Scriptural authority instead of a desire for self-preservation, economic safety, or even protection of one's culture. The Church's failures also teach us lessons about the dangers of power and fear. Just as the Church may have been influenced by the tax monies it received, and feared losing that support if it mounted strong resistance to the regime, we must discern when our position of power and related motivations may be misdirecting us. Connections to power lead to impure motives, and they push us away from love and justice to self-interest. As theologian James Cone writes,

> [W]e cannot find liberating joy in the cross by spiritualizing it, by taking away its message of justice in the midst of powerlessness, suffering, and death. The cross, as a locus of divine revelation, is not good news for the powerful, for those who are comfortable with the way things are, or for anyone whose understanding of religion is aligned with power. The religious authorities of Jesus's time were threatened by his teachings about the reign of God's justice and love, and the state authorities executed him as an insurrectionist.[69]

On Regulating Civility

Cone writes of the blindness of White Christians in America to the violence of White supremacy, citing the lynching tree and its unacknowledged similarities to the cross as an example. None of America's great theologians, he writes, say anything "of how the violence of White supremacy invalidated the faith of White churches. It takes a lot of theological blindness to do that, especially since the vigilantes were White Christians who claimed to worship the Jew lynched in Jerusalem."[70]

Historian Jemar Tisby's *The Color of Compromise* continues Cone's critique, condemning White churches for "passive complicity," silently sitting by in the face of horrific actions against Black people throughout this country's history.[71] Incomplete discernment has long contributed to maintaining the status quo: "all too often, Christians, and Americans in general, try to circumvent the truth-telling process in their haste to arrive at reconciliation."[72] Even when the discernment is in place and integrity requires massive change, many hesitate to make "the sacrifices that transformation entails."[73] What motivations—power, fear, discomfort—have kept so many from discerning and acting on the contradictions inherent in tolerating White supremacy and White privilege while also professing Christian faith? Indeed, as we discern right and wrong, we would do well to consider our blind spots regarding other marginalized groups—the poor, refugees and immigrants, women, the mentally ill, the LGBTQ+ community, the homeless, and the imprisoned.

Today, we must accept the challenge for much-needed self-critical examination that will lead to discerning practices of cultural engagement and determination of positive beliefs. We must translate that discernment to a language that brings hope and points to grace. Richard Stearns, retired president of World Vision, laments the current state of Christianity's negativity: "[W]e have become defined by those things we are *against* rather than those we are *for*. We're seen to be *against* homosexuality and gay marriage, *against* pornography and sexual promiscuity, *against* those who believe that global warming is a threat."[74] When these judgments become entwined with politics, the result leads to charges of hypocrisy and, even more damaging, loses the proclamation of Good News. So rather than use the political process to condemn, we need to begin by listening to the voices of the marginalized, the poor, the immigrant, and other victims of injustice.

Tisby's *The Color of Compromise* provides a good place to begin that listening, precisely because he challenges the American church's attachment to civility. When civility becomes elevated above integrity, the potential for damaging compromise, or worse yet, the silencing of differences, escalates into injustice. "[T]he most egregious acts of racism, like a church bombing," Tisby writes as he traces the history of racism in the American church, "occur within a context of compromise.... The refusal to act in the midst of injustice is itself an act of injustice. Indifference to oppression perpetuates oppression."[75] The American church has not always ordered its loves rightly, and Tisby cries out for change. He points out that there are many reasons the Church continues to practice a "complicit" rather than "courageous" Christianity, but, he argues, in doing so it "forfeits its moral authority by devaluing the image of God in people of color.... [I]t has *lost its integrity*" [emphasis added].[76] It is too easy to hide behind a veneer of civility to "get along," especially since that veneer can block out cries for justice, which may sound like uncivil speech. Such demands create discomfort for the majority and risk being labeled uncivil. Meanwhile, the marginalized remain marginalized because civility takes precedence over standing with integrity to fight for justice. Tisby cites a letter sent from prominent Birmingham clergymen to Martin Luther King Jr. during his time in jail in 1963 and in which they chastised King for his tactics. Tisby notes, "They did not realize that the talking and negotiating for which they advocated had been attempted and had yielded little to no progress. They denounced the violence that direct action would *supposedly* incite, but they did relatively little about the countless lynchings, church bombings, and beatings Black people across the nation suffered at the hands of segregationists."[77] When commitments to civility block our ability to listen, we lose our integrity and are blinded to injustice.

Tisby's narration of history and his calls to action strongly suggest that White Christians need to learn to accept certain words and actions they experience as uncivil as an invitation for positive change and self-critique. As rhetorician Raymie McKerrow asks, "[W]ho is determining what counts as civil? Keep in mind that within the councils of civility that have occurred in the past few years, those invited to the table have been the 'civil ones'— mostly White, mostly male, and always in a position to decry, denigrate and demean the actions of those not invited to the table."[78] Granted, Troup argues for a civility that is defined externally out of Jesus Christ's command to love thy neighbor. However, the danger of silencing some because their voices are uncivil points to an unwillingness on the part of Christians to listen and engage. McKerrow challenges us to consider when incivility may be a positive force for change.

Tisby's book is, we submit, precisely the kind of work Christians need if they are to have any integrity in the face of capitulation to systemic racism, bigotry, and marginalization of those without power. As social justice activist and attorney Brian Stevenson notes, "The true measure of our character is how we treat the poor, the disfavored, the accused, the incarcerated, and the condemned."[79] Tisby, McKerrow, and Stevenson's reflections should compel us to ask difficult questions in a posture of critical self-examination: Are we being appropriately engaged in cultural critique when an overwhelming number of evangelicals seem to be supporting policies that harm immigrant families, oppress people based on sexual identity or preference, and uphold systems originally designed to subjugate people of color? Are we truly discerning the path Jesus preached for the world when so many Christians do not seem bothered by their leaders' rhetoric of insult and hate, apparent support of White supremacy, and flaunting of immorality and greed?

At times, integrity may not call us to stand with the marginalized so much as stand against members of our own faith community, as *Christianity Today* editor Mark Galli did. Many evangelicals may see Galli's editorial calling for Trump's removal as an uncivil act, even though he describes this decision as one of conscience that fulfills his responsibility to "speak the truth."[80] The responses both in favor and against Galli's editorial were emotional, but we stand with his call to listen, to discern what is true, and to then take a stand rather than dogmatically clinging to sound bites. Did the Christians in Germany speak out enough when the Nazi regime encouraged hatred and violence against whole groups of people? Are we speaking out enough when we witness hatred toward and inhumane treatment of those marginalized in American society?

Conclusion

As today's Church faces deep political divides, growing socioeconomic gulfs, environmental degradation, and cultural change, to name just a few challenges, we need to pursue virtuous practices united in the integrity that make up our whole identity. We must practice discernment both individually and communally, identifying our blind spots and listening to other voices, particularly of those not in positions of power, civil or not. We must then live out our discernment with a willingness to speak out on why we have chosen that path, defining what we believe in instead of what we are against. We must actively stand for truth, valuing civility but not making it the end goal. We must break our passive complicity by speaking out, no longer watching silently in the face of injustice, nor clinging to power or political identity at the cost of integrity. The Barmen Declaration bears witness to contemporary Christians to stand "against the stream of 'culture Protestantism' and civil religion" and serves as a reminder of the integrity we need to stand courageously, and yes, even sacrificially, as faithful disciples of the Sovereign God.[81]

Chapter 8

Suffering and Civility

Rethinking the Role of the American Evangelical Tradition in Public Discourse and Public Life

Mark Allan Steiner

"Thus says the LORD of hosts, the God of Israel, to all the exiles whom I have sent into exile from Jerusalem to Babylon: Build houses and live in them; plant gardens and eat their produce. Take wives and have sons and daughters; take wives for your sons, and give your daughters in marriage, that they may bear sons and daughters; multiply there, and do not decrease. But seek the welfare of the city where I have sent you into exile, and pray to the LORD on its behalf, for in its welfare you will find your welfare.... For thus says the LORD: When seventy years are completed for Babylon, I will visit you, and I will fulfill to you my promise and bring you back to this place. For I know the plans I have for you, declares the LORD, plans for welfare and not for evil, to give you a future and a hope." (Jeremiah 29:4–7, 10–11, ESV)

Introduction

JEREMIAH 29:11 IS ARGUABLY one of the most commonly misquoted verses of Scripture in the American evangelical Christian community.[1] Lifted from its original context, American evangelicals commonly interpret the verse as a divine promise for temporal satisfaction or vindication on one's own terms. As such, the verse is frequently shared publicly as an inspirational "life verse," and the verse widely adorns Christian-themed merchandise and social media pages. In the full context of Jeremiah 29, though, the words of the prophet stand against precisely such consumeristic and individualistic concerns. Jeremiah admonishes the exiled Israelites to work for the good of the polity that brought them into exile and oppression, which is starkly opposed to the exiled Israelites' likely yearning for political deliverance and for the restoration of their land and their nation. This admonition was likely so disorienting, discouraging, and countercultural that Jeremiah included a specific warning in this passage not to believe the words of false prophets promising the kind of deliverance the people wanted. As such, Jeremiah's words likely felt much less like a promise and much more like a directive to suffer.

Such a directive to suffer was certainly as counterintuitive and countercultural for Jeremiah's original readers as it is for early twenty-first century American evangelicals, who have unwittingly embraced political and cultural tribalism. Indeed, such hyper-partisan and resentment-fueled tribalism dominates contemporary American public and political discourse, which has only intensified since the 2016 U.S. Presidential election.[2] While American evangelical Christians have frequently contributed to these dysfunctions,[3] I think it is also true that their theological resources can equip them to offer and practice a more edifying and productive alternative stance that embraces—not eschews—the kind of suffering that Jeremiah describes. This kind of suffering is, I suggest, an overlooked component of civility, but one that is necessary for a civility that can promote a robust, humane, and edifying democratic society.

To develop this overall idea, I first discuss the notion of civility in light of the contemporary American public and political context. More conventional notions of civility are insufficient to the challenges we currently face in mitigating and reversing the mistrust and tribal thinking that dominates our contemporary public and political lives. I then identify and explain three major ideas about suffering to show how a corrective and more robust framework for public/political civility can flow from a positive affirmation of suffering and the roles it can play in our individual and communal lives. Finally, I discuss how the contemporary public and political issues pertaining to racial justice and racial reconciliation can serve as a practical domain and model for public/political civility grounded in the idea of suffering.

Revisiting Civility and Trust

My claims about suffering and civility can be seen in recent conversations regarding the intersection of civility, Christianity, and virtue, particularly in the work of legal scholar Stephen L. Carter, theologian Richard Mouw, and rhetoric scholar Calvin L. Troup. In *Civility: Manners, Morals, and the Etiquette of Democracy*, Carter characterizes civility as a "pre-political" set of virtuous character traits, like respect and love for our "fellow citizens," which govern our interactions with others.[4] Civility that is rooted in love and respect then calls for "many sacrifices . . . for the sake of living together," sacrifices that demonstrate that our fellow citizens are "full equals, both before the law and before God."[5] For Carter, this more robust civility requires "a revival of all that is best in religion as a force in our public life."[6] Without religious traditions, he emphasizes, we will move "toward a world in which the only values that matter are the selfish and acquisitive values of politics and the market."[7] In *Uncommon Decency: Christian Civility in an Uncivil World*, Mouw argues for a "convicted civility" that rejects common conceptual pitfalls like relativism, crusaderism, and nationalism.[8] Instead, it embraces virtues including gentleness in speech, modesty about one's character and motives, empathy, and patience.

Similar to Carter and Mouw, Troup connects the Christian religious tradition with both civility and virtue. Drawing inspiration from Augustine's *City of God*, he recasts civility as dependent upon the virtue of humility and the practice of hospitality. By humility, Troup not only has in mind a concern for others—placing the focus of attention toward others rather than toward oneself—but also grounds this concern for others in love. Love demands a proper order to one's loves and a valuing of the right things in the right way. For Troup, love is what enables humility, or the capacity for leaders to bring themselves low and serve others. By hospitality, he has in mind the "exten[sion] [of] ourselves by opening our own households and living in our communities, not to the boundary of our personal preferences or comforts, but to the boundaries of God's law."[9] This extension involves not only initiative in reaching out to others, but also obedience to truth—a stance that, even when done in humility, may provoke opposition, scorn, reprisal, and undeserved ill-treatment.

Troup, Carter, and Mouw are helpful in several respects. First, these accounts of civility emphasize virtue, or what I would characterize as the necessary heart-attitude to practice public/political civility in any meaningful and productive way. Second, they highlight the need for inward self-reflection in a spirit of modesty, whether that takes the forms of sacrifice, transparency about motives, or humility. Third, they emphasize the need for a fundamental orientation to others that affirms their humanity. Carter's notion of sacrifice affirms the equality of others. Mouw's disavowal of crusaderism affirms the rights of others to live without violence.[10] Troup's notion of love affirms the solidarity one should have with others. However, I believe that the contemporary political and cultural conditions render these prescriptive accounts insufficient to the task of mitigating and reversing the dysfunctions that mar our public and political life together.

This insufficiency stems from two interrelated and contemporary problems to which American evangelical Christians, broadly speaking, have contributed. The first problem is an acute and profound lack of shared trust in our culture and in our polity. Divisions have always been a part of American life. What makes the situation in our own day different, though, is the degree to which cultural, demographic, and technological factors fundamentally inhibit our ability to see and hear people and ideas that are outside our spheres of familiarity and comfort. Philosopher Steve Wilkens and pastor Mark L. Sanford argue that the values of individualism and consumerism promote problematic character traits for many Americans, both Christian and non-Christian alike: egocentrism and personal comfort.[11] Individualism and consumerism, however, become even more problematic in our contemporary digital media-technological environment. Many social media platforms encourage egocentrism and comfort when they filter out those who are different from us. Digital technology makes it quite easy to never be exposed to, or to let alone cognitively and emotionally engage with, people and ideas that do not conform to what one already thinks and believes.[12] Individualism, consumerism, and digital technology also accompany the phenomenon of geographic self-segregation. Many neighborhoods and municipalities have increasingly become politically homogenous in ways that make it possible for people to interact with others of different political beliefs only rarely, if ever.[13] Furthermore, this profound homogeneity and self-segregation have been a staple of churches and other areas of religious life in America, particularly those that regard race.[14]

These cultural, technological, and demographic realities fundamentally inhibit shared trust. Literary scholar Wayne C. Booth emphasizes the importance of shared trust, which is built on "deep listening" and "probing for common ground."[15] To philosopher Eugene Garver, shared trust is at the heart of "practical reason" that can and should animate public and political discourse,[16] and differing political groups must together co-create trust if there is to be an ethical and productive public and political discursive climate.[17] But the cognitive and emotive contexts necessary for such motives are profoundly precluded when the overwhelming cultural temptation is to focus squarely on oneself and one's own needs and desires, and when it is all too easy to remain ignorant of the needs and desires of others.

The current state of tribalism also reflects and reinforces the absence of trust. For Wilkens and Sanford, tribalism erodes trust because this kind of thinking emphasizes power and control, sees only the incommensurability of values and truth claims across tribal lines, and elevates the needs and values of the tribe at the expense of other communities and groups. Perhaps most important, people captivated by this kind of thinking treat narratives of injury and marginalization as foundational to their identity, which only fuels moral outrage and self-justification.[18] The political rise of Donald Trump exacerbated such tribalism among American conservative evangelicals, over 80 percent of whom were reported as supporting Trump's presidency.[19] They support Trump not because he is like them, but because he vocally supports their tribal interests and is seen as someone who will protect them (and their understanding of what America should be) from the attacks and incursions of opposing tribes. He is seen as a "wrecking ball" to "political correctness" and as a "Cyrus" figure from the Old Testament—a "secular political leader" who is nonetheless used by God to usher in the goals of his people.[20] This magnification of tribal interest, and a self-serving confusion of tribal interest with public interest, can be seen in the recent advocacy of Messianic pastor Jonathan Cahn, who proclaimed a last-ditch "return" movement for faithful Christians to "return" the nation to God before the "window" of opportunity is permanently closed, and who organized a "National and Global Day of Prayer and Repentance" on September 26, 2020.[21]

The problem regarding the lack of shared collective trust is exacerbated by a second problem evident with American evangelicals. Put simply, they have responded to the political and cultural developments of the past several decades by clinging ever more tightly to dysfunctional expectations regarding their role in creating and sustaining political life. These expectations are sustained in part by a broadly Constantinian view of the relationship between the church and the state, in which Christian faithfulness in the public and political realm is seen as necessarily resulting in control over law and policy.[22]

This Constantinianism has taken different forms in American history. Church historian Mark Noll argues that the label "Christendom" characterizes both the U.S. as a nation and its people, and the Bible as a unique authority of meaning and argumentation in American public and political culture.[23] During the antebellum period, unfortunately, both pro-slavery and anti-slavery advocates appealed to the Bible and to divine providence in ways that magnified the dispute, casting the issue as a referendum on Christian civilization, and thereby hastened the recourse to civil war.[24]

Beginning in the last quarter of the twentieth century, this Constantinianism has taken the form of what has been commonly called the "Christian Right." With Francis Schaeffer's thinking about "Christian worldview" and secularism, and with the political activism of groups like Jerry Falwell's Moral Majority, conservative evangelicals were persuaded *en masse* not only to reengage in politics to "seize political power in the federal government,"[25] but also to do so with the purpose of reversing the moral decline brought about by secularism and feminism, and "to restore America to its Christian roots."[26]

In our own day, this Constantinianism all too easily interacts with the prevailing American cultural values of individualism and consumerism described above.[27] As such, American evangelicals not only generally expect that their tribal visions and values be established as the hegemonic norm for American public and cultural life, but also that the process by which they emerge "victorious" is straightforward, formulaic, gratifying in the short term, and does not involve any significant setbacks or struggles.

These Constantinian expectations have led American evangelicals to embrace one of two extremes in their approach to public and political life: triumphalism or withdrawal. Both extremes blind evangelicals to the need to work actively and across tribal lines to cultivate a shared trust that make civility possible. The first is a doubling down on the sort of Constantinian triumphalism described above, such that this approach becomes a defining indicator for Christian faithfulness in the public sphere. As historian John

Fea notes, the triumphalism in our own day is driven less by confidence and more by anger, fear, and resentment.[28] This fear-driven triumphalism helps in part to explain the degree to which evangelicals—particularly White conservatives—have embraced Donald Trump as someone whom they trust to protect them and their interests.

The second extreme is a retreat and withdrawal from public life, as seen recently in journalist Rod Dreher's *The Benedict Option* and former Roman Catholic archbishop of Philadelphia Charles Chaput's *Strangers in a Strange Land*. There is much to commend in Dreher's and Chaput's calls to "be the church" in truly authentic, communal, and countercultural ways. However, they emphasize such an oppositional and countercultural stance to the degree that it would be easy, all too easy, to neglect the tasks of reaching out to others and taking the initiative to foster relationship and dialogue. Creating discursive space, earning the right to be heard, and building trust: all these are tasks that require us to reach beyond just cultivating vibrant and authentic relationships within one's own tribe and with the truth.

Both of these stances, then, can unwittingly and too easily reinforce the deep mistrust of evangelicals by other tribes and communities. Something more radical is needed—something that evangelical Christian theological resources can provide.

Embracing Suffering

The something more radical I have in mind is an approach to public and political life that features an identity and heart-attitude that is grounded not merely in humility, but rather in humiliation. It flows out of a theological and practical perspective that sees suffering not just as an affirmative good in a number of important respects, but also as something fairly central to the practical expression of "know[ing] and liv[ing] Christianity in its authentic and divinely intended manner."[29] The broad approach I am proposing embraces suffering by affirming three major features about it. These major features of suffering connect in a foundational way to Christian identity and show it to be a corrective to the problems of trust and expectations identified above.

Suffering as Ontological Condition

First, this approach regards suffering as an ontological condition of being human. In theologian Timothy J. Basselin's study of Flannery O'Connor, he probes how the prominent Southern writer coped cognitively and emotionally with the lupus that imposed upon her pain, disability, and premature death. She articulates this alternative view of suffering.[30] O'Connor rejected the intellectual and cultural presuppositions that cast pain and suffering as irredeemably bad conditions to be mitigated and avoided at all costs: that human beings have the power to control their lives through the use of reason and action; that life is and should be predictable, formulaic, and responsive to our desires; and that happiness, conceptualized in profoundly therapeutic and consumeristic ways, is an inalienable right. She also saw suffering as a means to apprehend important and immutable realities of being human. Suffering brings into sharper relief the realities of human limitation and the need for grace from others and ultimately from God. Suffering directs us away from the temptation to see the limitations and frailties of others from a position of pity and dehumanizing sentimentality. Suffering brings questions of ultimate purpose into sharper focus, helpfully deemphasizing the vagaries of our mundane and provincial desires and expectations. Suffering uniquely places us in an emotional and ontological position of dependence, so that we can receive what is ultimately good.

In helping us to see ourselves as we really are, suffering can create possibility for us to escape the temptations to indulge in mistrust of others (particularly those outside of our communities and tribes) and in immodest expectations about public and political life. In apprehending more powerfully and more viscerally our limitations, we more easily assume a sober and modest stance about the certainty of our temporal/political visions and our ability to command them into reality—a stance that counters the temptation toward triumphalism. In seeing the limitations and frailties of others (as well as of ourselves), and in seeing the need for relationship and the mutual extension of grace that flows from our profound condition of dependence, we more easily assume a stance that can break down tribal barriers and create the possibility for meaningful trust.

Suffering as Flourishing

Second, this broad approach or framework conceptualizes suffering as fundamentally connected to human flourishing. Christian thinker Andy Crouch makes this countercultural connection in *Strong and Weak: Embracing a Life of Love, Risk and True Flourishing*, arguing for true flourishing as a "paradox" that embraces both "authority" and "vulnerability."[31] Rejecting common and hollow views of human flourishing as consumption, health, growth, affluence, or gentrification, Crouch understands flourishing as modeled on the life of Jesus, having a communal quality, and combining "the capacity for meaningful action" (true authority) with "exposure to meaningful risk" (true vulnerability).[32] True vulnerability, the more counterintuitive aspect of Crouch's view of flourishing, further implies the willingness to suffer. "*Vulnerable*," he writes, "at root means *woundable*—and any wound deeper than the most superficial scratch injures and limits not just our bodies but our very sense of self."[33] "Wounded," he continues,

> we are forced to become careful, tender, tentative in the way we move in the world, if we can still move on our own at all. To be vulnerable is to open oneself to the possibility—though not the certainty—that the result of our action in the world will be a wound, something lost, potentially never to be gained again.[34]

This sort of vulnerability connects us more profoundly with who we are and how we were made as God's image-bearers, and it does so in a way that helps us recognize and transcend the limitations of triumphalism, which operates from the assumption that flourishing flows out of strength and control—out of eliminating vulnerability rather than embracing it. This sort of vulnerability is also fundamental to more profound and authentic expressions of love. "[W]hat loves longs to be," Crouch declares, is "so committed to the beloved that everything meaningful is at risk."[35] "If we want flourishing," he emphasizes, we must embrace this risk.[36]

Suffering as Faithful Discipleship

Third, this broad approach centralizes Jesus's suffering and humiliation within an authentic expression of faith, community, and commonality. In his letter to the Philippians, the Apostle Paul encourages his readers to display a unity that emulates Jesus's experience of suffering and death.[37] In noting that Christ "emptied himself," Paul is spotlighting suffering in a superlative sense.[38] In Jesus's death, God's truest nature is "to pour himself out for the sake of others and to do so by taking the role of a slave." As such, he reveals "what it means for us to be created in God's image, to bear his likeness and have his 'mindset.' It means taking the role of the slave for the sake of others."[39] And all of this is meant not just as a personal exercise of sanctification, but also to accomplish edifying, humane, and productive communal work both inside and outside the church community. By inhabiting this framework of humiliation and self-emptying, members of the church community can collectively offer a profoundly countercultural witness against the individual and cultural impulse to "dominate" while also displaying a truly "'incarnational' demeanor."[40]

By doing so, evangelicals and others with a commitment to following Christ's example can meaningfully work to break down mistrust and the distinctively tribal identifications and motives that create and sustain that mistrust. They can more easily see that following Christ's example means seeing beyond one's own interests and the interests of like-minded and similarly situated people and communities, and in a profound and superlative way, hold in higher regard the interests and needs of others: people who think and feel differently, people with different backgrounds and experiences, people who have made mistakes, people who have in appearance or in reality done wrong and advanced falsehoods. Christ not only has shown grace to such people, but also has taken the initiative to actively engage and do good in the lives of such people. Internalizing and practicing Christ's example of suffering not only opens up the possibility of trust and common ground, but it also encourages the impulse not to engage in cultural retreat—the kind of retreat that abdicates the responsibility to share the wisdom, truth, and love that a community has with others, the kind of retreat that privileges being in relationship with and working for the good of one's own.

Suffering, Civility, and Racial Reconciliation

While there are many ways evangelicals can practice an authentic and powerful civility anchored in the embrace of suffering, one important area is in the pursuit of racial reconciliation. As sociologists of religion Michael O. Emerson and Christian Smith have pointed out, American evangelicals have tried and profoundly failed to address racial reconciliation in the second half of the twentieth century.[41] This profound failure is very much rooted not only in the norms and experiences of White American evangelical subculture but also in their epistemological and theological assumptions. In a variety of ways, evangelicals have been content to naturalize their own subcultural norms and, unfortunately, the broader American cultural norms of individualism and consumerism.

Doing this work in a more transformative way means first understanding and engaging—in an authentic and emotionally consubstantial way—the existential reality of the personal, political, and cultural suffering that Black Americans have faced throughout the history of the U.S., a reality that subcultural norms and theological assumptions have trained White evangelicals not to see. There was, before the Civil War, the suffering of chattel slavery and the race prejudice that authorized and reinforced it. In the post-Reconstruction period, Black Americans still faced suffering that was, in many ways, equal to or even worse than the suffering of chattel slavery.

The pervasive, systematic, and institutional ways in which suffering was inflicted upon African Americans has been amply studied and documented. Literary scholar Henry Louis Gates Jr., for instance, has recently offered a substantive study of the pervasive "religious" and "scientific" arguments employed to reinforce views of African Americans as subhuman—fit only for subservience and for control by others—and how these views were naturalized and reinforced in a wide array of popular cultural artifacts.[42] These views authorized a variety of systematic and oppressive acts in the post-Reconstruction period. Legal and political structures were set up that disenfranchised and segregated African Americans.[43] Lynching was a popularly celebrated and tacitly condoned campaign of domestic terrorism that led to the brutal and public murder of thousands of Black people in the decades following the end of Reconstruction.[44] Convict leasing, in which African Americans were incarcerated for unemployment or petty crimes and then leased out for involuntary servitude, created conditions arguably worse than slavery and persisted until well into the twentieth century.[45] In light of the patterns of mass incarceration that have taken shape over the past several decades, moreover, a credible case can be made that these conditions broadly extend to the present day.[46] Widespread real estate regulations and practices, including redlining, guaranteed that Black Americans would be segregated into poorer and isolated neighborhoods and ghettos, and that they would be systematically denied the opportunities to build wealth through real property that Whites have enjoyed.[47]

The sobering and morally serious truth is that, as a group, White American evangelicals have allowed themselves to be blinded to these historical and contemporary realities. They not only do not know the depth of suffering that the Black American community has endured over the full course of American history, but also (perhaps consequently) have a distorted view of suffering and how to see the nature of the adversity in their own lives. Without in any way minimizing this depth of suffering on the part of African Americans, White evangelicals can learn much about what suffering looks like by broadening their historical perspective along the lines very briefly described above.

But having a better cognitive understanding of what suffering has looked like in American history is just an initial step. To become deeply identified with this suffering, evangelicals need to better know what it feels like and what it means to inhabit the reality of the emotional exhaustion and oppression of Black suffering. Evangelicals also need to know how others have inhabited that reality and borne the yoke in ways that are theologically significant and life affirming. One way to start to do this is to take seriously the work of Black American theologians like James Cone and Howard Thurman. In *The Cross and the Lynching Tree*, Cone connects lynching with African American religious experience, such that suffering in a systematic and profoundly undeserved and dehumanizing way is a profound means to identify with Christ and the agonizing and undeserved suffering that he endured.[48] In *Jesus and the Disinherited*, Thurman draws upon the political and economic oppression systematically inflicted on the Black American community to understand the identity, purpose, and imperatives of Jesus in a counterculturally and arguably more authentically biblical way. He emphasizes that Jesus was a "poor Jew," economically and culturally disadvantaged,[49] whose words "were directed to the House of Israel, a minority within the Greco-Roman world, smarting under the loss of status, freedom, and autonomy, haunted by the dream of the restoration of a lost glory and former greatness," and whose message "focused on the urgency of a radical change in the inner attitude of the people."[50] In this way, Jesus was sociopolitically subversive, identified with people "with their backs against the wall,"[51] and practiced "a religion that was born of a people acquainted with persecution and suffering."[52]

This deep identification with the Black American experience—in the suffering and in the earnest work in drawing upon and growing from that suffering—can and should lead to concrete acts of suffering on behalf of others. In the case of advancing racial justice and racial reconciliation, this would involve an intentional emptying on the part of White evangelicals to empower Black Americans in ways that work to restore humanity and voice to them. Noting that repentance includes "dismantling" and "often means giving up something that is rightfully ours," pastor Ken Wytsma writes of the need for "giving up positions of power," for "passing along opportunity to others," for "actively and creatively making space for other voices," and for raising funds for groups and organizations promoting "the encouragement and development of leaders of color who often have a difficult time supporting funding."[53]

To be sure, work of this sort is simply not comparable in magnitude to the suffering that the Black American community has already endured over the centuries. In doing this public work of emptying and service, no one is going to be martyred. No one is going to be lynched. No one is going to be denied the opportunity for safe housing. No one is going to be summarily dehumanized in daily interactions and in the portrayals of popular culture. Even so, work that addresses racial injustice and creates the space for racial reconciliation involves the kind of emptying, the kind of exposure to and experience of risk and loss that are involved in suffering.[54] As such, it can stand as an example of how to engage in public and relational practices that exhibit a suffering-inflected approach to public and political civility.

The initial steps toward engaging in this kind of work have been taken recently within more conservative American evangelical denominations, particularly the Presbyterian Church in America (PCA), and in individual presbyteries (regional associations of churches) within the PCA. In 2018. The General Assembly of the PCA adopted a formal report of its *ad interim* committee on racial and ethnic reconciliation that, among other things, establishes the pursuit of racial reconciliation and racial justice on a structural level as activities not only consistent with the broad witness of Scripture, but also as a Scriptural mandate.[55] This view is also reflected in a formal report in the same year of an analogous committee in the Tidewater Presbytery of the PCA, which includes PCA churches from Richmond to Southeastern Virginia and Northeastern North Carolina.[56]

To be sure, though, these are the most preliminary of steps, and even these steps are being taken slowly and painfully. Even while the PCA's 2018 declarations were in many ways unprecedented, the PCA continues to be hampered by its own well-worn ways of seeing things, some of which Emerson and Smith highlighted in their study of earlier efforts at racial reconciliation: the tendency to see problems individualistically rather than systemically or structurally, the tendency to "over spiritualize" problems in ways that overshadow material causes and solutions, the aversion to listening to theological and cultural voices outside the confines of conservative White evangelicalism to gain greater insight, and the fear of embracing understandings and solutions that in any way smack of "Marxism" or "socialism" (as seen, for instance, in the contemporary public debates within the PCA and other conservative evangelical denominations over the nature and value of Critical Race Theory). Further and substantial progress will depend on the willingness to take concrete, persistent, and self-effacing steps to both promote justice and, over time, to earn the right to be heard and create a more authentically dialogic climate in which trust can be built. Embracing the perspective on civility and suffering outlined in this chapter, I believe, will precisely promote such action over time. Specifically for White evangelicals, particularly conservatives, the other major challenge to overcome is the perception that doing the things identified in this latter section of this chapter is inconsistent with their own theological commitments. Certainly, it is true that Black American religious expression and theological reflection have often appeared with ideas and perspectives that are decidedly on the Left of the political spectrum, and it is certainly fair to see theologians like Cone and Thurman espousing theological positions outside the bounds of evangelicalism. However, if theologians like Anthony B. Bradley are taken seriously, then this need not and should not be the case.[57] Put another way, evangelicals can edifyingly and powerfully engage the Black American community with a suffering-inflected civility, and they can do so in ways that affirm an embrace of the triune God, of a high view of the inspiration and authority of Scripture, and other important theological commitments. Indeed, the particular call to civility and suffering that I explicate in this chapter is meant not to disavow evangelical theology, but rather to more profoundly affirm it.

Conclusion

No one likes to feel pain, especially when it feels unearned or undeserved, and certainly no one likes to suffer. It cuts against our own human nature.

But even more profoundly, it cuts against American popular culture. And the fact that American evangelicals have so thoroughly resisted the idea of suffering—both individually and tribally—is more evidence of the extent to which, as political scientist and sociologist Alan Wolfe argues in *The Transformation of American Religion*, American Christianity has been profoundly co-opted by American culture. In this respect, the ability of American evangelicals to push beyond civility (and even, all too often, self-serving incivility) has been limited by an unwillingness to push beyond their self-serving instincts and their cultural lack of imagination.

As this chapter has hopefully shown, though, the willingness to affirm and practice suffering in the spirit of *diakonia* (or service) in a stance that embraces and engages others that pushes beyond humility to humiliation—and that embraces this degree of self-control, self-denial, and self-sacrifice—is important and even essential to move significantly toward the broad public and political goals that animate all the theorizing behind public civility. We need to enter into the lives and perspectives of others, but we need to do so in ways that are not only uncomfortable and disorienting, but also expose us to considerable and extended pain. We need to work to earn the right to be heard by others and build trust with others. But we need to do so not from a place of insisting on our own station and our rights, but from a place of giving those up and experiencing pain and loss on behalf of others with the same abiding spirit of *kenosis* (self-emptying) that Christ showed in his Incarnation and his death. As we do these things, we need to enter voluntarily and affirmatively into suffering for others (particularly for those unlike us) and for the public good. And for evangelicals, doing so is not a compromise of their faith and the advancement of what they see as divine purposes but is actually a profound, powerful, and uniquely countercultural affirmation of these commitments.

So let all of this be true in our own lives and in our communities. Let others see how we patiently, purposely, and resiliently suffer on behalf of others. Let others see how we break out of the provincial, individualistic, and consumeristic mentality that so dominates our popular and political cultures. And may all this truly change for the better the public and political life that we share together.

Chapter 9

Marginally Persuasive

Recovering the Cruciform Power of Prophetic Witness

John B. Hatch

"Then the chief priests and the Pharisees gathered a council and said, 'What shall we do? For this Man works many signs. If we let Him alone like this, everyone will believe in Him, and the Romans will come and take away both our place and nation.' And one of them, Caiaphas, being high priest that year, said to them, 'You know nothing at all, nor do you consider that it is expedient for us that one man should die for the people, and not that the whole nation should perish'" (John 11:47–50, NKJV).

"Jesus also suffered outside the city gate to make the people holy through his own blood. Let us, then, go to him outside the camp, bearing the disgrace he bore. For here we do not have an enduring city, but we are looking for the city that is to come" (Hebrews 13:12–14, NIV).

Introduction

Under brutal roman occupation in first-century Judea, the ruling Jewish council had good reason to fear losing "our place and our nation."[1] Yet in the name of saving God's people from a pagan crackdown, these religious leaders unwittingly "crucified the Lord of glory."[2] Fear, rooted in reliance on human power, blinded them to their true King. This is but one example of a pattern found across Scripture and human history. A millennium before Christ, the people of Israel feared perpetual threats and conquests from hostile neighbors, and thus clamored for the installation of a king, rather than relying on God to raise up deliverers when needed. Enticed by the allure of invulnerable power, they succumbed to what theologian Walter Brueggemann refers to as "royal consciousness," straying from their calling to be God's covenant community of freedom, justice, and compassion. In Saint Augustine's terms, they emulated the City of Man. In the words of the Hebrews passage above, they tried to make themselves "an enduring city" instead of "looking for the city that is to come."[3]

Three millennia later, White conservative evangelical Protestant Christians in the U.S. feared losing their freedom of public expression and institutional practice on such matters as sexuality, marriage, and abortion in an increasingly post-Christian culture. In response, the vast majority (81%) entrusted the nation's executive office to Donald Trump—a man who trafficked in a rhetoric of fear, relished incivility and scapegoating, and projected an image of invulnerable power.[4] While many evangelicals were initially wary, he won them over by embracing Republican policy priorities, promising to appoint pro-life Supreme Court justices, and identifying with their sense of being marginalized and persecuted.[5] Leading Right-wing Christian leaders heralded Trump's victory as the saving of Christian America; other evangelicals, however, have decried what they see as a subversion of the Church and its witness.[6]

As Calvin L. Troup observes in his address during the Forum 4:15 Unconference as presented in Chapter 1, present conditions in American culture work against civility and frequently make persuasion about contentious sociopolitical issues an exercise in futility. This situation is compounded when a group feels threatened and resorts to unprincipled power for protection. Taking contemporary conservative evangelicals during Trump's presidency as my case, I explore the challenge of maintaining a courageous and winsome witness in the face of the vulnerability and fear that naturally arise in an oft-hostile world. Specifically, I examine this situation through Walter Brueggemann's conceptions of royal consciousness and prophetic imagination, in tandem with René Girard's theory of the scapegoat. These conceptual lenses help us to see that biblical faith, consummating in Christ, aims to delegitimize and disarm the power-grabbing spirit of the world. They also afford insight into the sociopolitical character of conservative American evangelicalism, revealing that uncritical support for Trump by some evangelicals constitutes a paradoxical capitulation to the ways of empire in the name of saving God's commonwealth. This contradiction calls attention to the need to recover prophetic witness, beginning with marginality and the practice of lament. In light of Saint Augustine's wisdom and biblical insights, I conclude that Christians' greatest influence resides neither in exerting power nor deploying rhetoric, but rather in humbly lifting voices of lament with the marginalized, courageously loving one's enemies, and following Christ to the margins.

Scapegoating, Royal Consciousness, and Prophetic Imagination

To understand the challenge of Christian witness in society, let us begin with Girard's scapegoat theory and Brueggemann's account of prophetic imagination. According to Girard, since prehistoric times, human societies have resorted to unjust violence to establish and maintain order. While ancient myths about cultural origins cover up this injustice, the Bible exposes it. Similarly, Brueggemann shows that the imaginative visions of biblical prophets unmask the illegitimate claims of kings and empires and give hope to the oppressed. Brueggemann traces the development of prophetic consciousness through Scripture from the Exodus to the ministry of Jesus, who establishes a new kingdom of sacrificial love.

As Troup noted in Chapter 1, Saint Augustine observed that the City of Man is founded on fratricide and politically animated by social ambition. Augustine drew this conclusion both from Scripture and Roman legend. In the Book of Genesis, Cain envies Abel's divinely favored status, murders him, and founds a city. According to legend, the founder of Rome, Romulus, kills his sibling rival, Remus, while building the city. Girard's provocative thesis is that such legends are mythological reinterpretations of ancient acts of mob violence, and that prior to Christ, all civilizations use ordered violence to a keep lid on the chaos that might otherwise erupt from competing social desires.

According to Girard, human social desire is rooted in *mimesis*—imitation of others' desires—and this leads to rivalrous competition for any given object of social desire (such as honor and glory, which Augustine identifies as the motivating force of the Roman empire). In numerous origin myths from around the world, Girard found evidence suggesting that ancient kingdoms were born when the tensions of mimetic social desire spread like an infection through a primitive community until it reached an explosion-point of mob violence against a single victim. Having vented their envious desires in a unanimous act of murder, the community would suddenly experience a return to peace and order (often leading them to conclude that the murdered victim was really a god). Hoping to sustain this new state of order and avert future chaos, they would accord godlike authority to a king (who used violence to enforce laws and taboos) and designate priests to manage religious scapegoat rituals,[7] often involving human sacrifice.[8] Moreover, these societies mythologized the original violent event, whitewashing the murderers' guilt by attributing the scapegoat's death to the gods or indicating that the scapegoat had to be killed for violating a taboo.[9]

Girard found a marked departure from this pattern, however, when he examined Scriptural accounts: instead of obscuring the murderous roots of human civilizations, the Bible exposes them.[10] For instance, the story of Cain and Abel portrays Cain, the city-builder, as guilty of envy and murder and Abel as the innocent victim.[11] The well-known story of Joseph is another scapegoat narrative: Joseph enters the scene as a cocky adolescent who flaunts the divine favor he has received, and this unites his brothers against him in murderous envy. Scripture, however, clearly portrays Joseph as innocent and his brothers as guilty for selling him into slavery; despite their guilt, God brings about redemption for all of them to ensure Israel's future founding as a nation.[12] These and other biblical accounts, consummating in the narratives of Christ's Passion, highlight the innocence of the scapegoat and expose the diabolical nature of grasping for power and control through victimage.[13]

Girard's theory of cultural scapegoating and biblical revelation provides an enlightening backdrop for Brueggemann's dialectic between royal and prophetic consciousness. Running through Scripture, Brueggemann sees an evolving struggle between power-driven kingdoms and God's prophetically envisioned community.[14] Royal consciousness—the mindset of empire—is fixated on managing people and resources for the benefit of those in power. In the name of perpetuating order, it commits injustices, including military conquests and economic policies that take advantage of the vulnerable. In this way, the empire generates affluence and luxury, which numbs its citizens to the sufferings of the oppressed.[15] Royal consciousness resorts to a religion of triumphalism that cloaks oppression and injustice in an idolatrous smokescreen.[16] Prophetic imagination, however, sees through the smokescreen.

Biblical prophets challenge royal consciousness through discourses of criticizing and energizing. *Prophetic criticizing* exposes the falsehood and injustice of the present order and laments the destruction that is coming because of the sins of the kingdom or empire; the intense anguish of its lament pierces numbed hearts. Criticizing is followed by the second task of prophetic imagination: to energize others with the hope that a new reality is coming. Prophets use poetry to "cut through the despair" and foresee God's intervention to bring freedom and justice.[17] They also energize a *"politics of justice and compassion."*[18] Thus, to use Augustine's language, prophetic ministry calls forth a new commonwealth grounded in well-ordered loves instead of ambition and violence.

The connection between Girard's scapegoat mechanism and Brueggemann's dialectic becomes evident as we trace them through Scripture, from Israel's Exodus out of Egypt to the ministry of prophets in Israel to the life and death of Jesus. Ancient Egypt is the paradigm of royal consciousness, famous not only for its massive pyramids (built to preserve the glory of the Pharaohs forever), but also for its conscription of the Israelites into slave labor. Fearful of any threat to Egyptian power, Pharaoh treats this minority as a scapegoat, ordering that their male babies be killed at birth. Thus, Israel's prophetic imagination is born in lament, crying out to God for deliverance from bondage. Moses then comes with the prophetic message that God hears them, feels their pain, and intends to act. Through his prophet, God confronts the false gods of Egyptian power, overpowers them, and energizes the liberation of Israel. In the process, Moses's prophetic words forge a new kind of community based on a covenant of reverence for the transcendence of God, together with just treatment of one another, animated by love of neighbor.[19]

However, as the people of Israel settle in the Promised Land and grow in prosperity, they begin to emulate the royal consciousness of the surrounding nations. Beginning with King Saul,[20] this process comes to full fruition in Solomon, who creates a standing army, uses conscripted labor to build a palace and royal cities, and falls prey to idol worship through marriage-alliances with surrounding nations (or, through his enormous harem of foreign women).²¹ As Solomon's successors drift further into royal consciousness, some of them even adopt the abhorrent practice of sacrificing children to pagan gods.²² In response to all these corruptions of God's community, prophets arise, crying out against idolatry, injustice, and human sacrifice,²³ as well as the people's reliance on animal sacrifices to gain God's favor.²⁴ Among these prophets, Jeremiah epitomizes prophetic criticizing: he not only warns of the coming destruction of Jerusalem by the Babylonians but also lives to see this disaster.²⁵ The Book of Lamentations, which laments the horror of this event, is attributed to him. The prophet Isaiah, on the other hand, epitomizes energizing—but with a thread of sorrow. The second part of the Book of Isaiah (chapters 40–55) heralds a glorious new day but is woven through with the Songs of the Servant, who suffers unjust scapegoating on behalf of the people and so brings redemption and renewal.²⁶

Prophetic imagination reaches its climax in the ministry of Christ, who proclaims and inaugurates a kingdom of love while calling his followers to leave behind the ambitions and scapegoating impulses of the world.²⁷ Jesus hails from the margins of his society, conducts his ministry mainly outside the religious/political center (Jerusalem), and heralds a new kingdom in which the priorities of royal consciousness are inverted—where woe awaits the rich, the well-fed, the well-spoken-of, and blessing comes to the poor, the broken-hearted, the persecuted.²⁸ His mighty acts demonstrate these priorities: the blind see, the deaf hear, the lepers are cleansed, the demon-possessed are delivered, and the dead are raised.²⁹ Instead of ostracizing those whom society deems as "unclean" and "sinners," Christ's followers are to welcome them, forgive the repentant, and love their enemies.

Jesus's teachings and miracles critique the dominant value system that oppresses and excludes, and they herald a new community of inclusion and justice.³⁰ As the ultimate Prophet, Christ laments over Jerusalem, bewailing its age-old reliance on scapegoating violence to maintain power: "Jerusalem, Jerusalem, you who kill the prophets and stone those sent to you, how often I have longed to gather your children together, as a hen gathers her chicks under her wings, and you were not willing."³¹ On Palm Sunday, as Jesus and the other Passover pilgrims reach the outskirts of Jerusalem, he weeps over this so-called City of Peace.³² He knows that it will wreak violence upon him just as it did the other prophets, and it will eventually fall prey to violent destruction by the Romans.³³

The ministry of Jesus culminates in the cross—the ultimate refutation of royal consciousness. Viewing the Gospel accounts through the lens of scapegoat theory, Girard discovered that Christ's crucifixion turns the principle of victimage inside out. In the Gospels, Christ dies not as a sacrificial scapegoat demanded by God, but as the incognito King of Truth who draws the scapegoat mechanism into the light, willingly suffering and exposing its diabolical power.[34] All the elements of human civilizations' ubiquitous scapegoat mechanism are present and exposed as morally repugnant in the Gospels: for example, the notion that a killing is necessary to maintain order and secure the nation; the frenzy of the mob crying for blood; the friendship of former enemies (Pontius Pilate and Herod) through collaboration in victimization; and the falsehoods necessary to whitewash the murder.[35] Having recently given vent to prophetic lament outside the gate of Jerusalem, Jesus now carries his cross to the hill of execution just outside the city, where he cries out in anguish and offers up his life.

The resurrection, however, resoundingly vindicates the truth of Christ's righteousness and kingship and exposes the falsehood of humans' royal consciousness. Christ founds the new community, the Kingdom of God, not on dead scapegoats but on the "living sacrifices" of self-giving love.[36] This kingdom comes not through force of arms, but through Christ-followers' proclamation and demonstration of the Gospel, as they follow their Master to the margins, serving the lost and least. Their prophetic witness is *cruciform*, conformed to the way of the cross.

The Troubled Legacy of the Christian Right

When Brueggemann's and Girard's insights are applied to the phenomenon of evangelical support for Donald Trump, they reveal a paradox: in the name of saving God's commonwealth, many Christians have capitulated to the ways of empire. From its inception in the 1970s, the Religious Right movement raised a prophetic voice for family values. At the same time, however, it remained somewhat captive to royal consciousness regarding race and culture. In our contemporary moment, the balance of this tension has shifted toward royal consciousness, as seen in fear and callousness toward vulnerable outsiders, acceptance of Trump's troubling character, and a drift toward embracing raw power.

For decades, conservative Christian activism advanced under the banner of family values.[37] To a considerable extent, this signals a commitment to defend Judeo-Christian households from the intrusive and controlling tendencies of federal bureaucracy. As Troup observes in Chapter 1 of this book, the well-ordered loves that characterize commonwealth are nurtured first and foremost in households—not only biological families, but also especially in the spiritual households of the Church. In this light, Christ-followers have reason to be wary of government overreach into local and family life. The Christian homeschool movement exemplifies grass-roots resistance to government management and control, reasserting the centrality of family to the education and nurture of children. In 1994, homeschoolers exercised outside influence by flooding Congress with phone calls opposing a proposed amendment to a federal bill on education. The Armey Amendment would have required every full-time teacher, including homeschool parents, to be certified by the state—in effect, making most homeschooling illegal. Not only did the barrage of protest overwhelm congressional telephone switchboards to the point of shutdown, but also it led to the defeat of the Armey Amendment by an overwhelming margin.[38]

Overall, however, the balance of power in the nation has trended away from families and local communities toward large cities, multinational corporations, and state or federal bureaucracy. Thus, a key reason for the rise of Trump on an anti-elite, anti-big-government platform is a national erosion of commonwealth, particularly in rural areas that had known community cohesion most deeply. "Make America Great Again" may be heard as a call to restore the Judeo-Christian values, time-honored traditions, and thriving small communities of the nation's past.

Yet the "great" America of that bygone era—including its churches—was widely complicit and invested in the ways of empire, particularly with regard to race. While the federal government may have intruded less into the lives of White citizens, the nation was built on the stolen lands (and lives) of Indigenous Americans and the forced labor of African Americans—emblems of empire and royal consciousness. For a century after the abolition of slavery, many states and local communities still maintained a rigid and oppressive racial hierarchy through unjust segregation laws and discriminatory policies. White Christian communities participated in a home-grown form of scapegoating: lynching any African American who seemed to threaten the racial order.[39] Unbelievably, they did so *under the banner of the cross*,[40] missing how the true King had repudiated all such scapegoating. Many of these practices ended only through the intervention of the federal government. Sadly, even the anti-abortion movement, dedicated to the sanctity of human life and the defense of the most vulnerable, originated in the 1970s as part of southern evangelicals' strategy to protect de facto racial segregation in schools.[41] However, many pro-lifers today have no awareness of or allegiance to those origins.[42]

As the Christian Right has roots in both commonwealth and racialist empire, so conservative evangelical support for Donald Trump is rife with moral contradictions. I give examples from his first three years of presidency. On the one hand, Trump has appointed federal judges who oppose abortion and align with the political values of the Religious Right, and he has cut both taxes and federal regulations. However, there is tragic irony in potentially saving unborn lives only to cut away safety nets and support systems that would help make life endurable for poor children, many of whom are people of color. Separating innocent Central American children from their parents and holding them in cramped, unsanitary facilities for months as a deterrent against illegal immigration goes against Moses's call to love the foreigner.[43] Still worse, it treats children as scapegoats for the nation's problems. Likewise, when Trump's supporters accept or embrace his stereotyping of brown-skinned asylum-seekers and illegal immigrants as dangerous criminals (when statistics show they are actually less likely to commit crimes[44]), they are complicit in verbal scapegoating. Hence, the historical tension between family values and racialist empire persists in the Trump era.

Moreover, in terms of presidential character, Trump embodies a definitive shift toward royal consciousness. Nepotism, financial conflicts of interest, careless disregard for Constitutional checks and balances, an evident wish for greater autocratic power, expressed admiration of brutal dictators, constant and exaggerated self-praise, influencing foreign powers to act against his political opponents—these bespeak a heart given to royal ambition.[45] While some of these qualities are not unique to Trump among U.S. presidents, they uniquely pervade and define his presidency. An unparalleled profusion of lies, exaggerations, and personal attacks on his critics numb citizens' consciousness.[46] Referring to the press as "The Enemy of the People" mirrors the way in which fascist dictators scapegoat journalists to rally their supporters. Yet many evangelical leaders speak scarcely a word against this president, instead falling in line with his rhetoric whenever he casts the enemy as anyone who justly exposes or criticizes his wrongs.

The tragic irony in evangelicals' unswerving loyalty to such a leader is that in the months and years after the election, as evidence of his moral, intellectual, and verbal unfitness for the presidency mounted up, their political choice was no longer between Trump and a liberal, pro-choice Democrat. Rather, it was between Trump and Vice President Pence—a strongly conservative Christian with executive political experience as governor, a far better grasp of Constitutional governing, and a much better record of moral integrity prior to the election. With a little prophetic imagination, mainstream evangelical leaders might have recognized that once the election was won by the Republican ticket, they could safely marshal their millions of followers to call on Trump to either repent of his lying and corruption, incivility and scapegoating, or resign (at which time the vice president would take his place)—thus emulating the homeschool movement's grassroots power demonstrated in the 1990s. But instead, as of this writing, Trump has been able to consistently rely on their loyalty, love, and even hero-worship.[47] As conservative columnist Michael Gerson laments, "Evangelicals have been reshaped into the image of Trump himself."[48]

This capitulation to royal consciousness stems both from fear and the allure of power. White Christians (including evangelicals) have enjoyed democratic voice and pride of place in the U.S. for more than two centuries. In recent decades, however, they have experienced moderate threats to their freedoms and privileges.[49] Fearful of these threats, some evangelical leaders now argue that politics is about raw power, not character, and what matters is that they have a strongman on their side.[50] To conservative evangelical pundit David French, however, this position reflects a shocking loss of perspective: "The American evangelical church isn't so weak that it needs Trump's version of secular salvation. The early persecuted church would be stunned at the modern American church's immense political strength."[51] Failing to see this, some prominent evangelicals now implicitly cast themselves in the mold of the Jewish captives in Babylon and Persia and view Donald Trump as a modern-day Cyrus—a pagan emperor who is on their side.[52] However, given that Trump gained office through the votes of Christians (after having blatantly displayed autocratic tendencies not seen in previous presidential contenders), a very different biblical analogy is far more applicable: Israel opting for a king when they were overcome by fear of enemy attacks and the allure of pagan royal consciousness.[53]

In the Scriptural account of Saul's rise to the throne (1 Samuel 8), God reprimands the people through the prophet Samuel, saying that they have faithlessly rejected their true King by clamoring for a king like their pagan enemies have. Similarly, David French chides the evangelical church for putting fear of Democrats over faith in God, "acting as if it needs Trump to protect it. That's not courageous. It's repulsive. And so long as this fear continues, expect the church's witness to degrade further."[54] To use another analogy, if Trump is like Pontius Pilate or Caesar, devoted to power at the expense of truth, then Trump's evangelical advisors/cheerleaders have become rather like the Jewish ruling council of that time (the Sanhedrin)—more concerned with preserving their power under the present regime than protecting the integrity of their witness. As French laments, this has taken a tremendous toll on their credibility. Observing that some evangelical leaders have spoken out against Democrats' errors and sins while ignoring the same sins in Trump, French writes: "We should pray for presidents, critique them when they're wrong, praise them when they're right, and never, ever impose partisan double standards. We can't ever forget the importance of character, the necessity of our own integrity, and the power of the prophetic witness."[55] Rather than conforming to a president who thrives on marginalizing and scapegoating others, Christians are called to follow their Master, who identified with the marginalized, lamented the blindness of those in power, and gave himself over to become their scapegoat so their eyes could be opened to God's love.

Marginality, Lament, and Persecution

If White evangelical Christians in the U.S. are to regain a genuine prophetic witness, then they must turn away from royal consciousness to embrace marginality, recover lament, and accept persecution when persuasion is not possible. As Brueggemann points out, prophets typically arise from the margins of society; moreover, their calling makes them marginal figures, who neither sit comfortably inside the centers of power nor stand outside casting verbal stones from a safe distance.[56] In fact, prophets themselves frequently become the scapegoats of society, as mentioned in Jesus's lament over Jerusalem. Such has been the fate of French, whose critiques of evangelical support for Trump have drawn the wrath of fellow evangelicals and led some conservatives to brand him a Left-wing collaborator.[57] Prophetic witnesses are caught between their compatriots in the thrall of royal consciousness and God's coming community of freedom, justice, and compassion. They offer words and displays of anguish for those who have been seduced by empty power, and they pray for their repentance. Thus, prophetic discourse is humble and hospitable, inviting all who hear to heed its lament, turn from triumphalism, and enter in.

Indeed, embracing marginality goes hand-in-hand with a recovery of lament.[58] According to Old Testament scholar Glenn Pemberton, lament makes up 40 percent of the psalms but less than 20 percent of Presbyterian, Baptist, and Church of Christ hymnals.[59] Avoidance of lament is especially pronounced in the White American church, particularly among evangelicals. Missiologist Soong-Chan Rah observes, "For American evangelicals riding the fumes of a previous generation's assumptions, a triumphalist theology of celebration and privilege rooted in a praise-only narrative is perpetuated by the absence of lament and the underlying narrative of suffering that informs lament."[60] This is not the case, however, in the Black church tradition, which was forged in the fires of racist marginalization and oppression.[61] Thus, recovering a robust practice of prophetic lament will require White evangelicals (especially the well-to-do among them) to repent of smugness and intently listen to, learn from, and identify with Christians from minority groups and the margins. It might entail some discomfort or loss of reputation; but the Master said, "Whoever wants to be my disciple must deny themselves and take up their cross and follow me."[62] The author of Hebrews highlights the social import of this command: "Let us, then, go to him outside the camp, bearing the disgrace he bore."[63]

What might it look like for White evangelicals in the U.S. to recover prophetic lament for a nation—and a Church—largely given over to royal consciousness? Thankfully, there are a few recent exemplars that demonstrate how lament can pierce the numbness and triumphalism of royal consciousness in our time. Rah, for instance, wrote a lament over racism in America patterned after Lamentations 5. Here is an excerpt:

> 8 Our ancestors sinned the great sin of instituting slavery;
> they are no more—but we bear their shame.
> 9 The system of slavery and institutionalization of racism ruled
> over us, and there is no one to free us from their hands.
> 10 We get our bread at the risk of our lives
> because of guns on the streets. . . .
> 13 Young men can't find work because of unjustly applied laws;
> boys stagger under the expectation that their lives are destined for jail.
> 14 The elder statesmen and civil rights leaders are gone from the

city gate; young people who speak out their protest through
music are silenced.
15 Trust in our ultimate triumph has diminished;
our triumphant dance has turned to a funeral dirge.
16 Our sense of exceptionalism has been exposed.
Woe to us, for we have sinned![64]

Other examples come from *The Gospel Coalition*, which hosts a blog of prayers for lamenting. One of these decries abortion within a frame of compassion: "We long for the Day when 'death shall be no more' . . . including the death of unborn children. . . . Show us how to care for women and men whose stories have been marked by abortion—either as victims or agents. May our love be more notorious than our rhetoric, and a non-anxious presence mark our undaunted protest . . ."[65] Another prayer on this blog laments violence in the world today:

> How long, O Lord, until you return and put an end to *all* violence—whether it's in the streets of Syria or the villages of Iraq; the highways of Arizona or the business district of Manhattan? How long before there's no more warring nations, or even divisive personalities. . . .
>
> We *yearn*, *crave*, and *long* for the Day when peace will be our governor and well-being our ruler. . . .
>
> Until that Day, Jesus, help us to live *by the gospel*, not by the sword —by the way of your cross, not by the ways of mere men. . . .[66]

Notice how this lament transcends partisanship by decrying all forms of violence. It even recognizes divisive personalities as a form of violence, thus cutting through indifference toward the fractious rhetoric practiced by men like Trump. It stands against royal consciousness and aspires to a cruciform life, exemplifying an orientation that is needed in an age when many Christians' public witness has become more conformed to Trump than to Christ.

In the aftermath of the 2016 presidential election, Christian blogger John Pavlovitz lamented what I have characterized as the rise of royal consciousness among fellow Christians. In a post titled "Here's Why We Grieve Today," he explains that many citizens' anguish was "not about losing an election," but about such phenomena as "religion being weaponized . . . crassness and vulgarity and disregard for women . . . a barricaded, militarized, bully nation . . . an unapologetic, open-faced ugliness."[67] Pavlovitz goes on to clarify: "it is not only that these things have been ratified by our nation that grieve us . . . it's knowing that these things have been amen-ed by our neighbors, our families, our friends, those we work with and worship alongside."[68] In a subsequent post titled "White Evangelicals, This is Why People Are Through With You," Pavlovitz writes not with a tone of anger, but of deep anguish at the misjudgments he believes evangelicals have made and the credibility they've lost. At the end of the post, he writes: "I know it's likely you'll dismiss these words . . . But I had to at least try to reach you. It's what Jesus would do."[69] Pavlovitz does not rely on clever reasoning or ingratiating appeal to convince his audience; in fact, he admits to having little confidence in the effectiveness of his words. Perhaps that is because royal consciousness works against persuasion toward truth when the truth challenges its hold on power.

In circumstances where persuasion is limited or futile, Christ-followers need to remember the wisdom of Saint Augustine and the example of early Christians, who expected to be marginalized and persecuted—even martyred. Before Augustine's conversion to Christ, he was a master teacher and practitioner of rhetoric in the Roman Empire, using it for personal gain. Later, as a theologian and bishop, he placed this knowledge in the service of the Church, much like Aristotle had done for the Greek city-state. Yet Saint Augustine ultimately relied on Christ's transformative power of mind-and-heart-change, which works through apparent weakness.

In his treatise *On Christian Doctrine*, Augustine commends rhetoric as a worldly treasure that can be put to God's service.[70] His rationale is that the tools of rhetoric, like military weapons, are used by both sides in the battle of truth versus falsehood, and it would be wrong to leave truth "unarmed against lying."[71] Eight centuries before Augustine, Aristotle made a similar argument, noting that truth is more defensible than falsehood and ought to be defended by rhetorical means.[72] Aristotle identified three primary means of persuasion to be used by those at the centers of cultural and political power: *ethos* (credibility based on perceived character, competence, and goodwill), *logos* (sound, audience-oriented reasoning), and *pathos* (appealing to audience emotions). Christ embodied divine *ethos*, *logos*, and *pathos* at the margins of society through miraculous healing, prophetic proclamation, and willing suffering.

The climax of Jesus's prophetic ministry—the cross—reveals the inadequacy of traditional rhetoric to break the spell of royal consciousness. In the Gospel narratives, the pious and highly educated members of the Sanhedrin are not open to Christ's truthful persuasion; instead, they welcome false testimony in support of trumped-up charges against him, in order to rid themselves of a threat to their power. In response, Christ offers courageous, silent suffering as a witness to his Truth. Pilate is so accustomed to exercising ruthless power on behalf of the Roman Empire that he cynically asks Jesus, "What is truth?"[73] He ultimately yields to the mob's demand for crucifixion while knowing there is no truth in the charges against Jesus. This paradigmatic example shows that both pagan politicians and pious believers are susceptible to the spirit of falsehood and scapegoating when their control feels threatened and they succumb to fear. When royal consciousness has stopped ears and numbed hearts, and the bloodlust of scapegoating has possessed the mob, civility may be of no avail, and the "good [person] skilled in speaking" may not be able to gain a fair hearing.[74] Nonetheless, one can stand as a witness to Truth and grieve for those who will not take it to heart. As shown in Troup's Chapter 1 in the current volume, Saint Augustine enjoined Christians to speak truth with humility while showing general respect for the laws and customs of local culture. When Divine Law requires Christ's followers to disobey human law, there may be the opportunity to argue their case—and this should be done with civility—but there is no promise that their rhetoric will persuade.

Both Jesus and the early Church remind Christians that their calling and duty is not to win arguments but to stand as a *martyros*—the New Testament Greek word for "witness," from which the English word *martyr* is derived. In other words, Christians should expect that their testimony may cost them their property, their comfort, or even their lives. Yet civility and love remain incumbent upon them in such circumstances. Rather than indulging in fear or resentment, Saint Augustine says that followers of Jesus should have compassion toward leaders who feel compelled by their laws and taboos to marginalize or persecute them. In the first centuries of Christianity, it was Christ-followers' courageous virtue and love in the face of Roman persecution that convinced many onlookers that Jesus was the true King. Loving one's enemies is the ultimate negation of royal consciousness and the ultimate influencer for the kingdom of God. The practice of lament prepares the way, for it is more about identification than persuasion as it empathizes with a people caught in royal consciousness.

Indeed, the One who wept over Jerusalem on Palm Sunday also prayed for his murderers on Good Friday: "Father, forgive them, for they do not know what they are doing."[75]

Conclusion

Unless Christians understand and embrace the theo-political, anti-scapegoating import of the cross, they are in danger of treating the crucifixion as a talisman for individual salvation, while remaining captives to royal consciousness in their civic and communal life. The present challenge, then, for White American Christians accustomed to cultural privilege, is to cease conforming to the world—that is, to the twisted *logos* of royal consciousness—and "be transformed by the renewing of your mind."[76] In other words, the Church must be baptized into a prophetic consciousness—recovering the marginal practice of lament and living into the hope of God's coming kingdom of compassion and justice. Only then can there be a true Gospel influence in society. Only at the margins of human order, in humility, weakness and apparent foolishness, can the full power of the crucified *Logos* (the divine Word-made-flesh) be realized.[77] With this mindset, Christ-followers can respond to a hostile culture (or church) with passion, civility, and even empathy. When loyalty to an earthly leader or party seems to have become the defining mark of "Christian" ethos, when sound logos fails and the pathos of the refugee no longer moves the Church at large, Christ-followers have occasion to embrace the margins and give voice to prophetic lament—and rediscover that "the foolishness of God is wiser than human wisdom, and the weakness of God is stronger than human strength."[78]

CONCLUSION
FOR GOD, ALL THINGS ARE POSSIBLE

Conclusion

For God, All Things Are Possible

A More Substantive Christianity for the Twenty-first Century

NAAMAN WOOD AND SEAN CONNABLE

Introduction

I (NAAMAN) ONCE ATTENDED A LECTURE (for which class, I cannot recall) by Black theologian Willie James Jennings, and he offered this analysis on Christianity and slavery. I am paraphrasing, but this is close to what I remember him saying:

> In the pre-antebellum period, slavemasters preached the gospel to enslaved people. The enslaved often had one of three reactions. Some rejected what the slavemaster said. Others outwardly accepted Jesus but only as a means of survival. Perhaps inwardly and secretly, these two groups kept their traditional religions their peoples carried with them across the ocean. But some heard what the slavemasters said, and they believed. Some of these believers knew that the slavemaster used Jesus to assault their dignity and humanity and rejected that version of the gospel. Instead, they found within the story of Jesus that God could do for them something the slavemaster never intended: in the midst of the most inhumane treatment, God could give them life.

Jennings, we think, articulates not only a problem that was endemic to Christianity in the past but also is still with us today, a split between orthodoxy and orthopraxy. Orthodoxy describes the limited set of content that is thought of as right Christian teaching. Traditionally, the Apostles' and Nicene Creeds are the backbone of orthodoxy, uniting Catholic, Protestant, and Orthodox Christians throughout the world and in different time periods. Orthopraxy is right Christian behavior. Jennings's example demonstrates that American Christians have a history, and we would argue a present, where we might affirm the content of an orthodox faith, but we fail to live a life of Christian orthopraxy. Because worship is part of orthopraxy, we think it is safe to say that the Jesus the slavemasters worshipped was, to use terms from Mark A. E. Williams's Chapter 2, only the appearance of Jesus, whereas the Jesus the enslaved worshipped was, at the very least, a far more substantive one.

This split between orthodoxy and orthopraxy—between the substance and appearance of Christian faith—is the split we think Christians need to deal with. Although we are borrowing terms from Williams, we want to acknowledge that we are transposing them from the way he uses the terms. Williams retains the classical rendering: appearances are the realities we witness here on earth, where substances are their connection to reality in the mind of the Triune God. Here we retain the two terms but use them to describe Christian life. When Christians are able to hold together orthodoxy and orthopraxy, then, we assert, they are living the truest, most substantive form of Christian life. In the example Jennings offered, the enslaved Christians who believed in the Jesus who gave them life amid a death-dealing world lived a more substantive life than their slavemasters. When Christians divorce orthodoxy from orthopraxy, like the slavemasters did, the appearance of Christianity ensues. Nearly every chapter in this book points to suffering in the lives of oppressed people groups, and those realities continually pose a problem to Christian faith. The question we want to grapple with is this one: Will we allow our orthodoxy to produce an orthopraxive response to that suffering, a response that befits a substantive faith, or will we minimize or deny that suffering, embracing instead only the mere appearance of Christianity?

We conclude this book arguing that if Christians want to have anything meaningful to say about the matter of civility and the conditions of hospitality and humility, then we will have to refuse the appearance of civility and embrace its substance. To support this claim, this concluding chapter unfolds in two sections. The appearance of civility is a problem that is present in the key arguments Christians make about civility. Referring to the authors we discussed in the introduction—Richard Mouw, Tim Muehlhoff, Os Guinness, and Calvin L. Troup—they perhaps unintentionally display two problems: a desire for homogeneous eschatology and an indifference to injustices. We think the revelation of John of Patmos and the insights of Abraham Joshua Heschel on the Hebrew prophets offer a corrective to homogeneity and indifference. To put orthodoxy and orthopraxy back together, Christians must, against our indifference, develop in our communities that same sensitivity that the prophets had toward suffering. For the prophets, the entire cosmos was at stake in the most mundane injustice. Christians must also, against our desire for homogeneity, imagine and live into a diverse, pluralist future that we, White Christians especially, embrace as both a good future and God's future. Next, when viewed in light of these two problems, the chapters in this volume point toward some of the substantive conditions Christians need to acknowledge and the substantive resources Christians need to embrace to resist the appearance of civility. To our minds, the chapters foreground the substantive problem of colonialism; race, sex, and class; and Christian nationalism. But they also suggest the recovery of theological resources to engage these problems, particularly the recovery of resistance and land, the Incarnation, and Jesus's aphorism, the "first will be last" in Matthew 19:30 (NIV).

The Appearance of Civility

As you (dear reader) have walked alongside us, perhaps you have noticed, as we have, that many of these chapters explored forms of violence—colonial violence; fascism; inequities of race, sex, and class; and politics. We arrive at the question: Are civility, hospitality, and humility sufficient to deal with a world of such violence, a violence that many Christians have actively participated in or allowed to transpire? As editors of this volume, we fear we come to the conclusion, "No." The intervening chapters have convinced us there are conditions behind hospitality and humility that must be addressed. And if we do not address them, then there will be little chance that Christians will inhabit the humility and hospitality necessary for civility to be possible. These chapters urge us, as editors, to reconsider the Christian reflections on civility from our introduction. While Mouw, Muehlhoff and

Langer, Guinness, and Troup are thoughtful, timely, and helpful, we now see two important limitations in their perspectives.

Because both Mouw and Muehlhoff see pluralism as a problem to be solved, their writing suggests that they, perhaps unwittingly, affirm a homogeneous eschatology. Mouw speaks about the difficulty Christians experience, for example, when mosques appear "in our neighborhoods,"[1] or New Age people show up in our schools or business. He suggests that Christians need, in this pluralistic climate, to be convicted about the truth and to be civil to others. They need to have a convicted civility. Muehlhoff suggests that Christians, as a group, are a "counterpublic," or countercultural group who live outside of the norms of American culture.[2] With Christians positioned as outsiders to mainstream culture, Muehlhoff and Langer offer theoretical and practical advice on how Christians can communicate more effectively against the tensions that pluralism creates. While neither Mouw nor Muehlhoff and Langer claim explicitly that the world would have less conflict if there were less diversity, there is something of this desire for homogeneity in their assumption that pluralism is a problem to be solved. If the diversity of a pluralistic world is a problem to be solved, such solving imagines a future that is less problematic—that is, less diverse, less pluralistic, and, by definition, more homogenous. Put differently, to assume that pluralism is a problem is also to assume that the future would be better if those people over there were more like us. This assumption suggests a Christianity that imagines a homogeneous eschatological future, a time in which everyone will conform more closely to who we are.

The desire for homogeneity should be a problem for Christians, because the Bible imagines eschatology, or God's good future, as a way of belonging that is, foundationally, pluralistic and diverse in nature. In the Book of Revelation, Chapter 7, John of Patmos sees a vision of God's good future. The author says, "I looked, and behold, a great multitude that no one could number, from every nation (*ethnos*), from all tribes and peoples and languages, standing before the throne and before the Lamb."[3] Growing up in a Pentecostal church, I (Naaman) was taught to look at this passage and see one thing, the kind of triumphalism Mark Allan Steiner in Chapter 8 argues is so very problematic. In God's good future, I was taught that we are many, and we are victorious. It was not until much later in my life that someone (who I now cannot remember) pointed out the middle part of the verse. While the Greek word *ethnos* is often translated into English

Conclusion

as "nation" or "Gentiles," it is helpful to remember that nation-states as we think of them today were not really part of the ancient world.

What the author is likely trying to communicate with the word *ethnos* is the diversity of the people gathered at the foot of Jesus's throne. For Jews of Jesus's time, this way of belonging would have been a difficult teaching to accept, because Gentiles were unclean and did not follow the ways of God. But as the Book of Acts demonstrates so clearly, the Spirit is often drawing Jesus's followers into belonging with people they would rather not be in community with. Think of the first words Peter says when he enters the Gentile Cornelius's home, "[I]t is unlawful for a Jew [Peter] to associate with or to visit a Gentile [Cornelius]."[4] The Spirit has different plans for Peter and the rest of the Jewish followers of Jesus.[5] By the time John writes his vision, he transposes the pluralism of Acts into his Apocalypse. The future is good, because God brings diverse peoples into a state of belonging with each other, here within the intimacy of worship.

Because the Bible imagines God's good future as a pluralistic future, Christians have the theological resources to refuse to see pluralism as a problem, but without that resource, Mouw and Muehlhoff's reflections on civility make unintentional room for violence. As theological resource, when Jesus puts the world to rights, what that includes is the reality to refuse pluralism as problematic. In John's Apocalypse, all the peoples of the world bring themselves fully into communion with Jesus and each other. There is no sense that everyone in this scene looks the same, sounds the same, worships God the same. There is no homogeneity. Rather, Jesus preserves ethnic, linguistic, and, dare we say, cultural diversity in God's good future. Without that pluralism, the future would be neither good nor God's. When Mouw and Muehlhoff assume that pluralism is a problem to be solved, we are forced to say that assumption is, unfortunately, antithetical to a Biblical vision of God's good future. It unwittingly assumes that the Spirit desires belonging, as Peter assumed in Acts, as homogeneous. It unwittingly assumes that Jesus's eschatological achievement will include only homogeneous Jesus followers. What nearly every chapter in this book demonstrates is that when Christians have historically desired homogeneity and have allied themselves with political power to achieve that desire, we have participated in and perpetuated violence against people who are not like us. We want to make this clear—Mouw and Muehlhoff never advocate for violence. However, without addressing the implicit desire for homogeneity in their framework, we do not believe their thinking will produce a civil social space. It will create the appearance of civility, a civility in which Christians in the present will repeat the mistakes of Christians in the past. We will make room for violence.

Guinness and Troup do well to avoid the idea that pluralism is a problem, but their writing betrays a related issue—an indifference to injustice. Guinness implies that a plain reading of the Founding Fathers can lead to the kind of pluralism that will protect both White evangelicals and everyone else. Maximal pluralism for everyone will permit social spaces for Christians to be fully Christian in the public sphere, in the exact way it will preserve that same space for all other faith and non-faith groups. Of all the reflections on civility, this one strikes us as the most counterintuitive for many Christians, but also the most daring. It also strikes us as the most promising for a civil future. Troup also sees pluralism as something to be embraced. In his reading of Augustine, the commonwealth is, by its very nature, a pluralistic space in which all ethnic, cultural, and racial groups can flourish and find peace. Like Guinness, Troup has convinced us that Christians can embrace pluralism as foundational to our future, a future that can make space for everyone in our civic and political communities. However, within or alongside these affirmations of plurality, there are places that, if unexamined, will, like the ideas of Mouw and Muehlhoff and Langer, inhibit the means by which pluralism and civility can be achieved.

In his discussions on civility, Guinness displays what we take to be an unintentional indifference to racial injustices. In reference to the Founding Fathers, Guinness does not acknowledge the racial injustices in the lives of the framers or the inequalities they placed in the Constitution. This precise topic came up at our most recent unconference in 2021 hosted by the Christianity and Communication Studies Network (www.theccsn.com). After his keynote address on how Christian division emerged during the Civil War era, historian of American Christianity Mark Noll took questions from his online audience. When an audience member raised the topic of racism and the Founding Fathers, Noll said in response, "As to the question of whether the Founding Fathers were incidentally racist or intentionally racist, we must say the latter."[6] We bring up Noll because he is, by all accounts, one of the leading historians of Christianity working today. He is not a liberal. He does not want to excoriate Christians or make unfair, unreasonable historical claims. He is not only an incredibly capable historian, but he also is a sensible, reasonable, and clear-minded academic.

Conclusion

He has come to the historical conclusion that many Christians resist: Racism is foundational to the crafting of the Constitution and therefore to our nation. As legal scholar Alan Jenkins eloquently argues, "The framers of the Constitution achieved exactly what they set out to achieve with respect to race, which was maintaining the institution of slavery. Indigenous people were given even less attention and subsequently the Constitution allowed for their repeated relocation and attempted genocide."[7] This does not mean the thinking of the Founding Fathers cannot be used to craft a pluralistic vision like the one for which Guinness advocates. Rather, if the founding documents of the U.S. have, indeed, begotten the racial inequality we see today, then unless some intervention is made on the realities of those injustices (and the constitution itself), it is highly unlikely Guinness's vision will achieve anything other than the appearance of civility. It will, in effect, make room for the injustices the founders preserved. Therefore, to create the conditions for a pluralistic civility, the intentional racism that founded the country must be addressed. Our understanding of Guinness is that he offers no such interventions.

Troup also displays an unintentional indifference, this time to both racial and economic injustices, which occur during his references to justice, activism, and family dinners. Far from nitpicking these passing references, they let us see "under the hood," as it were, of Troup's framework to catch a glimpse of what civility looks like in a lived life. As his framework suggests, lived life in households and on the streets is the essence of a commonwealth. He argues that love, not justice, is what is needed to build a pluralistic commonwealth, because justice divides people rather than unifies them. Troup suggests that Jesus's parables demonstrate the point. Justice divides the sheep from the goats[8] and the wheat from the tares.[9] Because commonwealths are built on shared realities and shared loves, the division justice brings cannot be foundational to humility, hospitality, or civility. Similarly, Troup rejects activist rhetoric. When discussing the way civility plays out in the books of Acts and Daniel, he claims the figures in those texts were not "movement people or political activists. They are not carrying banners and saying, 'You are all messed up, and you do not know what is going on.' Instead, they plainly say, 'Here we stand. We know our stance is not a comfortable thing for you, and we cannot do anything else but stand here. We cannot accommodate this.' We must follow Christ."[10] He also regrets the reality that the condition of the family dinner is all but missing from contemporary society. Such a practice is, perhaps, the primary place individuals learn to disagree with one another. This daily, private practice is one of the key conditions that make rhetorical training in civility truly effective in public life. Without practices like the family dinner, there can be no real civility.

Taken together, these passages suggest an unintentional indifference to the experience of those people who face racial and economic injustice. First, in undervaluing of justice, political movements, and advocacy, Troup's commonwealth seems to us like a place that would not welcome a figure like Martin Luther King Jr. To our minds, King's Christian faith and experience as a Black man in a racist society led to his public action as a movement person and a political activist, precisely what Troup claims is problematic. He engaged in divisive rhetoric, particularly in the form of public speeches and prophetic acts that demonstrated two important realities. White America was, first, deeply mistaken about who they claimed they were (i.e., "You are all messed up"[11]), and second, White America did not know—or did not want to know—about the injustice in their own country (i.e., "You do not know what is going on"[12]). To King's mind, those White Americans who posed the greatest threat to him were not those who were explicitly racist. Rather, moderate Whites, many of whom included Christians, posed the greatest harm to the Black community. In his "Letter from Birmingham Jail," King writes that

> the Negro's great stumbling block in his stride toward freedom is not the White Citizen's Counciler or the Ku Klux Klanner, but the White moderate, who is more devoted to "order" than to justice; who prefers a negative peace which is the absence of tension to a positive peace which is the presence of justice . . . Shallow understanding from people of good will is more frustrating than absolute misunderstanding from people of ill will. . . . I have been so greatly disappointed with the White church and its leadership. . . . In the midst of blatant injustices inflicted upon the Negro, I have watched White churchmen stand on the sideline and mouth pious irrelevancies and sanctimonious trivialities.[13]

Troup's 2017 call for a commonwealth without divisive rhetoric or public action strikes us as uncomfortably similar to what King found so disappointing in the 1960s. If we follow King, a commonwealth can only be a commonwealth to the extent that justice is established, particularly through individuals and groups brave enough to offer decisive, prophetic speech and action.

We affirm, along with King, that a contemporary commonwealth is only possible to the extent that White American Christians change in the most profound ways. Even a cursory reading of books by Christian authors like sociologists Michael O. Emerson and Christian Smith's *Divided by Faith: Evangelical Religion and the Problem of Race in America*, historian Jemar Tisby's *The Color of Compromise: The Truth about the American Church's Complicity in Racism*, Austin Channing Brown's memoir *I'm Still Here: Black Dignity in a World Made for Whiteness*, Biblical scholar Esau McCaulley's *Reading While Black: African American Biblical Interpretation as an Exercise in Hope*, and many others demonstrates so clearly that White American Christians have refused to hear King's voice. What the mere existence of these books suggests is that we Christians, as a group, remain indifferent to the suffering that racialized minorities experience in this country and in our institutions.

We see a similar indifference in Troup's desire for something as mundane as a family dinner. In tracing the development of the family dinner, historian Simone Cinotto argues that the inequalities of both race and class limited the historical practice in profound ways. "The ideal of the proper family mealtime," he notes, "originally devised by the Victorian middle class, gained cultural hegemony in modern America, but with the partial exception of the 1950s, only a minority of American families could ever live by it."[14] Fleshing out the claim, Cinotto recounts that during the Industrial Era of the early twentieth century:

> Racism in hiring left many black men unemployed and channeled black women into domestic jobs. This, in addition to the high rates of mortality among black males, caused the proportion of black families headed by unmarried or widowed women to soar. Women often juggled to balance wage work with domestic chores and child care, with scant possibility of success. The frequent cohabitation of relatives outside the nuclear family and unrelated boarders was yet another structural factor differentiating urban poor black households' mealtimes from those of the middle class.[15]

Because racial and economic inequalities like the ones Cinotto mentions are still a part of life for many Black, Indigenous, and other people of color (BIPOC), it is no stretch to imagine that similar structural factors create the conditions in which the poor BIPOC might possess neither the time nor the resources of White middle-class Americans to engage in anything like a regular family dinner. Hence, to bemoan the absence of the practice of a family dinner without reference to these limiting factors displays a similar form of indifference to those who suffer racial and economic injustice.

A similar indifference exists in Muehlhoff and Langer's *Winsome Conviction: Disagreeing without Dividing the Church*. They rightfully say that the conflicts Christians experience today are "embedded in a social context made of groups of people, institutions we are part of, and treasured histories and legacies that are passed from person to person and generation to generation. . . . Without even knowing it, our social context can blind us to facts or numb us to the suffering of those from a different context."[16] Langer goes on to say how his predominately white education blinded him "to the deep racism inherent in our language choices and even what subjects were neglected" in his education.[17] However, the reality that racism exists or that our predominately homogenous formations might impact us as Christians is never addressed in any substantial or practical way. There is no real sense that these historical or social inequalities matter to civility in any way that should alter the way Christians understand themselves, their world, or their place in it, much less the way we imagine civility.

This indifference should be a problem for Christians, first, because of the writing of the Old Testament prophets. When I (Naaman) was in my twenties, I read the entire Bible for the first time in my life. What shocked and shook me was the way nearly all the prophets spoke about the plight of those who suffered injustice. My churches and Christian universities never really took the words of the prophets with any seriousness. Because we never believed that God desired justice, we remained indifferent to it. While the prophets had touched me deeply, my Christian formation did not give me the language to speak about what the prophets said until I read the work of Jewish theologian and rabbi Abraham Joshua Heschel, most notably in his monumental study simply titled *The Prophets*. Heschel brought into words what I felt about the prophets but could never articulate. What the prophets say still stands as a challenge to Christians today.

Heschel argues that part of what the prophetic tradition articulates at nearly the outset of the Bible is this: "indifference to evil is worse than evil itself . . . Cain's question 'Am I my brother's keeper?'(Genesis 4:9) and his implied negative response must be regarded among the great fundamental evil maxims of the world."[18] Set in this framework of indifference, the heart of Cain's problem is not that he murdered his brother. Rather, it is that he does not care that he has murdered his brother. If he cared, then perhaps he would have interpreted God's question "Where is your brother Abel?" as an invitation to confession, repentance, and living a different form of life. It is his indifference to his brother's suffering that is the true evil. When I (Naaman) lecture about indifference, the White Christian students to whom I speak often protest. "Certainly," they claim, "the one who harms is the one who has performed the most evil." It is difficult to persuade them otherwise. After one of these class lectures, a Black student approached me. He spoke to me in quiet tones, as though he did not want any of the White students to hear him. "I was born in Rwanda, but I have grown up in Canada my whole life," he said. "But my parents are still there, and they remember the genocide. I think they would agree with what you said today. Part of the way a genocide takes place is that people remain indifferent to the suffering around them." My heart sank that White Christians created the conditions where their Black brother did not feel safe to speak up in class. And my heart sank that his proximity to suffering had produced in him a lived experience that makes this Biblical truth credible. But his words reminded me what both Heschel (a German-born Jew who fled genocide) and my student (a Rwandan-born immigrant who fled genocide) both share. They know that indifference is a necessary component for injustices of all kinds to transpire.

If indifference is a moral problem, then the prophets offer to us a solution: an infinite sensitivity to those who suffer. "The more deeply immersed I became in the thinking of the prophets," Heschel writes, "the more powerfully it became clear to me what the lives of the prophets sought to convey: that morally speaking there is no limit to the concern one must feel for the suffering of human beings."[19] As a result of their sensitivity, when prophets speak, they speak in extreme ways. For example, if prophets look at a city and see one starving orphan, they are "scandalized, and rave as if the whole world were a slum [sic]."[20] Their language also extends beyond cities or nation or worlds. For the prophets, "even a minor injustice assumes cosmic proportions," because such a reality poses a threat to the entire existence of humanity and the world.[21] As goes one poor, hungry child, so goes all of humanity, the entire earth, and the whole cosmos. The universe is at stake, the thinking goes, if one child goes hungry.

If this way of looking at the world seems too interdependent for most Christians, then this brings us to the second reason Christians should find indifference to be a problem. Heschel's understanding of what is at stake in the reality of injustice comes into clearer focus when Christians apply what he is saying to Jesus, the one prophet whom Christians profess to be the Godhead bodily. Part of what is implicit in the Gospels is precisely this reality. The existence and salvation of all humanity, the world, the cosmos, was at stake in the death of a single, poor, Jewish prophet who lived his entire life under Roman colonial injustice. As the Gospel of Luke tells us, this prophet was both poor and homeless. Precisely as a poor person, he pronounces woes upon the rich and blessings upon the poor. As the Gospel of Matthew says, Jesus claims that what happens to the most vulnerable among us—the prisoner, the naked, the hungry, the thirsty—happens to him, precisely because this prophet was a prisoner stripped naked, who cried out for thirst on the cross, and who was starving in the wilderness. If what Matthew communicates is true, then what happens to the poor and oppressed everywhere and anywhere in the world happens to Jesus. Our indifference to them is, in fact, indifference to the one whom we say we worship and adore. If the redemption of the cosmos is at stake in the life of this one poor Jewish prophet, and if this poor Jewish prophet says what happens to the poor happens to him, then perhaps we should take Heschel seriously when he claims that the cosmos, the world, and humanity is at stake in one suffering person.

Taken together, the problems of a homogeneous eschatology and indifference to injustice sit at the heart of the appearance of civility Christians tend to inhabit. However, Christians possess, within our tradition, two important resources to resist such problems. First, we must develop in our communities that same sensitivity the prophets possessed, for whom the entire cosmos was at stake in the most mundane injustice. As a result, we must do what Cain could not bring himself to do. We must listen to those who have died unjust deaths, like Abel, and to those who live lives under the weight of injustice, like Jesus. We must breathe in their words as though our life depended on them. And then we must let those voices have a say in what we think reality is. If we want a future that is more just for people who are not White American Christians, then we must develop the prophets' sensitivity to suffering.

Second, we must imagine a diverse, pluralist future that is both good and God's, and we must live into that reality in the present. For many of us,

CONCLUSION

imagining a pluralist future is fearful. We fear different bodies and different cultures and different languages because they complicate or disrupt how our present world works for us. We also fear belonging to those who are different from us, because it would change the world we want to see when we look at our churches, at our institutions, at our cities, at our neighborhoods, and at our own households. Because of that fear, many Christians have built fences and walls to hedge others out, policies and laws to push others away, and we do so in the name of civility and peacemaking. If Christians live into the plurality of God's good future, then it will, in fact, disrupt our present world. It will radically alter our churches, institutions, neighborhoods, and—perhaps most importantly—our households. But the good news is this: God's future is better than our present, and it is better than anything we can possibly imagine. If we desire a taste of that good future, then we must, as the author of Hebrews tells us, grasp it by faith, because, the author says, "faith is the substance of things hoped for, the evidence of things not seen."[22] If White Christians engage in the task of trying to belong to others who are not like them, then we must, by faith, embrace a future we cannot imagine. "Without faith" of this kind, the writer tells us, "it is impossible to please God."[23] Many of the chapters in this volume help us grapple with substantive problems that Christians must deal with if, by faith, we want to live into God's good future. And it is to those insights that we now turn.

Substantive Problems, Substantive Resources

When considered in light of the problems of a homogeneous eschatology and indifference to injustice, the chapters in this volume point toward at least some of the substantive conditions or problems with which Christians need to grapple. We think that a proper grappling with these problems will help us embrace the sensitivity that the prophets possessed and live into God's good, diverse, and pluralist future. It will also enable Christians to inhabit the humility and hospitality Troup rightly calls for in Chapter 1. And here we, the editors of this book, need to be clear. We do not speak for the authors of the chapters you have read. We do not assume that they will agree with our situating of their work. Nevertheless, to our minds, the chapters foreground the substantive problem of colonialism; race, sex, and class; and Christian nationalism, but they also suggest the recovery of theological resources to engage those problems, particularly the recovery of resistance and land; the Incarnation; and Jesus's aphorism, the "first will be last" in Matthew 19:30 (NIV).

We begin with the problem of Christians entangled with colonialism. In Susangeline Y. Patrick's call to inhabit a reverse and covenantal hospitality (Chapter 4), her brief account of Christian mission suggests, rather strongly we might add, that Christianity, by and large, already has capitulated to the forces of empire that Troup urged us so desperately to resist. Colonialism, it seems, is one of the key substantive problems in which Christians are enmeshed and have yet to rectify. My (Naaman's) Chapter 5 argues that the realities of Residential Schools and the Sixties Scoop suggest that colonialism is a force that has limited and continues to limit the taking on of virtues, like love or humility. Colonialism is such a powerful force that it traffics as our common sense. However, empire and colonialism are not death sentences.

As Susangeline Y. Patrick's chapter demonstrates, there were Christians who resisted the forces of empire, who stood with and learned from Indigenous peoples. Those saints can be models for us, if only we take time to study and emulate them. Likewise, Patrick points out that the land is one of the substantive conditions of our existence. Part of what she suggests is that we can, if we so choose, stop treating the land as a resource to exploit. Rather, as the writer of Genesis 2:15 points out, we can take up a posture of service to the land.[24] Because all that we could possibly offer to others in hospitality comes from the land, we should not exploit it. Rather, in a posture of true humility, we should see ourselves in service to that upon which we depend. In grappling with the problem of colonialism, we have the opportunity to resist it through both learning from Christians who have gone before us and taking up a posture of service to God's creation.

While several chapters articulate just how deeply Christians have not considered the substantive problems of race, sex, and socioeconomics, they also open an opportunity to recover more deeply the doctrine of the Incarnation. Jaime Harris (Chapter 6) points to several problems that keep Christians from engaging in civility, especially with members of the LGBTQ+ community: we often misperceive ourselves as a persecuted minority, our communities often benefit from incivility with others, and many accounts of civility impose unilateral conditions on civil dialogue. Mark Allan Steiner (Chapter 8) notes that current accounts of civility do not adequately deal with mistrust and tribal thinking common today. Suffering, he contends, can serve as an antidote, particularly as it relates to racial justice

Conclusion

and racial reconciliation. Michelle Shockness's work (Chapter 3) suggests that Christians often lack an awareness of socioeconomic conditions that inhibit our ability to be truly hospitable and to let others be hospitable to us. However, because all these substantive problems are, fundamentally, related to the particular bodies we inhabit, our recovery of the doctrine of the Incarnation has the potential to provide dignity to a plurality of bodies.

The fourth-century Church Father Gregory of Nazianzus offered one of the classic doctrinal statements on the Incarnation, "The unassumed is the unhealed."[25] What he means is that only those elements of humanity that Jesus has assumed, or taken on or inhabited, can be healed or redeemed. In traditional reflection, Jesus's own suffering and death means that, through Jesus's Incarnation, or taking on of human flesh, our own suffering and death can be healed. Upon closer examination, there are all kinds of particularities to Jesus's bodily Incarnation that shed light on the injustices he experienced. As a Middle Eastern Jew, Jesus likely incarnated a brown body, what today we might call a marginalized body. Because Jesus was born without significant financial resources, Jesus grew up poor, what today we might call a body at risk. Because Jesus was born under the weight of the Roman Empire, Jesus's body suffered colonial oppression, what today we might call a colonized body. Jesus's body suffered unjust imprisonment and death at the hands of law enforcement, not unlike the bodies of George Floyd or Daunte Wright. And, presumably, Jesus never married, thus defying the expectations for so-called expected duties of procreation and marriage. Jesus's sexual body did not represent a so-called normal body of his time (or our time for that matter). Because of the particularities of Jesus's body—his race, sexuality, and low socioeconomic standing—we can take seriously Jesus's words from Matthew 25:45. What happens to "the least," meaning what happens to those bodies who are, like Jesus's, rejected and marginalized, happens to Jesus himself. The Incarnation provides a way to treat all these bodies with the dignity of Jesus, one whom we worship as our Savior and Lord.

Finally, these chapters suggest that Christians have not faced the substantive problem of Christian nationalism, but that problem suggests an opportunity to take more seriously Jesus's teaching of "the first" and "the last." Annalee R. Ward and Mary K. Bryant (Chapter 7) argue that when German Christians capitulated to German nationalism, what was needed was not mere civility. The Barmen Declaration demonstrated that integrity can sometimes produce needed uncivil speech. John B. Hatch (Chapter 9) outlines how American evangelicalism has also capitulated to nationalism and the forces of empire through its uncritical support for President Donald Trump. However, against this clinging to power, we suggest that Christians learn again what Jesus said about "the first" and "the last."

In the Gospels of Matthew, Mark, and Luke, there are four passages that culminate with variations on Jesus's phrase, "many who are first will be last, and the last will be first."[26] In interactions with a rich man, for example, Jesus tells the man to sell all his possessions and follow him, but he refuses to do so.[27] The disciples are shocked at Jesus's words, because they, perhaps like the rich man himself, see wealth as an asset rather than a liability. But Jesus will have none of this kind of thinking. He concludes his interaction with his disciples saying that, in his community, there will be a different economy at work. "[M]any who are first," like the rich man, "will be last, and the last," meaning those without wealth or power, "will be first." For many Christians, our nationalism functions for us like the wealth of the rich man. It is that power, that sense of security and safety, that we do not want to give up. We must, like Jesus invites the rich man to do, find productive ways to divest ourselves of the security we think nationalism provides, precisely because, like the rich man, it is what keeps us from following the poor, brown-skinned, Middle Eastern man who died at the hands of an empire. We must, in essence, follow the example of Jesus's disciples. "Look," Peter says to Jesus, "we have left everything. . . ."[28] How to divest ourselves of political power, how to leave everything, is an open question. But when we reflect on the chapters in this volume, it is likely one of the most important tasks for twenty-first century Christians.

When we try to imagine a substantive Christianity that has tarried with the problem of colonialism; race, sex, and class; and Christian nationalism, we are, honestly, not sure what to imagine. We do not think we have the power, with our limited imaginations, to project what that Christianity looks like. We hope the chapters in this book have articulated some coordinates, some essential issues, that we must grapple with if we want to keep orthodoxy and orthopraxy together. That we cannot imagine this future does not mean that we are without hope, because we remember what Jesus said to his disciplines about the rich man:

> "Truly I tell you, it will be hard for a rich person to enter the kingdom of heaven. Again I tell you, it is easier for a camel to go through the eye of a needle than for someone who is rich to

Conclusion

enter the kingdom of God." When the disciples heard this, they were greatly astounded and said, "Then who can be saved?" But Jesus looked at them and said, "For mortals it is impossible, but for God all things are possible."[29]

The same is true for us. If the future is left to us, then a substantive Christianity is impossible. But for God, all things are possible.

Endnotes

Introduction

[1] Richard Mouw, *Uncommon Decency: Christian Civility in an Uncivil World* (Downers Grove, IL: InterVarsity Press, 1992), 16.

[2] Ibid., 15.

[3] Ibid., 11–12.

[4] Richard Mouw, *Adventures in Evangelical Civility: A Lifelong Quest for Common Ground* (Grand Rapids, MI: Baker Books, 2016), iBooks.

[5] Tim Muehlhoff, *I Beg to Differ: Navigating Difficult Conversations with Truth and Love* (Downers Grove, IL: InterVarsity Press, 2014), iBooks.

[6] Ibid.

[7] Ibid.

[8] Tim Muehlhoff and Richard Langer, *Winsome Persuasion: Christian Influence in a Post-Christian World* (Downers Grove, IL: IVP Academic, 2017), 17–21.

[9] Tim Muehlhoff and Richard Langer, *Winsome Conviction: Disagreeing without Dividing the Church* (Downers Grove, IL: IVP Academic, 2020), 38.

[10] Ibid., 39.

[11] Ibid., 40.

[12] Ibid., 41.

[13] Ibid., 44.

[14] Os Guinness, *The Case for Civility: And Why Our Future Depends on It* (New York: HarperCollins, 2008), 135.

[15] Ibid., 136.

[16] Os Guinness, *The Global Public Square: Religious Freedom and the Making of a World Safe for Diversity* (Downers Grove, IL: InterVarsity Press, 2013), 13.

[17] Ibid., 15.

[18] While a full understanding of Guinness's eight steps is outside the scope of this chapter, we paraphrase them as an invitation for further reflection and investigation. They are as follows: (1) Soul freedom is good for everyone (Ibid., 27); (2) Ignoring our differences puts the future at risk (Ibid., 45); (3) Freedom of thought, conscience, religion, and belief are primary (Ibid., 63); (4) Trivial limitations of freedom matter immensely (Ibid., 98); (5) The models of the public square we currently inhabit produce bad ends (Ibid., 121); (6) The current responses to religion in public life disregard freedom of thought and conscience (Ibid., 132); (7) Civility will take place when the

greatest number of people experience soul freedom (Ibid., 180); and (8) Religious and secular leaders need to start with the declaration of principles they need to achieve soul freedom (Ibid., 193).

[19] While not directly relevant to the work here, we wanted to offer one interpretation of Kant's phrase "the conditions of the possibility of . . . " Earlier in the Enlightenment, philosopher René Descartes offered a rationalist account of human knowing. Such an account claimed that humans could know the world through reason alone, that is, through concepts or categories. This meant that the human did not need to go out and have direct, experiential contact with the world to know it. See Fredrick Copelston, *A History of Philosophy, Volume VI: Wolff to Kant* (New York: Paulist Press, 1960), 273. Kant is trained in this rationalist tradition, and for most of his life, he affirmed it. Later in his life, however, he takes a critical turn. Kant argues that there is no getting around experience in our knowledge of the world. It is essential. However, there are concepts or categories that come before our experiences of the world that make experience possible. There are "conditions of the possibility of experiences." Immanuel Kant, *Critique of Pure Reason*, trans. and eds. Paul Guyer and Allen W. Wood (Cambridge: Cambridge University Press, 1998), A94, B127, 225. Hence, Kant reformulates the terms of Descartes as a means of rejecting his rationalism. For more on the significance of this phrase and his critical turn, see Jennifer Mensch, "The Key to All Metaphysics: Kant's Letter to Herz, 1772," *Kantian Review* 12 (2007): 109–127; Claude Piché, "Kant on the 'Conditions of the Possibility' of Experience," in *Transcendental Inquiry: Its History, Methods and Critiques*, eds. Halla Kim and Steven Hoeltzel (London: Palgrave MacMillian, 2016), 1–20; "Gadamer on Kant," *Philosophy Overdose*, accessed May 15, 2021, https://www.youtube.com/watch?v=w3V5B6k6Mms. Grant Bartley, host, "The Hidden World of Immanuel Kant," *Philosophy Now: A Magazine of Ideas*, accessed May 16, 2021, https://philosophynow.org/podcasts/The_Hidden_World_of_Immanuel_Kant.

[20] Kant, *Critique of Pure Reason*, A95, 225. It is important to note that this is a paragraph that only appeared in the first edition of the *Critique of Pure Reason*. He cut it from latter editions of the text. Given the nature of how philosophy generally narrates the significance of the phrase (see previous note), we thought this obscure passage proved a better way of illustrating what Troup does.

[21] Luke 19:41–2, NRSV.

[22] Leon Morris, *Luke: An Introduction and Commentary* (Grand Rapids, MI: Eerdmans, 1988), 306.

[23] Charles L. Childers, "The Gospel According to St. Luke," in *Beacon Bible Commentary*, Vol. 6 (Kansas City, MO: Beacon Hill Press of Kansas City, 1964), iBooks.

[24] Fred B. Craddock, *Luke: Interpretation: A Bible Commentary for Teaching and Preaching* (Louisville, KY: Westminster John Knox Press, 2009), iBooks.

[25] Walter L. Liefeld and David W. Pao, "Luke," in *The Expositor's Bible Commentary: Luke-Acts*, Vol. 10 (Grand Rapids, MI: Zondervan, 2007), iBooks.

[26] Joel B. Green, *The Gospel of Luke: The New International Commentary on the New Testament* (Grand Rapids, MI: Eerdmans, 1997), iBooks.

[27] Ibid.

[28] If there is a condition for the possibility of civility in Guinness, then it might take the form of a diverse public sphere free from coercion and leadership able to engage in self-critique.

[29] Matthew 25:40–45, NRSV

ENDNOTES

Chapter 1

[1] Jacques Ellul, *The Presence of the Kingdom*, 3rd edition (Colorado Springs, CO: Helmers and Howard, 1989), 91–93.

[2] Jacques Ellul, *The Humiliation of the Word*, trans. Joyce Main Hanks (Grand Rapids, MI: Eerdmans, 1985), 210–214.

[3] Michael B. Salwen and Michael Dupagne, "The Third-Person Effect: Perceptions of the Media's Influence and Immoral Consequences," *Communication Research* 26, no. 5 (October 1999): 525–526.

[4] Admittedly, what Hauser implies is slightly different from Troup's emphasis. Hauser says, "My extended family taught me that you do not require a university education to be an informed citizen and that you should never forget the realities of the neighborhood in which you were raised. I thank my parents, grandparents, aunts, and uncles for including me in their spirited conversations, expecting me to think before speaking and treating my opinions seriously." Gerard A. Hauser, *Vernacular Voices: The Rhetoric of Publics and the Public Sphere* (Columbia, SC: University of South Carolina Press, 1999), xii.

[5] Maggie Jackson, *Distracted* (Amherst, NY: Prometheus Books, 2008), 63.

[6] Calvin L. Troup and Christina L. McDowell Marinchak, "Niceness, Flattery, and Deceit," *Western Journal of Communication* 82, no. 1 (2018): 65–69.

[7] Philip Hamburger, *Separation of Church and State* (Cambridge, MA: Harvard University Press, 2004), 290; Joseph S. Moore, *Founding Sins: How a Group of Anti-Slavery Radicals Fought to Put Christ into the Constitution* (Oxford: Oxford University Press, 2016), 154–156.

[8] Moore, *Founding Sins*, 1.

[9] Isaiah 66:6, ESV.

[10] Isaiah 66:12, ESV.

[11] Zechariah 8:4–5, ESV.

[12] Jacques Kelly, "Cool Summer Tradition Returns When Porch Awning Is Unfurled," *The Baltimore Sun*, June 15, 1997, https://www.baltimoresun.com/news/bs-xpm-1997-06-15-1997166201-story.html; "Your Turn: Favorite Porch Stories," *NPR*, August 14, 2006, https://www.npr.org/templates/story/story.php?storyId=5644464; John Blake, "'Lord of the Flies' Comes to Baltimore," *CNN*, May 4, 2015, https://www.cnn.com/2015/05/02/us/lord-of-the-flies-baltimore.

[13] Matthew 13:24–30, ESV.

[14] Matthew 13:47–50, ESV.

[15] Matthew 25:31–46, ESV.

[16] Matthew 22:37–39, ESV.

[17] Jean Bethke Elshtain, *Augustine and the Limits of Politics* (Notre Dame, IN: University of Notre Dame Press, 1996), 39–40.

[18] Augustine, *The City of God against the Pagans*, trans. and ed. R. W. Dyson (Cambridge: Cambridge University Press, 1998), 19.14.

[19] Alasdair MacIntyre, *After Virtue: A Study in Moral Theory*, 2nd edition (Notre Dame, IN: University of Notre Dame Press, 1984), 177.

[20] Augustine, *City of God*, 19.14–16.

[21] Augustine, *Confessions of St. Augustine*, trans. John K. Ryan (New York: Doubleday, 1960), 3.8–9; *On Christian Doctrine*, trans. D. W. Robertson Jr. (New York: Macmillan, 1958), 3.8.21–3.14.22.

[22] Matthew 20:28, Mark 10:45, ESV.
[23] Augustine, *City of God*, 19.14.
[24] Augustine, *Saint Augustine: Letters, Vol. 1 (1–82)*, The Fathers of the Church: A New Translation, Vol. 12, trans. Sister Wilfrid Parsons, S.N.D. (Washington, DC: The Catholic University of America Press, 1951), 167.
[25] Augustine, *City of God*, 11.2, 15.22.
[26] C. S. Lewis, *Screwtape Letters with Screwtape Proposes a Toast*, revised edition (New York: Macmillan, 1982), Letter 14.
[27] Daniel 6:1–28, ESV.
[28] Acts 23:1–5, ESV.
[29] Daniel 3:8–18, ESV.
[30] Philippians 2:6, ESV.
[31] Matthew 11:28–30, ESV.
[32] Isaiah 55:1, ESV.

Chapter 2

[1] Calvin L. Troup, "Humility and Hospitality: Two Conditions Necessary for the Possibility of Civility," in *Humility and Hospitality: Changing the Christian Conversation on Civility*, eds. Naaman Wood and Sean Connable (Pasco, WA: Integratio Press, 2022), 7.

[2] Sancti Aurelii Augustini, *de Civitate Dei*, 5th edition, eds. Bernhard Dombart and Alfons Kalb (Leipzig: B.G. Teubner, 1981), 19.21.

[3] Ibid.

[4] Historian R. A. Markus tried to argue that Augustine's view of government anticipated and laid the foundation for the secular, multicultural state; that argument has not held up under review. See G. J. P. O'Daly, *Augustine's City of God: A Reader's Guide* (Oxford: Oxford University Press, 1999), 207. See especially the remarks at footnote 25 and the various sources cited there.

[5] The concept of substance is complex, interacting with theories of matter, forms, and *teloi* that develop and rework their definitions across centuries. From Plato to Vico and Hume, isolating substances was a—often *the*—central focus of the educational enterprise. In Plato's view, the human soul was capable of perfecting itself via intense discipline so that it could absolutely know the nature of the substances. Plato also held matter to be inherently corrupting. Both of these perspectives are vigorously rejected in Augustine, adjudicated by the core Christian dogmas of human sinfulness and the Incarnation. Throughout this chapter, when I use the words substance, substantive, or substantial, I am referring to this complex interaction of ideas.

[6] Bruce Cockburn, "Rumours of Glory," recorded August 1980, track 2 on *Humans*, True North Records, CD.

[7] Augustine, *de civitate Dei*, 19.21.

[8] This transition is the crucial fulcrum in the chapter and perhaps in all of Book 19. It is here that Augustine moves his focus from the civic appearance of justice to a more encompassing Christian view of the substance of justice as it really is, dwelling in the heart and mind of God.

[9] Augustine, *de civitate Dei*, 19.21.

[10] Ibid., 19.6.

Endnotes

[11] See Peter Brown's decisive commentary on this interwoven nature of redemption in *Augustine of Hippo: A Biography* (Berkeley, CA: University of California Press, 2000). See Chapters 29–31 on the Pelagian controversy, especially pages 373–377. Brown focuses on the interweaving of knowledge (broadly understood) and love (i.e. on the consubstantiation of intellect and feeling) as a central outcome of redemption, and this perfect interweaving (which can never be complete in this life) is what Saint Augustine means by free will.

[12] Augustine, *de civitate Dei*, 19.24.

[13] And this forbidden choice makes the heavenly citizens terribly inconvenient to the inhabitants of the earthly city, as Troup notes in Chapter 1 of the current volume.

[14] Augustine, *de civitate Dei*, 19.24.

[15] This is also Anselm's view, and the foundation of his ontological argument for the existence of God in the *Monologion* and the *Proslogion*.

[16] Augustine, *de civitate Dei*, 19.14.

Chapter 3

[1] Arlie Hochschild's concept of emotional labor influenced my reflections on the concept of labor as drawn on in this work. Arlie R. Hochschild, *The Managed Heart: Commercialization of Feeling* (Berkeley, CA: University of California Press, 1983).

[2] Canadian Association of Social Workers, *CASW Code of Ethics* (Ottawa, ON: CASW, 2005), 4.

[3] Ibid.

[4] Allison D. Murdach, "What Happened to Self-Determination?", *Social Work* 56, no. 4 (October 2011): 371.

[5] Ibid.

[6] Ibid., 372.

[7] Terry A. Wolfer, David R. Hodge, and Janessa Steele, "Rethinking Client Self-Determination in Social Work: A Christian Perspective as a Philosophical Foundation for Client Choice," *Social Work & Christianity* 45, no. 2 (2018): 18.

[8] Andrew J. McCormick, "Self-Determination, the Right to Die, and Culture: A Literature Review," *Social Work* 56, no. 2 (April 2011): 125.

[9] Donna Baines, "Bridging the Practice-Activism Divide: Advocacy, Organizing and Social Movements," in *Doing Anti-Oppressive Practice: Social Justice Social Work*, ed. Donna Baines (Winnipeg: Fernwood Publishing, 2017), 93.

[10] Lena Dominelli, *Anti-Oppressive Social Work Theory and Practice* (New York: Palgrave Macmillan, 2002), 121.

[11] Ibid. See also Gary C. Dumbrill and June Ying Yee, *Anti-Oppressive Social Work: Ways of Knowing, Talking, and Doing* (Oxford: Oxford University Press, 2019), 300–301.

[12] Christine D. Pohl, "Responding to Strangers: Insights from the Christian Tradition," *Studies in Christian Ethics* 19, no. 1 (2006): 93, https://doi.org/10.1177/0953946806062287.

[13] Hebrews 13:2, NIV.

[14] Matthew 25:31–40, NIV.

[15] Christine D. Pohl, *Making Room: Recovering Hospitality as a Christian Tradition* (Grand Rapids, MI: Eerdmans, 1999), 121–122.

[16] Ibid., 120.

ENDNOTES

[17] Ibid.

[18] Amanda Sackreiter and Tonya D. Armstrong, "Radical Hospitality: Welcoming the Homeless Stranger," *Social Work & Christianity* 37, no. 2 (2010): 208.

[19] Ibid.

[20] Pohl, *Making Room*, 31.

[21] Ibid.

[22] Andrew Shepherd, *The Gift of the Other: Levinas, Derrida, and a Theology of Hospitality* (Eugene, OR: Wipf and Stock, 2014), 54–55.

[23] See Baines, *Doing Anti-Oppressive Practice*. See also Lena Dominelli, "Deprofessionalizing Social Work: Anti-Oppressive Practice, Competencies and Postmodernism," *The British Journal of Social Work* 26, no. 2 (1996): 153–175.

[24] Karen Morgaine and Moshoula Capous-Desyllas, *Anti-Oppressive Social Work Practice: Putting Theory into Action* (Thousand Oaks, CA: Sage, 2015), 24.

[25] Ibid.

[26] *CASW Code of Ethics*, 4.

[27] Revelation 3:20, NIV.

Chapter 4

[1] Here, I acknowledge my use of "American Christians" as inclusive of various ethnicities and cultural backgrounds in the U.S. While the majority of harmful modes of hospitality are often performed by White individuals or groups, American Christianity is more than just White Christianity. Christians in America include diverse groups such as Nepalese American Christians in Texas, Black Christians in Missouri, Karin/Burmese Christians in Indiana, and many other Christian communities with diverse cultural backgrounds.

[2] Noble David Cook, "Requerimiento," in *Encyclopedia of Latin American History and Culture*, eds. Jay Kinsbruner and Erick D. Langer, 2nd edition, vol. 5 (New York: Charles Scribner's Sons, 2008), 522–523.

[3] Mark A. Noll, *A History of Christianity in the United States and Canada*, 2nd edition (Grand Rapids, MI: Eerdmans, 2019), 15.

[4] Thomas Thorowgood proposed a connection between the Indigenous people in New England and the Jews. Thomas Thorowgood, *Ievves in American, or, Probabilities That the Americans Are of That Race. With the Removall of Some Contrary Reasonings, and Earnest Desires for Effectual Endeavours to Make Them Christian* (London: Printed by W.H. for Tho. Slater, 1650; Ann Arbor, MI: Text Creation Partnership, 2011), 4–6. Portuguese Rabbi Menasseh ben Israel (1604–1657) also promoted the belief that Indigenous people were Jews being scattered in America. Manasseh ben Israel and Moses Wall, *The Hope of Israel*, 2nd edition (London: Printed by R.I. for L. Chapman, 1652).

[5] Craig Ott, Stephen J. Strauss, and Timothy C. Tennent, *Encountering Theology of Mission: Biblical Foundations, Historical Developments, and Contemporary Issues* (Grand Rapids, MI: Baker Academic, 2010), 172.

[6] Ibid., 171.

[7] Dana Robert, *Christian Mission: How Christianity Became a World Religion* (Malden, MA: Wiley-Blackwell, 2009), 51.

[8] L. Daniel Hawk and Richard L. Twiss, "From Good: 'The Only Good Indian Is a Dead Indian' to Better: 'Kill the Indian and Save the Man' to Best: 'Old Things Pass

Endnotes

Away and All Things Become White!' An American Hermeneutic of Colonialization," in *Evangelical Postcolonial Conversations: Global Awakenings in Theology and Praxis*, eds. Kay Higuera Smith, Jayachitra Lalitha, and L. Daniel Hawk (Downers Grove, IL: IVP Academic, 2014), 53.

[9] James A. Sandos, *Converting California: Indians and Franciscans in the Missions* (New Haven, CT: Yale University Press, 2007), 57, 98.

[10] Samson Occom, *A Choice Collection of Hymns and Spiritual Songs* (New London, CT: Press of Thomas and Samuel Green, 1774).

[11] William Wallace Tooker, *John Eliot's First Indian Teacher and Interpreter, Cockenoe-de-Long Island: And the Story of His Career from the Early Records* (New York: F. P. Harper, 1896), 12–13.

[12] Howard L. Harrod, *Mission Among the Blackfeet* (Norman, OK: University of Oklahoma Press, 1971), 22.

[13] Edward E. Andrews, *Native Apostles: Black and Indian Missionaries in the British Atlantic World* (Cambridge, MA: Harvard University Press, 2013), 127, 185–186.

[14] Gustavo Gutiérrez, *Las Casas: In Search of the Poor of Jesus Christ* (Maryknoll, NY: Orbis Books, 1993); Francisco de Vitoria, *Las Relecciones De Indis Y De Iure Belli*, ed. notes Javier Malagón Barceló (Washington, DC: Unión Panamericana, 1963).

[15] Mark A. Noll, *Turning Points: Decisive Moments in the History of Christianity* (Grand Rapids, MI: Baker Academic, 2000), 215.

[16] A. J. Langguth, *Driven West: Andrew Jackson and the Trail of Tears to the Civil War* (New York: Simon & Schuster, 2010), 265.

[17] *Lives of Missionaries, Greenland: Hans Egede: Matthew Stach and His Associates* (London: Society for Promoting Christian Knowledge, 1860), 52.

[18] Craig Ott, Steven J. Strauss, and Timothy C. Tennent, *Encountering Theology of Mission* (Grand Rapids, MI: Baker Academic, 2010), 169.

[19] Kwame Nkrumah, *Neo-Colonialism: The Last Stage of Imperialism* (Bedford, UK: Panaf Books, 1987), xiii.

[20] Ibid., x–xi.

[21] Tsenay Serequeberhan, *The Hermeneutics of African Philosophy: Horizon and Discourse* (New York: Routledge, 1994), 13–14.

[22] Exceptions to this misperception sometimes include countries like South Korea, Japan, and Singapore.

[23] Gary B. Ferngren, *Medicine & Health Care in Early Christianity* (Baltimore, MD: John Hopkins University Press, 2009), 95.

[24] Ibid., 97–104.

[25] Ibid., 103.

[26] Mary C. Earle, *The Desert Mothers: Spiritual Practices from the Women of the Wilderness* (New York: Morehouse, 2007), 73.

[27] Steve Corbett and Brian Fikkert, *When Helping Hurts: How to Alleviate Poverty without Hurting the Poor and Yourself* (Chicago, IL: Moody, 2009), 51.

[28] Janice E. Perlman, *Favela: Four Decades of Living on the Edge in Rio De Janeiro* (New York: Oxford University Press, 2009), 318.

[29] Bryant Myers, *Walking with the Poor: Principles and Practices of Transformational Development* (Maryknoll, NY: Orbis Books, 1999), 86–87.

[30] Amos Yong, *Hospitality and the Other: Pentecost, Christian Practices, and the Neighbor* (Maryknoll, NY: Orbis Books, 2008), 101–102.

[31] Ibid., 124.

Endnotes

[32] See Hebrews 13:12. See also Jonathan Wilson-Hartgrove, *Strangers at My Door: A True Story of Finding Jesus in Unexpected Guests* (New York: Convergent Books, 2013), 5; Richard Beck, *Stranger God: Meeting Jesus in Disguise* (Minneapolis, MN: Fortress Press, 2017), 2.

[33] Stanley H. Skreslet, "Comprehending Mission: The Questions, Methods, Themes, Problems, and Prospects of Missiology," *American Society of Missiology Series, No. 49* (Maryknoll, NY: Orbis Books, 2012), 184–185.

[34] Andrew Arterbury, *Entertaining Angels: Early Christian Hospitality in Its Mediterranean Setting* (Sheffield: Sheffield Phoenix Press, 2005), 190.

[35] Amy Oden, *And You Welcomed Me: A Sourcebook on Hospitality in Early Christianity* (Nashville, TN: Abingdon, 2011), 109.

[36] While it is outside of the scope of this chapter, Christians can seek opportunities to reduce waste, wean from excessive consumerism and the use of single-use plastic, and creatively partner with people and groups who are intentional about how to live in ways less harmful to the land.

[37] Robert D. Lupton, *Toxic Charity: How Churches and Charities Hurt Those They Help, and How to Reverse It* (New York: HarperOne, 2011), 62.

[38] Robert D. Putnam, *Bowling Alone: The Collapse and Revival of American Community* (New York: Touchstone Books, 2001), 21.

[39] Dana L. Robert, *Faithful Friendships: Embracing Diversity in Christian Community* (Grand Rapids, MI: Eerdmans, 2019), 20.

[40] Deepa Narayan and Patti Petesch, *Voices of the Poor: From Many Lands* (New York: World Bank and Oxford University Press, 2002), 490.

[41] Alvaro L. Nieves, "Applied Research Strategy for Christian Organizations," in *This Side of Heaven: Race, Ethnicity, and Christian Faith*, eds. Robert J. Priest and Alvaro L. Nieves (New York: Oxford University Press, 2007), 309.

Chapter 5

[1] This chapter was originally to be written by postcolonial historian Dr. Deanne van Tol. While her name is not listed as author, I want to acknowledge her immense contribution to the work here. Van Tol outlined the chapter and articulated its conceptual moves and sources. She originated the chapter's thesis on the colonial conditions that limit the embodiment of virtues. She laid out Hall's concept of mutually constituted identities and Crysdale's multiple healing meanings as ways of understanding more fully our lived lives. She also worked tirelessly in researching and identifying key moments from the CRCNA's denunciation of the Doctrine of Discovery. That her schedule did not permit her to finish the chapter should not underplay her vital contribution. The chapter would, simply put, not exist without her insight, expertise, and creativity.

[2] "Portrait Of: Author Julia Alvarez," *Latino USA*, September 10, 2019, accessed July 31, 2020, https://www.npr.org/2019/09/09/758995158/a-portrait-of-author-julia-alvarez.

[3] Ibid.

[4] Ibid.

[5] Ibid.

[6] Saint Augustine, *The City of God*, trans. Marcus Dods, D.D. (New York: The Modern Library, 1993), 19.4.

Endnotes

[7] Ibid.

[8] "Prime Minister Stephen Harper's Statement of Apology," *CBC*, June 11, 2008, accessed July 31, 2020, https://www.cbc.ca/news/canada/prime-minister-stephen-harper-s-statement-of-apology-1.734250.

[9] Truth and Reconciliation Commission of Canada, *Honouring the Truth, Reconciliation for the Future, Volume One: Summary, Final Report of the Truth and Reconciliation Commission of Canada* (Toronto: James Lorimer and Company), vi.

[10] Ibid., viii, xi.

[11] Ibid., v.

[12] Ibid., 138. "In Canada, 52.2 percent of children in foster care are Indigenous, but account for only 7.7 percent of the child population according to Census 2016." These rates suggest that the Sixties Scoop never truly ended. To reduce the number of Indigenous children in the system, Canada passed the "Act Respecting First Nations, Inuit and Métis Children, Youth and Families (S.C. 2019, c. 24)," which went into effect January 1, 2020. As of July 2020, there is no evidence rating the effectiveness of the act. "Reducing the Number of Indigenous Children in Care," *Government of Canada*, February 20, 2020, accessed July 31, 2020, https://www.sac-isc.gc.ca/eng/1541187352297/1541187392851.

[13] Holly A. McKenzie, Colleen Varcoe, Annette J. Browne, and Linda Day, "Disrupting the Continuities Among Residential Schools, the Sixties Scoop, and Child Welfare: An Analysis of Colonial and Neocolonial Discourses," *The International Indigenous Policy Journal* 7, no. 2 (2016): 6, http://ir.lib.uwo.ca/iipj/vol7/iss2/4. It is important to note the impact racism and Residential Schools had in creating the conditions for the so-called bad parenting. Many child welfare services did not understand or respect Indigenous cultures and interpreted Indigenous cultural norms as inferior. Hence, the implicit racism of White child welfare workers likely contributed to misperceptions of bad parenting. Furthermore, the abuse and dislocation that Indigenous peoples experienced at Residential Schools caused profound harm that extended from one generation to the next, what has been described as generational or historical trauma. The separation of Indigenous children from their families deprived Indigenous households of their traditional parenting role models and encouraged an impaired capacity to parent in healthy ways. For Indigenous survivors who coped with the trauma of abuse, many developed substance abuse issues. When compounded with lack of parental role models, these two factors put parents at risk for so-called parental incompetence and emotional unavailability. See Maria Yellow Horse Brave Heart, "The Historical Trauma Response among Natives and its Relationship with Substance Abuse: A Lakota Illustration," *Journal of Psychoactive Drugs* 35, no. 1 (January–March 2003): 9. Children of survivors tended to be at risk themselves for substance abuse and suicide. Therefore, the generational or historical trauma of Residential Schools helped create the Indigenous households of the Sixties Scoop the government deemed as unfit. The Canadian government and Canadian churches failed to acknowledge that their collaboration produced these so-called deficient households. As Indigenous filmmaker Alanis Obomsawin rightly claims, welfare agents often overlooked the reality that in Indigenous communities, "every child has many mothers." Alanis Obomsawin, dir., *Richard Cardinal: Cry from a Diary of a Métis Child*, National Film Board of Canada, accessed June 23, 2020, https://www.nfb.ca/film/richard_cardinal/.

[14] David Fanshel, *Far from the Reservation: The Transracial Adoption of American Indian Children* (New Jersey: The Scarecrow Press, 1972), iii, quoted in Sarah Wright

Cardinal, "Beyond the Sixties Scoop: Reclaiming Indigenous Identity, Reconnection to Place, and Reframing Understandings of Being Indigenous" [PhD diss., University of Victoria, 2017], 21.

[15] McKenzie et al., "Disrupting the Continuities," 7.

[16] Ibid.

[17] Raven Sinclair, "Identity Lost and Found: Lessons from the Sixties Scoop," *First Peoples Child & Family Review* 3, no. 1 (2007): 70.

[18] Cardinal, "Beyond the Sixties Scoop," 110.

[19] Ibid., 120.

[20] Ibid., 112.

[21] Linnell Secomb, "Empire and the Ambiguities of Love," *Cultural Studies Review* 19, no. 2 (September 2013): 199, accessed September 27, 2019, http://epress.lib.uts.edu.au/journals/index.php/csrj/index.

[22] Saint Augustine, *The City of God*, 2.21. See also John M. Warner and John T. Scott, "Sin City: Augustine and Machiavelli's Reordering of Rome," *Journal of Politics* 73, no. 3 (July 2011): 860.

[23] Robert A. Williams Jr., *Savage Anxieties: The Invention of Western Civilization* (New York: St. Martin's Press, 2012), 17.

[24] Georg Wilhelm Friedrich Hegel, *Phenomenology of Spirit*, trans. Terry Pinkard (Cambridge: Cambridge University Press, 2018), 113. Judith Butler makes it clear that this relationship is violent. See her *Subjects of Desire: Hegelian Reflections in Twentieth-Century France* (New York: Columbia University Press, 1987), 38.

[25] Franz Fanon, *Black Skin, White Masks*, trans. Richard Philcox (New York: Grove Press, 1952, 2008), xiii–10. In the first few pages of the book, Fanon implicates several dichotomies, including metropole/colony, White/Black, and colonizer/colonized.

[26] Allan A. Boesak, *Black and Reformed: Apartheid, Liberation, and the Calvinist Tradition* (Eugene, OR: Wipf and Stock, 1984), 1–10. Writing on the limitations of traditional Western theology, he claims that White theology has never taken seriously the Black experience because to be non-White is to be regulated to a nonperson, a negation.

[27] Willie James Jennings, "Disfigurations of Christian Identity: Performing Identity as Theological Method," in *Lived Theology: New Perspectives on Method, Style, and Pedagogy*, eds. Charles Marsh, Peter Slade, and Sarah Azaransky (Oxford: Oxford University Press, 2017), 76. Jennings notes that aesthetic judgements are a byproduct of global capitalism. Therefore, what we know as beauty is that quality that circulates around the acquisition of objects that consumers desire.

[28] Gloria Anzaldúa, *Borderlands/La Frontera: The New Mestiza*, 4th edition (San Francisco: Aunt Lute Books, 2012), 58–59. Anzaldúa affirms that this key dichotomy fueled and continues to fuel much of the colonial violence we presently inhabit.

[29] Steven Newcomb, *Pagans in the Promised Land: Decoding the Doctrine of Christian Discovery* (Golden, CO: Fulcrum, 2008), 68–69.

[30] Ibid.

[31] Linda Tuhiwai Smith, *Decolonizing Methodologies: Research and Indigenous Peoples*, 2nd edition (New York: Zed Books, 2012), 21–29. For Smith, the terms need not only describe people. Things, concepts, perceptions, places, and practices, for example, can all be colonized, including but not limited to time, imagination, history, society, and research. This also means that all these things can be decolonized.

[32] Ann Laura Stoler, "Tense and Tender Ties: The Politics of Comparison in North American History and (Post) Colonial Studies," *The Journal of American History* 88, no.

3 (December 2001): 832.

[33] Catherine Hall, *Civilizing Subjects: Metropole and Colony in the English Imagination 1830–1867* (Chicago, IL: University of Chicago Press, 2002), 9.

[34] Ibid., 10.

[35] Ibid., 13.

[36] James Baldwin, "Stranger in the Village," in *Collected Essays* (New York: The Library of America, 1998), 119.

[37] Ibid.

[38] Cynthia S.W. Crysdale, *Embracing Travail: Retrieving the Cross Today* (New York: Continuum, 2000), 5.

[39] Ibid.

[40] Ibid.

[41] Ibid., 6.

[42] This point is an essential feature of evangelical theology and piety, which often goes unnamed. However, the popular hymn "How Deep the Father's Love" precisely articulates this reading. In speaking of the crucifixion, Christians sing, "It was my sin that held him there," and "My sin [was] upon his shoulders." Stuart Townsend, "How Deep the Father's Love for Us," track 11 on *Ultimate Collection*, Integrity Music, 2013, iTunes.

[43] Crysdale, *Embracing Travail*, 8.

[44] Ibid.

[45] David C. Steinmetz, "The Superiority of Pre-Critical Exegesis," *Theology Today* 37, no. 1 (1980): 26–38.

[46] Ibid., 33.

[47] Ibid, 34.

[48] Ibid.

[49] Ibid., 34–35

[50] Ibid., 35.

[51] Truth and Reconciliation Commission of Canada, *Honouring the Truth*, 427.

[52] Doctrine of Discovery Task Force, "Creating a New Family: A Circle of Conversation on the Doctrine of Christian Discovery" (Grand Rapids, MI: The Christian Reformed Church in North America, 2016), 6–7, accessed July 27, 2020, https://www.crcna.org/sites/default/files/doctrine_of_discovery.pdf. This account of the Doctrine of Discovery takes seriously the work of scholars like Indigenous legal scholar Steven T. Newcomb, particularly in his book *Pagans in the Promised Land*. Focusing on a series of cases issued by the Marshall Supreme Court, Newcomb recounts how the court uses these edicts as legal precedent to dispose Indigenous peoples of their land. He rightly describes two key realities: the effect the edicts had in Western history and the logics of the court that can be rightly ascribed to the wider project of colonization. The CRCNA's historical narration owes much to Newcomb's narration. This work is slightly different from readings of papal edicts in their original, historical context. For example, as theologian Damian Costello points out, colonial empires were not "dependent on the Church for its legitimacy." That is to say, empires did not require the sanction of the Pope to engage their colonial conquests. They "nevertheless utilized religious channels. . . . Thus, Ferdinand, through the papal bulls and royally sponsored apologies, constructed a type of divine sanction for a campaign won by military force." See Damian Costello, "Revisiting the *Requerimiento*: Fealty, Unsacred Monarchy, and Political Legitimacy," in *Weaving the American Catholic Tapestry: Essays in Honor of William L. Portier*, eds. Derek C. Hatch and Timothy R. Gabrielli (Eugene, OR: Pickwick, 2017), 194–196.

[53] Newcomb, *Pagan in the Promised Land*, 84.
[54] Ibid.
[55] Doctrine of Discovery Task Force, "Creating a New Family," 10.
[56] Ibid. For a more detailed analysis of Ginsberg's decisions affecting Indigenous peoples, see Carole Goldberg, "Finding the Way to Indian Country: Justice Ruth Bader Ginsburg's Decisions in Indian Law Cases," *Ohio State Law Journal* 70, no. 4 (2009): 1003–1035.
[57] Doctrine of Discovery Task Force, "Creating a New Family," 39.
[58] Ibid.
[59] Ibid.
[60] "Thursday, June 16–PM Session 1–Synod 2016," *CRCNA–Christian Reformed Church in North America*, June 22, 2016, accessed August 1, 2020, https://www.youtube.com/watch?v=4YBKvfSbSuQ&list=PLOuKlnOF5iTDe2U8f-0cCv0yr4eqk9O88&index=5.
[61] Ibid.
[62] Cornelius Plantinga Jr., *Engaging God's World: A Reformed Vision of Faith, Learning, and Living* (Grand Rapids, MI: Eerdmans, 2002), 15.
[63] Doctrine of Discovery Task Force, "Creating a New Family," 22.
[64] Ibid.
[65] Ibid.
[66] Ibid., 38.
[67] Ibid., 40.
[68] Ibid., emphasis original.
[69] Mark Charles, "Race, Trauma, and the Doctrine of Discovery," *The January Series of Calvin University*, January 19, 2017, accessed August 1, 2020, https://www.youtube.com/watch?v=fYZ2rj2Jooc&t=2s.
[70] "Thursday, June 16–PM Session 2–Synod 2016," *CRCNA–Christian Reformed Church in North America*, June 22, 2016, accessed August 1, 2020, https://www.youtube.com/watch?v=2xCqy2Oewl4&list=PLOuKlnOF5iTDe2U8f-0cCv0yr4eqk9O88&index=4.
[71] Charles, "Race, Trauma, and the Doctrine of Discovery."
[72] Ibid.
[73] H. Richard Niebuhr, *The Meaning of Revelation* (Louisville, KY: Westminster John Knox Press, 1941, 1968, 2006), 61.
[74] Ibid.
[75] Isaiah 55:8, NRSV.
[76] Mark 5:27, NRSV.

Chapter 6

[1] W. E. B. Du Bois, *The Souls of Black Folks* (New York: Dover Publications, 1994), 2.
[2] "In U.S., Decline of Christianity Continues at Rapid Pace: An Update on America's Changing Religious Landscape," *Pew Research Center* (October 17, 2019), https://www.pewforum.org/2019/10/17/in-u-s-decline-of-christianity-continues-at-rapid-pace/.
[3] Michael Lipka, "A Closer Look at America's Rapidly Growing Religious 'Nones,'" *Pew Research Center*, May 13, 2015. http://pewrsr.ch/1L1D5KW.
[4] "In U.S., Decline of Christianity Continues at a Rapid Pace," *Pew Research*

Center, October 17, 2019, https://www.pewforum.org/2019/10/17/in-u-s-decline-of-christianity-continues-at-rapid-pace/.

[5] Ibid.

[6] Ibid.

[7] Robert P. Jones, Daniel Cox, E.J. Dionne Jr., William A. Galston, Betsy Cooper, and Rachel Lienesch, "How Immigration and Concerns about Cultural Changes Are Shaping the 2016 Election: Findings from the 2016 PRRI/Brookings Immigration Survey," *Public Religion Research Institute*, June 23, 2016, https://www.prri.org/wp-content/uploads/2016/06/PRRI-Brookings-2016-Immigration-survey-report.pdf.

[8] "White Evangelicals See Trump as Fighting for Their Beliefs, Though Many Have Mixed Feelings about His Personal Conduct," *Pew Research Center*, March 12, 2020, https://www.pewforum.org/2020/03/12/white-evangelicals-see-trump-as-fighting-for-their-beliefs-though-many-have-mixed-feelings-about-his-personal-conduct/.

[9] Ibid.

[10] Philip S. Gorski, "Historicizing the Secularization Debate: An Agenda for Research," in *The Handbook of the Sociology of Religion*, ed. Michele Dillon (Cambridge: Cambridge University Press, 2003), 110. Gorski also notes the exceptions: "In a few countries, such as Ireland and Poland, levels of belief and practice are still very high; in others, however, such as Sweden and Denmark, they are quite low." Ibid.

[11] Mark Chaves, "Secularization as Declining Religious Authority," *Social Forces* 72, no. 3 (1994): 750.

[12] Ibid.

[13] Heidi A. Campbell and Stephen Garner, *Networked Theology: Negotiating Faith in Digital Culture* (Grand Rapids, MI: Baker Academic, 2016), 73–75.

[14] It is important to note the majority of these incidents of harassment occur in countries where Christians are a majority—not a minority—of the population. See Katayoun Kishi, "Christians Faced Widespread Harassment in 2015, but Mostly in Christian-Majority Countries," *Pew Research Center*, June 9, 2017, http://pewrsr.ch/2s59PCw. It is also important to note that while Christians experience discrimination globally, they have devoted immense resources to infringing upon the human rights of LGBTQ+ individuals around the world, as well as in the same countries where Christians report harassment. See Kapya Kaoma, "Globalizing the Culture Wars: U.S. Conservatives, African Churches, and Homophobia," *Political Research Associates*, December 1, 2009, http://www.politicalresearch.org/2009/12/01/globalizing-culture-wars.

[15] Candida R. Moss, *The Myth of Persecution: How Early Christians Invented a Story of Martyrdom* (New York: HarperCollins, 2013), 247.

[16] Ibid., 11.

[17] Ibid., 250.

[18] Ibid.

[19] Robert P. Jones et al., "How Immigration and Concerns," 2016.

[20] Franklin Graham, "The War on Christmas Is a War on Christ," *Decision: The Evangelical Voice of Today*, November 25, 2014, https://decisionmagazine.com/war-christmas-war-christ/.

[21] George Yancey, "Has Society Grown More Hostile Towards Conservative Christians? Evidence from ANES Surveys," *Review of Religious Research* 60 (2018): 85, https://doi.org/10.1007/s13644-017-0303-8.

[22] Ibid., 88.

[23] Ibid., 89.

Endnotes

[24] Conrad Hackett and David McClendon, "Christians Remain World's Largest Religious Group, But They Are Declining in Europe," *Pew Research Center*, April 5, 2017, http://pewrsr.ch/2o5CXFL.

[25] "In U.S., Decline of Christianity Continues at Rapid Pace," *Pew Research Center*.

[26] Brian J. Grim and Melissa E. Grim, "The Socio-economic Contribution of Religion to American Society: An Empirical Analysis," *Interdisciplinary Journal of Research on Religion* 12, no. 3 (2016): 27.

[27] Brian Kluth, "State of the Plate," *Evangelical Council for Financial Accountability*, http://www.ecfa.org/Documents/News/20-Truths-About-Tithers-Executive-Summary-eBook-Report.pdf. Whether or not Kluth's methods are reliable, the rhetoric of wealth is what is, perhaps, most interesting here. Far from an economically marginalized group, this survey suggests a Christian self-understanding as resource rich.

[28] Madeline St. Amour, "Giving Growth Slows," *Inside Higher Ed*, February 6, 2020, accessed July 9, 2020, https://www.insidehighered.com/news/2020/02/06/college-and-university-fundraising-rises-growth-slows-down.

[29] "Faith on the Hill: The Religious Composition of the 116th Congress," *Pew Research Center*, January 3, 2019, https://www.pewforum.org/2019/01/03/faith-on-the-hill-116/. Whether or not all evangelicals might consider these convictions as always real, such identifications reveal a deeper reality. Many politicians find Christianity to be more viable politically than other religions, like Islam, or no religion. Even if such identifications are cynically political, they reveal the reality that Christian convictions possess political power, even if that power is shifting and decreasing.

[30] "White Evangelicals See Trump," *Pew Center Research*, 2020. This number slipped to 78 percent in the 2020 election. See Gregory A. Smith, "White Christians Continue to Favor Trump over Biden, But Support Has Slipped," *Pew Research Center*, October 13, 2020, https://pewrsr.ch/3709QMp.

[31] Steven Waldman and the Working Group on Information Needs of Communities, *The Information Needs of Communities: The Changing Media Landscape in a Broadband Age* (Federal Communications Commission), 186, https://transition.fcc.gov/osp/inc-report/INoC-11-Religious-Broadcasting.pdf.

[32] "Lobbying for the Faithful," *Pew Research Center*, May 15, 2012, https://www.pewforum.org/2011/11/21/lobbying-for-the-faithful-exec/.

[33] Moss, *The Myth of Persecution*, 252.

[34] Ibid.

[35] Ibid.

[36] Yancey, "Has Society Grown," 88. See also George Yancey, "Who Has Religious Prejudice? Differing Sources of Anti-Religious Animosity in the United States," *Review of Religious Research* 52, no. 2 (2010): 159–171.

[37] Rodney Stark and Roger Finke, *Acts of Faith: Explaining the Human Side of Religion* (Berkley, CA: University of California Press, 2000), 197.

[38] See, for example, Roger Finke and Rodney Stark, *The Churching of America, 1776–2005: Winners and Losers in our Religious Economy* (New Brunswick, NJ: Rutgers University Press, 2005). See also Stark and Finke, *Acts of Faith*. See also Laurence R. Iannaccone, Roger Finke, and Rodney Stark, "Deregulating Religion: the Economics of Church and State," *Economic Inquiry* 35, no. 2 (1997): 350–364.

[39] Finke and Stark, *The Churching of America*, 249–250.

[40] Laurence R. Iannaccone, "Why Strict Churches Are Strong," *American Journal of Sociology* 99, no. 5 (March 1994): 1203.

ENDNOTES

⁴¹ Lewis A. Coser, *The Functions of Social Conflict* (New York: Routledge, 1956, 2001), 87. See also Iannaccone, "Why Strict Churches," 1203–1205. See also James K. Wellman Jr. and Kyoto Tokuno, "Is Religious Violence Inevitable?" *Journal for the Scientific Study of Religion* 43, no. 3 (2004): 292.

⁴² Finke and Stark, *The Churching of America*, 283.

⁴³ Ibid., 3.

⁴⁴ Melanie White, "An Ambivalent Civility," *Canadian Journal of Sociology/Cahiers Canadiens de Sociologie* (2006): 452–454.

⁴⁵ Ibid., 453.

⁴⁶ Ibid.

⁴⁷ Todd Stillman, "Civility," in *Encyclopedia of Social Theory*, ed. George Ritzer (Thousand Oaks, CA: Sage Publications, 2005), 103.

⁴⁸ Ibid.

⁴⁹ Thomas Reese, "Pope to Gay Priests: Be Celibate or Get Out," *National Catholic Reporter*, December 7, 2018, https://www.ncronline.org/news/opinion/signs-times/pope-gay-priests-be-celibate-or-get-out.

⁵⁰ See for example, Ariel Shidlo and Michael Schroeder, "Changing Sexual Orientation: A Consumers' Report," *Professional Psychology: Research and Practice* 33, no. 3 (2002): 249–259, accessed July 10, 2020, https://doi.org/10.1037/0735-7028.33.3.249. See also Robert L. Spitzer, "Can Some Gay Men and Lesbians Change Their Sexual Orientation? 200 Participants Reporting a Change from Homosexual to Heterosexual Orientation," *Archives of Sexual Behavior* 32 (October 2003): 403–417. For a personal account of the harm of such ministries, see Garrard Conley, *Boy Erased: A Memoir* (New York: Riverhead Books, 2016).

⁵¹ See for example Deborah Lolai, "'You're Going to Be Straight or You're Not Going to Live Here': Child Support for LGBT Homeless Youth," *Tulane Journal of Law and Sexuality* 24, no. 35 (2015): 35–97.

⁵² Cornel West, "Introduction: The Radical King We Don't Know," in *The Radical King: Martin Luther King Jr.*, ed. Cornel West (Boston, MA: Beacon Press, 2012), iBooks.

⁵³ Martin Luther King Jr., "Letter from Birmingham Jail." in *The Radical King*.

⁵⁴ Ibid.

⁵⁵ Ibid.

Chapter 7

¹ Theologian Arthur Cochrane's excellent history of the Barmen Declaration details the rise of the "German Christians" and how their "union of Christianity, nationalism, and militarism was taken for granted." See Arthur C. Cochrane, *The Church's Confession under Hitler* (Philadelphia: Westminster Press, 1962), 50. "German Christians" joined with Nazi party members and campaigned on the "belief that 'race, nationality, and the nation [are] orders of life granted and entrusted to us by God, for whose preservation God's law requires us to strive.'" By appealing to God's natural laws and Romans 13, they believed they were in the center of God's will (83). Furthermore, "German Christians" accepted the Aryan principle and would not even consider dissent at its National Synod (111).

² Hubert G. Locke, ed., *The Church Confronts the Nazis: Barmen Then and Now* (Lewiston, NY: Edwin Mellen Press, 1984), 14.

ENDNOTES

[3] Ibid., 1–15; for the full contemporary version of the Barmen Theological Declaration, see the Presbyterian Church's *Book of Confessions*, https://www.pcusa.org/site_media/media/uploads/oga/pdf/boc2016.pdf, 279–284.

[4] Shelley Baranowski, *The Confessing Church, Conservative Elites, and the Nazi State* (Lewiston, NY: E. Mellen Press, 1986); Shelley Baranowski, "The Confessing Church and Antisemitism: Protestant Identity, German Nationhood, and the Exclusion of the Jews," in *Betrayal: German Churches and the Holocaust*, eds. Robert P. Ericksen and Susannah Heschel (Minneapolis, MN: Augsburg Fortress Press, 1999); Robert P. Ericksen and Susannah Heschel, *Betrayal: German Churches and the Holocaust* (Minneapolis, MN: Augsburg Fortress Press, 1999), 10.

[5] Richard J. Evans, *The Third Reich in Power, 1933–1939* (New York: Penguin, 2005), 4.

[6] Ibid., 5.

[7] Ibid., 6.

[8] Ramathate Dolamo, "Karl Barth's Contribution to the German Church Struggle against National Socialism," *Studia Historiae Ecclesiasticae* 36, no. 1 (2010): 3.

[9] Baranowski, *The Confessing Church*, 26.

[10] Ibid.

[11] Robert T. Osborn, *The Barmen Declaration as a Paradigm for a Theology of the American Church* (Lewiston, NY: Edwin Mellen Press, 1991), 35.

[12] Ibid., 4–11.

[13] Ibid., 23.

[14] Ibid., 25.

[15] Victoria Barnett, *For the Soul of the People: Protestant Protest against Hitler* (New York: Oxford University Press, 1992), 30.

[16] Rolf Ahlers, *The Barmen Theological Declaration of 1934: The Archeology of a Confessional Text* (Lewiston, NY: Edwin Mellen Press, 1986), 7.

[17] Klaus Scholder, *The Churches and the Third Reich: Preliminary History and the Time of Illusions 1918–1934*, vol. 1, trans. John Bowden (Philadelphia: Fortress Press, 1988), 257.

[18] Ahlers, *The Barmen Theological Declaration of 1934*, 9.

[19] Robert A. Krieg, "The Vatican Concordat with Hitler's Reich: The Concordat of 1933 Was Ambiguous in Its Day and Remains So," *America Magazine*, September 1, 2003, https://www.americamagazine.org/faith/2003/09/01/vatican-concordat-hitlers-reich-concordat-1933-was-ambiguous-its-day-and-remains.

[20] Cochrane, *The Church's Confession under Hitler*, 74.

[21] Ibid., 50.

[22] Ibid., 76.

[23] Ibid., 83.

[24] Ibid., 90.

[25] Scholder, *The Churches and the Third Reich*, 378–79; Ahlers, *The Barmen Theological Declaration of 1934*, 7.

[26] Cochrane, *The Church's Confession under Hitler*, 91.

[27] Baranowski, *The Confessing Church, Conservative Elites, and the Nazi State*, 46–52.

[28] Cochrane, *The Church's Confession under Hitler*, 53–54.

[29] Ibid., 51.

[30] Ibid., 56–65.

Endnotes

[31] Ibid., 82–85.

[32] Ibid., 102.

[33] Discontent within the church led to Confessional Synods at Berlin, Dortmund, and Ulm, all of which preceded the Barmen Synod. See Bishop of Chichester, "Foreword" to *The Significance of the Barmen Declaration for the Ecumenical Church*, eds. Hans Herbert Walther Kramm and J. O. Cobham, Theology Occasional Papers 5 (London: Society for Promoting Christian Knowledge, 1943), 5. Also notable to the Confessing Church's struggle are Heinrich Vogel's *8 Articles of Evangelical Doctrine* (Cochrane, *The Church's Confession under Hitler*, 124), the Tecklenburg Confession, and publications in the series *Theologische Existenz Heute*, the series *Bekennende Kirche*, and articles in the periodical *Evangelishe Theologie* (Ibid., 126). The church and state divide was also debated in theological faculties with numerous statements issued in favor of the German Church and opposed to it (Ibid., 126-128).

[34] Peter Longerich, *Holocaust: The Nazi Persecution and Murder of the Jews* (New York: Oxford University Press, 2010), 33–39.

[35] Kenneth C. Barnes, *Nazism, Liberalism, and Christianity: Protestant Social Thought in Germany and Great Britain, 1925–1937* (Lexington, KY: University Press of Kentucky, 2015), 95.

[36] Cochrane, *The Church's Confession under Hitler*, 108–9. Martin Niemöller, according to Barth, was "the embodiment of Barmen" (110).

[37] Ibid., 111.

[38] Randall L. Bytwerk, *Bending Spine: The Propagandas of Nazi Germany and the German Democratic Republic* (East Lansing, MI: Michigan State University Press, 2004), 1.

[39] Niemöller originally tried to work with the Nazi regime to resolve his concerns with State Interference, but in January 1934, shortly after the "muzzling" order had been decreed (Cochrane, *The Church's Confession under Hitler*, 129), Niemöller spoke up during a meeting with forty other church leaders and Hitler. The Gestapo had listened in on a phone call an hour earlier, where, as Niemöller described it, a colleague joked about Hitler. This was raised as a concern about Niemöller, and although Niemöller attempted to reassure him, Hitler reprimanded him, saying, "You leave the care of the Third Reich to me." As the meeting ended, Niemöller approached Hitler and responded with a reproach of his own: "Neither you nor any power in the world is in a position to take from us Christians and the Church the responsibility God has laid upon us" (130–31). Niemöller soon found himself under investigation and the leader of the German Christian Church disciplined and dismissed him (132).

Because of his continued public opposition to the encroaching State, Niemöller was finally arrested in 1937 and then acquitted (Ibid., 110). After his release in 1938 he was immediately re-arrested by the Gestapo as Hitler's special prisoner. He spent the next seven years, until the end of the war, in Sachsenhausen and Dachau concentration camps (Evans, *The Third Reich in Power*, 231, 232). The poem "Then They Came for Me" is attributed to Niemöller.

[40] "Richard Mouw Speaks About Convicted Civility," *Reformed Church in America*, June 10, 2017, accessed May 2, 2022, https://www.rca.org/richard-mouw-speaks-about-convicted-civility/.

[41] Compromise has its place even in practicing integrity. The partisan politics of current practices shows how difficult it is to get anything done when people refuse to compromise. But the willingness to compromise can quickly lead to a loss of one's

integrity if the discernment process has been weak.

[42] Damian Cox, Marguerite LaCaze, and Michael Levine, "Integrity," in *The Stanford Encyclopedia of Philosophy*, ed. Edward N. Zalta, Spring 2017 (Stanford, CA: Metaphysics Research Lab, Stanford University, 2017), https://plato.stanford.edu/archives/spr2017/entries/integrity/.

[43] Barbara Killinger, *Integrity: Doing the Right Thing for the Right Reason*, 2nd edition (Montreal: McGill-Queen's University Press, 2007), 29.

[44] Stephen L. Carter, *Integrity* (New York: HarperCollins, 1996), 39.

[45] Ibid., 61.

[46] Ibid., 7.

[47] J. L. Austin, *How to Do Things with Words* (London: Oxford University Press, 1962). See also John R. Searle, *Speech Acts: An Essay in the Philosophy of Language* (Cambridge: Cambridge University Press, 1969).

[48] "Boundaries are essential to the life of the church and its ministry, in order to preserve the church's core identity and mission." Arden F. Mahlberg and Craig L. Nessan, *The Integrity of the Body of Christ: Boundary Keeping as Shared Responsibility* (Eugene, OR: Wipf and Stock, 2016), 23.

[49] Mark Galli, "Trump Should Be Removed from Office," in *Christianity Today*, December 19, 2019, https://www.christianitytoday.com/ct/2019/december-web-only/trump-should-be-removed-from-office.html.

[50] Proverbs 9:10, NIV.

[51] Philippians 1:9–11, NIV.

[52] Gregory Spencer, *Awakening the Quieter Virtues* (Downers Grove, IL: InterVarsity Press, 2010), 32.

[53] Carter, Integrity, 27.

[54] Spencer, *Awakening the Quieter Virtues*, 23.

[55] Evans, *The Third Reich in Power, 1933–1939*, 224.

[56] Ruth W. Grant, *Hypocrisy and Integrity: Machiavelli, Rousseau, and the Ethics of Politics* (Chicago, IL: University of Chicago Press, 1997), 2.

[57] Thomas Forsyth Torrance, "Karl Barth: Swiss Theologian," in *Encyclopedia Britannica*, June 25, 2019, https://www.britannica.com/biography/Karl-Barth.

[58] We must credit Stephen Carter's work. Carter first called the Barmen Declaration an act of integrity. Stephen L. Carter, *Civility* (New York: HarperCollins, 1998), 274–76.

[59] Incivility becomes an option only when discernment is also truly in place. Discernment can be hampered by echo chambers and unwavering loyalty to public leaders, many of whom have embraced the spread of misinformation to support their own agendas. Thus, discernment requires research of diverse sources, prayer, and wisdom to determine the truth.

[60] Busch, *The Barmen Theses Then and Now*, 11.

[61] Randall L. Bytwerk, *Bending Spine*, 6; Gerhard Hahn, "The Cross of Christ and the Swastika," trans. Randall L. Bytwerk (Grand Rapids, MI: German Propaganda Archive, Calvin University, 2010), https://research.calvin.edu/german-propaganda-archive/christuskreuz.htm. This 1934 pamphlet by Gerhard Hahn titled *The Cross of Christ and the Swastica* states, "We see in Adolf Hitler the Führer sent to us by God" (today everyone sees that, and it is probably no longer blasphemy!)

[62] Karl Barth, *JA und NEIN, Karl Barth zum Gedaechtnis* (1967), dir. by Heinz Knorr and Calwer Verlag. Karl Barth on the Confessing Church (Bekennende Kirche),

Endnotes

https://www.youtube.com/watch?v=drq9hz5tYDI

[63] Barmen Theological Declaration, cited in Cochrane, *The Church's Confession under Hitler*, 257.

[64] Ibid.

[65] Susannah Ticciati, "The Scriptural Logic of Barmen and the Jewish Question," in *Reading Scripture as a Political Act: Essays on the Theopolitical Interpretation of the Bible*, eds. Matthew A. Tapie and Daniel Wade McClain (Minneapolis, MN: Fortress Press, 2015), 264.

[66] Baranowski, *The Confessing Church*, 59.

[67] If the Barmen Declaration is an act of integrity, then why did it not address the "Jewish Question"? Ticciati notes, "Barth himself later wrote to Eberhard Bethge, 'I myself have long felt guilty that I did not make [the Jewish] problem [Die Judenfrage] central [entscheidend], at least public, in the two Barmen declarations of 1934 which I had composed'" (Ticciati, "The Scriptural Logic of Barmen and the Jewish Question," 260). In earlier tracts and papers, Barth had included the issue of racism in the church (Ahlers, *The Barmen Theological Declaration of 1934*, 248, n. 20), but while negotiating between different denominational emphases, it did not come out in the 1934 Barmen version (Ticciati, "The Scriptural Logic of Barmen and the Jewish Question," 252, n. 4). Notice that the fifth point in the Declaration might point to the Aryan clause by suggesting the government was not ruling responsibly for all its subjects, but Hans Asmussen's lecture, which the synod bound to the Declaration as authoritative, "downplays any hint of political activism" (Ibid., 267). That does not mean that as the Declaration spread, others did not draw the conclusion that the Confessing Church opposed the Aryan clause.

[68] Eberhard Jügel, *Christ, Justice, and Peace: Toward a Theology of the State in Dialogue with the Barmen Declaration*, trans. D. Bruce Hamill and Alan J. Torrance (Edinburgh: T & T Clark, 1992), 15.

[69] James H. Cone, *The Cross and the Lynching Tree* (Maryknoll, NY: Orbis Books, 2011), 156.

[70] Ibid., 159.

[71] Jemar Tisby, *The Color of Compromise: The Truth about the American Church's Complicity in Racism* (Grand Rapids, MI: Zondervan, 2019), 151.

[72] Ibid., 15.

[73] Ibid.

[74] Richard Stearns, *The Hole in Our Gospel: What Does God Expect of Us?* (Nashville, TN: Thomas Nelson, 2009), 229.

[75] Tisby, *The Color of Compromise*, 14–15.

[76] Ibid., 24.

[77] Ibid., 137.

[78] Raymie McKerrow, "The Limits of Civility," *Vital Speeches of the Day* 67, no. 9 (February 15, 2001): 3.

[79] Bryan Stevenson, *Just Mercy* (New York: Random House, 2014), 18.

[80] Emma Green, "How Trump Lost an Evangelical Stalwart," *The Atlantic*, December 19, 2019, https://www.theatlantic.com/politics/archive/2019/12/christianity-today-trump-removal/603952/.

[81] Alan J. Torrance, "Introductory Essay," in *Christ, Justice and Peace: Toward a Theology of the State in Dialogue with the Barmen Declaration*, ed. Eberhard Jüngel (London: T & T Clark, 1992), xii.

ENDNOTES

Chapter 8

[1] In using the terms "evangelical" and "American evangelical," I have in mind the broad religiocultural community that is grounded in particular theological distinctives, as explicated by Mark Noll and James Davison Hunter. See Mark Noll, *American Evangelical Christianity: An Introduction* (Malden, MA: Blackwell, 2001); James Davison Hunter, *American Evangelicalism: Conservative Religion and the Quandary of Modernity* (New Brunswick, NJ: Rutgers University Press, 1983).

[2] See, for instance, Ben Sasse, *Them: Why We Hate Each Other—and How to Heal* (New York: St Martin's, 2018); Catherine Rampell, "Americans Are Burning Down the House," *Washington Post*, July 10, 2017, https://www.washingtonpost.com/opinions/americans-are-burning-down-the-house/2017/07/10/7b522ea6-65af-11e7-a1d7-9a32c91c6f40_story.html; James Davison Hunter, *To Change the World: The Irony, Tragedy, and Possibility of Christianity in the Late Modern World* (New York: Oxford University Press, 2010), and *Before the Shooting Begins: Searching for Democracy in America's Culture War* (New York: Free Press, 1994).

[3] See, for instance, John Fea, *Believe Me: The Evangelical Road to Donald Trump* (Grand Rapids, MI: Eerdmans, 2018); Stephen L. Carter, *God's Name in Vain: The Wrongs and Rights of Religion in Politics* (New York: Basic Books, 2000).

[4] Stephen L. Carter, *Civility: Manners, Morals, and the Etiquette of Democracy* (New York: Basic Books, 1998), xi–xii.

[5] Ibid., 11.

[6] Ibid., 18.

[7] Ibid., 19.

[8] Richard Mouw, *Uncommon Decency: Christian Civility in an Uncivil World* (Downers Grove, IL: InterVarsity Press, 1992), 12.

[9] See Chapter 1 in this volume.

[10] Ibid., 31, 53–55.

[11] Steve Wilkens and Mark L. Sanford, *Hidden Worldviews: Eight Cultural Stories That Shape Our Lives* (Downers Grove, IL: InterVarsity Press, 2009), 27–60.

[12] See, for instance, Anthony G. Wilhelm, *Democracy in the Digital Age: Challenges to Political Life in Cyberspace* (New York: Routledge, 2000); Natalie Jomini Stroud, *Niche News: The Politics of News Choice* (New York: Oxford University Press, 2011).

[13] See Bill Bishop, *The Big Sort: How the Clustering of Like-Minded America Is Tearing Us Apart* (New York: Houghton Mifflin Harcourt, 2008).

[14] See Michael O. Emerson and Christian Smith, *Divided by Faith: Evangelical Religion and the Problem of Race in America* (New York: Oxford University Press, 2000).

[15] Wayne C. Booth, *The Rhetoric of Rhetoric: The Quest for Effective Communication* (Malden, MA: Blackwell, 2004), 10–11.

[16] Eugene Garver, *For the Sake of Argument: Practical Reasoning, Character, and the Ethics of Belief* (Chicago, IL: University of Chicago Press, 2004), particularly 13–43.

[17] Eugene Garver, "How Can a Liberal Listen to a Religious Argument? Religious Rhetoric as a Rhetorical Problem," in *How Should We Talk about Religion? Perspectives, Contexts, Particularities*, ed. James Boyd White (Notre Dame, IN: University of Notre Dame Press, 2006), 164–93.

[18] Wilkens and Sanford, *Hidden Worldviews*, 139–59. James Davison Hunter also addresses the connections among perceived victimization, moral outrage, and moral

Endnotes

self-justification with his invocation of Nietzsche's notion of "ressentiment" (*To Change the World*, 107–8).

[19] Gregory A. Smith, "White Christians Continue to Favor Trump over Biden, But Support Has Slipped," *Pew Center Research*, October 13, 2020, accessed May 7, 2021, https://www.pewresearch.org/fact-tank/2020/10/13/white-christians-continue-to-favor-trump-over-biden-but-support-has-slipped/.

[20] Fea, *Believe Me*, 131–132.

[21] See Jonathan Cahn's website, https://thereturn.org.

[22] See, for instance, Rodney Clapp, *A Peculiar People: The Church as Culture in a Post-Christian Society* (Downers Grove, IL: InterVarsity Press, 1996), particularly 22–28.

[23] Mark A. Noll, *In the Beginning Was the Word: The Bible in American Public Life, 1492–1783* (Oxford: Oxford University Press, 2016), 3–17.

[24] See Mark Noll, *The Civil War as a Theological Crisis* (Chapel Hill, NC: University of North Carolina Press, 2006).

[25] Fea, *Believe Me*, 60.

[26] Ibid.

[27] See, for instance, Skye Jethani, *The Divine Commodity: Discovering a Faith beyond Consumer Christianity* (Grand Rapids, MI: Zondervan, 2009); John F. Kavanaugh, *Following Christ in a Consumer Society*, 3rd edition (Maryknoll, NY: Orbis, 2006); Vincent J. Miller, *Consuming Religion: Christian Faith and Practice in a Consumer Culture* (New York: Contiunuum, 2003); Alan Wolfe, *The Transformation of American Religion: How We Actually Live Our Faith* (Chicago, IL: University of Chicago Press, 2003).

[28] Fea, *Believe Me*.

[29] Hunter, *American Evangelicalism*, 9.

[30] Timothy J. Basselin, *Flannery O'Connor: Writing a Theology of Disabled Humanity* (Waco, TX: Baylor University Press, 2013).

[31] Andy Crouch, *Strong and Weak: Embracing a Life of Love, Risk and True Flourishing* (Downers Grove, IL: InterVarsity Press, 2016), 10–11.

[32] Ibid., 28–29, 33, 35–41.

[33] Ibid., 41.

[34] Ibid., 41–42, emphasis in original.

[35] Ibid., 48.

[36] Ibid.

[37] Philippians 1:27–2:4, NIV.

[38] Philippians 2:7, NIV.

[39] Gordon D. Fee, *Paul's Letter to the Philippians* (Grand Rapids, MI: Eerdmans, 1995), 214.

[40] Frank Thielman, *The NIV Application Commentary: Philippians* (Grand Rapids, MI: Zondervan, 1995), 128–129.

[41] Michael O. Emerson and Christian Smith, *Divided by Faith: Evangelical Religion and the Problem of Race in America* (New York: Oxford University Press, 2000).

[42] Henry Louis Gates Jr., *Stony the Road: Reconstruction, White Supremacy, and the Rise of Jim Crow* (New York: Penguin Press, 2019), particularly 55–77, 125–57. For a sustained discussion of the religious justifications for post-Reconstruction "redemption"—and the more general ways in which Christian theology was used in the post-Reconstruction period to valorize the Confederate cause at the expense of African Americans—see Charles Reagan Wilson, *Baptized in Blood: The Religion of the Lost Cause, 1865–1920*, 2nd edition (Athens, GA: University of Georgia Press, 2009).

Endnotes

⁴³ See, for instance, Ken Wytsma, *The Myth of Equality: Uncovering the Roots of Injustice and Privilege* (Downers Grove, IL: InterVarsity Press, 2017), 55–56.

⁴⁴ See, for instance, Wytsma, *The Myth of Equality*, 69; James H. Cone, *The Cross and the Lynching Tree* (Maryknoll, NY: Orbis Books, 2011), 3.

⁴⁵ See, for instance, Wytsma, *The Myth of Equality*, 50–54; David M. Oshinsky, *Worse Than Slavery: Parchman Farm and the Ordeal of Jim Crow Justice* (New York: Free Press, 1996), 34–84.

⁴⁶ See, for instance, Michelle Alexander, *The New Jim Crow: Mass Incarceration in the Age of Colorblindness*, revised edition (New York: Free Press, 2012).

⁴⁷ See, for instance, Wytsma, *The Myth of Equality*, 72–79.

⁴⁸ Cone, *The Cross and the Lynching Tree*, 3.

⁴⁹ Howard Thurman, *Jesus and the Disinherited* (1949; reprint, Boston: Beacon Press, 1996), 6ff.

⁵⁰ Ibid., 11.

⁵¹ Ibid., 3.

⁵² Ibid., 2.

⁵³ Wytsma, *The Myth of Equality*, 177.

⁵⁴ It should be made clear that in this example the suffering that is required is on the part of Whites and White evangelicals. From the standpoint of justice, it is not proper to ask the Black American community to suffer more to help realize the possibility of racial reconciliation, as they have suffered too much already. Given the context and the history surrounding this issue, the responsibility is properly on Whites and White evangelicals to learn how to bear some of the profound burdens of racism—not as a means to "save" Black Americans, but as a means to follow Christ.

⁵⁵ See "Report of the Ad Interim Committee on Racial and Ethnic Reconciliation to the Forty-Sixth General Assembly of the Presbyterian Church in America," June 2018, https://www.pcahistory.org/topical/race/2018_report_ethnic_and_racial_reconciliation.pdf.

⁵⁶ See "Ad Interim Committee on Racial Reconciliation Report," in "14th Stated Meeting of the Tidewater Presbytery Docket," unpublished document, June 7, 2018.

⁵⁷ See Anthony B. Bradley, *Liberating Black Theology: The Bible and Black Experience in America* (Wheaton, IL: Crossway, 2010). For other examples of similar and more contemporary work, see Vince L. Bantu, *A Multitude of All Peoples: Engaging Ancient Christianity's Global Identity* (Downers Grove, IL: IVP Academic 2020); Drew G. I. Hart, *Who Will Be a Witness? Igniting Activism for God's Justice, Love, and Deliverance* (Harrisonburg, VA: Herald Press, 2020); Esau McCaulley, *Reading While Black: African American Biblical Interpretation as an Exercise in Hope* (Downers Grove, IL: IVP Academic, 2020); Jemar Tisby, *The Color of Compromise: The Truth about the American Church's Complicity in Racism* (Grand Rapids, MI: Zondervan, 2019).

Chapter 9

¹ John 11:47–50, NKJV

² 1 Corinthians 2:8, NIV.

³ Hebrews 13:12–14, NIV.

⁴ Sarah Pulliam Bailey, "White Evangelicals Voted Overwhelmingly for Donald Trump, Exit Polls Show," *The Washington Post*, November 9, 2016, https://www.

Endnotes

washingtonpost.com/news/acts-of-faith/wp/2016/11/09/exit-polls-show-white-evangelicals-voted-overwhelmingly-for-donald-trump/?utm_term=.c7fe2bef8eb7.

[5] It is important to note that many voted not so much *for* Trump as *against* Hillary Clinton. See Ed Stetzer and Andrew MacDonald, "Why Evangelicals Voted Trump: Debunking the 81%," *Christianity Today*, October 18, 2018, https://www.christianitytoday.com/ct/2018/october/why-evangelicals-trump-vote-81-percent-2016-election.html.

[6] For example, see Michael Gerson, "Franklin Graham Has Played His Ultimate Trump Card," *The Washington Post*, June 3, 2019, https://www.washingtonpost.com/opinions/franklin-graham-has-played-his-ultimate-trump-card/2019/06/03/22a50b18-862b-11e9-98c1-e945ae5db8fb_story.html; Michael Gerson, "Evangelicals Are Naked Before the World," *The Washington Post*, June 27, 2019, https://www.washingtonpost.com/opinions/evangelicals-are-naked-before-the-world/2019/06/27/463e87b4-991a-11e9-8d0a-5edd7e2025b1_story.html; David French, "Evangelicals Are Supporting Trump out of Fear, Not Faith," *Time*, June 27, 2019, https://time.com/5615617/why-evangelicals-support-trump/.

[7] See René Girard, "Mimesis and Violence," in *The Girard Reader*, ed. James G. Williams (New York: Crossroad, 1996), 9–19; René Girard, *Things Hidden Since the Foundation of the World*, trans. Stephen Bann and Michael Meteer (Stanford, CA: Stanford University Press, 1987).

[8] For an example from Aztec culture, see Gil Bailie, *Violence Unveiled: Humanity at the Crossroads* (New York: Crossroad, 1995), 99–107. See also René Girard, *Violence and the Sacred*, trans. Patrick Gregory (Baltimore, MD: Johns Hopkins University Press, 1977), 104–11.

[9] See Girard, "Mimesis and Violence," 14–15.

[10] See René Girard, "The Bible's Distinctiveness and the Gospel," in *The Girard Reader*, ed. James G. Williams (New York: Crossroad, 1996), 148–57.

[11] Genesis 4:1–17, NIV.

[12] Genesis 37, 41–42, 45, NIV.

[13] Girard, "The Bible's Distinctiveness and the Gospel."

[14] Walter Brueggemann, *The Prophetic Imagination*, 40th Anniversary edition (Minneapolis, MN: Fortress Press, 2018), 6.

[15] Ibid., 26–27, 41.

[16] Ibid., 6, 28–29.

[17] Ibid., 63.

[18] Ibid., 6, emphasis in original.

[19] Ibid., 7–9, 14–19. For a few Biblical examples, see also Exodus 3:7–8, 15, 20:1–17, 22:20–21; Leviticus 19:9–18, 33–37, Deuteronomy 10:18; Deuteronomy 15:7–8, and Deuteronomy 16:18–20, NIV.

[20] See I Samuel 8:4–22, 10:17–25, 15:10–23, 18:5–15, 19:1–2, NIV.

[21] See Brueggemann, 23–25; I Kings 6:38–7:1, 9:10–23, 11:1–8, NIV.

[22] See 2 Kings 16:1–3, 21:1–6, NIV.

[23] For example, see Jeremiah 32:30–35, NIV.

[24] For example, see Amos 5:10–15, 21–24; Hosea 6:6; Isaiah 1:11–17, NIV.

[25] Brueggemann, 48: Jeremiah 52, NIV.

[26] Isaiah 52:13–53:12, NIV.

[27] See Brueggemann, *Prophetic Imagination*, 82.

[28] See Luke 6:20–26, Matthew 5:1–12, NIV.

[29] See Luke 7:20–22, NIV.

[30] For example, contravening the rules of the religious leaders with his compassion, Jesus healed on the Sabbath; touched an "unclean" leper and an "unclean" dead girl to heal them; offered "living water" to a despised Samaritan woman; saved a woman caught in adultery from being stoned; offered good news to the poor and oppressed and penitent sinners; ate with tax collectors and other "sinners," and harshly critiqued the empty, heartless piety of the religious leaders.

[31] Luke 13:34, NIV.

[32] Jerusalem means "city of peace."

[33] See Luke 19:41–44, NIV.

[34] See John 18:19–24, 28–40, NIV.

[35] Girard, "The Bible's Distinctiveness and the Gospel," 165–68; René Girard, "The Nonsacrificial Death of Christ," in *The Girard Reader*, ed. James G. Williams (New York: Crossroad, 1996), 177–188.

[36] Romans 12:1, NIV.

[37] See Seth Dowland, *Family Values and the Rise of the Christian Right* (Philadelphia, PA: University of Pennsylvania Press, 2015).

[38] Emi Kolawole, "Congress to Outlaw Homeschooling?", FactCheck.org, A Project of the Annenberg Public Policy Center, April 4, 2008, https://www.factcheck.org/2008/04/congress-to-outlaw-homeschooling/.

[39] See Jamelle Bouie, "Christian Soldiers," *Slate*, February 10, 2015, https://slate.com/news-and-politics/2015/02/jim-crow-souths-lynching-of-blacks-and-christianity-the-terror-inflicted-by-whites-was-considered-a-religious-ritual.html.

[40] The Ku Klux Klan famously used a burning cross to symbolize its supposedly Christian zeal.

[41] Randall Balmer, "The Real Origins of the Religious Right," *Politico Magazine*, May 27, 2014, https://www.politico.com/magazine/story/2014/05/religious-right-real-origins-107133?o=3.

[42] Ibid.

[43] Miriam Jordan, "U.S. Shutters Warehouse Where Migrants Were Kept in 'Cages,'" *The New York Times*, November 25, 2020, https://www.nytimes.com/2020/11/25/us/border-migrant-children-cages-ursula-warehouse.html.

[44] See Alex Nowrasteh, "Illegal Immigrants and Crime—Assessing the Evidence," *Cato Institute*, March 4, 2019, https://www.cato.org/blog/illegal-immigrants-crime-assessing-evidence.

[45] Moreover, Trump has long evidenced an obsession with the glitz and glamor of royalty. See Nina Burleigh, "Trump's Obsession with the Royals and Their Golden Lifestyle Dates Back Decades," *NBC News*, June 5, 2019, https://www.nbcnews.com/think/opinion/trump-s-obsession-royals-their-golden-lifestyle-dates-back-decades-ncna1013911?cid=sm_npd_nn_fb_ma&fbclid=IwAR3VcFfbclq7Yc0_iy63SRYxljTGQGcis7e6SH4p5A5KInSR4koyQAg51Vs.

[46] For a science-based account of this process, see Maria Konnikova, "Trump's Lies vs. Your Brain," *Politico Magazine*, January/February 2017, https://www.politico.com/magazine/story/2017/01/donald-trump-lies-liar-effect-brain-214658.

[47] Ralph Reed spoke for many evangelicals when he said, "'There has never been anyone who has defended us and who has fought for us, who we have loved more than Donald J. Trump. No one!'" Peter Wehner, "The Deepening Crisis in Evangelical Christianity," *The Atlantic*, July 5, 2019, https://www.theatlantic.com/ideas/archive/2019/07/evangelical-christians-face-deepening-crisis/593353/?utm_

campaign=the-atlantic&utm_source=facebook&utm_content=edit-promo&utm_medium=social&utm_term=2019-07-05T10%3A00%3A16.

[48] Michael Gerson, "Evangelicals Have Been Reshaped into the Image of Trump Himself," *The Washington Post*, October 28, 2019, https://www.washingtonpost.com/opinions/evangelicals-have-been-reshaped-into-the-image-of-trump-himself/2019/10/28/f37f5154-f9c0-11e9-ac8c-8eced29ca6ef_story.html.

[49] David French identifies such threats: "The left wants 'nones' to facilitate access to abortifacients and contraceptives, it wants Christian adoption agencies to compromise their conscience or close, and it even casts into doubt the tax exemptions of religious education institutions if they adhere to traditional Christian sexual ethics. These issues are legally important, and there are reasons for evangelicals to be concerned." French, "Evangelicals Are Supporting Trump out of Fear."

[50] For instance, in 2018, Liberty University President Jerry Falwell Jr. tweeted, "Conservatives & Christians need to stop electing 'nice guys.' They might make great Christian leaders but the United States needs street fighters like @realDonaldTrump at every level of government b/c the liberal fascists Dems are playing for keeps & many Repub leaders are a bunch of wimps!" (https://twitter.com/jerryfalwelljr/status/1045853333007798272?lang=en). Similarly, Sohrab Ahmari regards "[c]ivility and decency" as "secondary values" and argues that conservatives should "fight the culture war with the aim of defeating the enemy and enjoying the spoils in the form of a public square re-ordered to the common good and ultimately the Highest Good." Sohrab Ahmari, "Against David French-ism," *First Things*, May 29, 2019, https://www.firstthings.com/web-exclusives/2019/05/against-david-french-ism.

[51] Ibid.

[52] Katherine Stewart, "Why Trump Reigns as King Cyrus," *The New York Times*, December 31, 2018, https://www.nytimes.com/2018/12/31/opinion/trump-evangelicals-cyrus-king.html.

[53] See French, "Evangelicals Are Supporting Trump out of Fear."

[54] Ibid.

[55] David French, "Franklin Graham and the High Cost of the Lost Evangelical Witness," *National Review*, April 25, 2019, https://www.nationalreview.com/2019/04/franklin-graham-and-the-high-cost-of-the-lost-evangelical-witness/.

[56] See Brueggemann, *Prophetic Imagination*, xxx–xxxi.

[57] See Nancy French, "What Happened after My Husband Was Attacked For Critiquing Franklin Graham's Pete Buttigieg Tweets," *The Washington Post*, May 9, 2019, https://www.washingtonpost.com/religion/2019/05/09/what-happened-after-my-husband-was-attacked-critiquing-franklin-grahams-pete-buttigieg-tweets/; Tyler O'Neil, "Bizarre: Mainstream Conservative Leaders Are Gunning for David French," *PJ Media*, June 5, 2019, https://pjmedia.com/trending/the-bizarre-conservative-twitter-mob-gunning-for-david-french/.

[58] In recent decades, a cadre of theologians and Bible scholars have begun the work of recovering lament. For example, see Kathleen D. Billman and Daniel L. Migliore, *Rachel's Cry: Prayer of Lament and Rebirth of Hope* (Cleveland, OH: United Church Press, 1999); Sally A. Brown and Patrick D. Miller, eds., *Lament: Reclaiming Practices in Pulpit, Pew, and Public Square* (Louisville, KY: Westminster John Knox Press, 2005); Soong-Chan Rah, *Prophetic Lament: A Call for Justice in Troubled Times* (Downers Grove, IL: InterVarsity Press, 2015).

[59] Glenn Pemberton, *Hurting with God: Learning to Lament with the Psalms*

(Abilene, TX: Abilene Christian University Press, 2012), Kindle loc. 441–45.

[60] Rah, *Prophetic Lament*, 24.

[61] See Jemar Tisby, *The Color of Compromise: The Truth about the American Church's Complicity in Racism* (Grand Rapids, MI: Zondervan, 2019); James H. Cone, *The Cross and the Lynching Tree* (Maryknoll, NY: Orbis, 2013).

[62] Mark 8:34, NIV.

[63] Hebrews 13:13, NIV.

[64] Rah, "Prophetic Lament," 210–211.

[65] Scotty Smith, "A Prayer for Lamenting the Death of Unborn Children," *The Gospel Coalition*, August 25, 2015, https://www.thegospelcoalition.org/blogs/scotty-smith/a-prayer-for-lamenting-the-death-of-unborn-children/.

[66] Scotty Smith, "A Prayer for Lamenting Violence and Longing for Its End," *The Gospel Coalition*, September 13, 2015, https://www.thegospelcoalition.org/blogs/scotty-smith/a-prayer-for-lamenting-violence-and-longing-for-its-end/.

[67] John Pavlovitz, "Here's Why We Grieve Today," *John Pavlovitz: Stuff That Needs to Be Said*, November 9, 2016, https://johnpavlovitz.com/2016/11/09/heres-why-we-grieve-today/.

[68] Ibid.

[69] John Pavlovitz, "White Evangelicals, This Is Why People Are Through with You," *John Pavlovitz: Stuff That Needs to Be Said*, January 24, 2018, https://johnpavlovitz.com/2018/01/24/white-evangelicals-people/.

[70] Saint Augustine famously uses the analogy of the Israelites in Exodus taking gold and silver items from the idolatrous Egyptians, which were then put to use in creating the tabernacle of Yahweh. See Saint Augustine, *On Christian Doctrine*, trans. D. W. Robertson, Jr. (New Jersey: Prentice-Hall, 1958), 75.

[71] Ibid., 118.

[72] See Aristotle, *On Rhetoric: A Theory of Civic Discourse*, 2nd edition, trans. George A. Kennedy (Oxford: Oxford University Press, 2006), 3.

[73] John 18:38, NIV.

[74] Quintilian, *Institutes of Oratory*, trans. John Selby Watson, eds. Curtis Dozier and Lee Honeycutt (Creative Commons), 637.

[75] Luke 23:34, NIV.

[76] Romans 2:2, NIV.

[77] In John 1:1–14, NIV. "Word" (alluding to Christ) is a translation of the Greek *logos*.

[78] 1 Corinthians 1:25, NIV.

Conclusion

[1] Richard Mouw, *Uncommon Decency: Christian Civility in an Uncivil World* (Downers Grove, IL: InterVarsity Press, 1992), 16.

[2] While it is outside the scope of our chapter, it is important to note the larger context in which these claims take place. In many ways, the homogeneity of dominant Western culture has some rootage in a secularized and colonial Judeo-Christian ideology. Therefore, claims that pluralism is a problem are indicative of the Christian persecution complex Jaime Harris discussed in Chapter 6. The persecution complex reframes dominant culture to justify or rationalize the call for homogeneity.

Endnotes

[3] Revelation 7:9, NRSV.

[4] Acts 10:28, NRSV.

[5] Like Peter, Jesus also calls the apostle Paul to a conversion of his imagination with reference to Gentiles. Paul describes his Jewish pedigree (Philippians 3:4b–6, NRSV) and there is no evidence in the Biblical text that he, or any of the other disciples for that matter, ever stopped being faithful Jews. However, he retains a deep cultural flexibility as he bears witness to Jesus, both to his Jewish community and among the Gentiles. Part of what he carries out, particularly from the Jerusalem Council in the Acts of the Apostles, is not imposing Jewish cultural practices—like observances of holy days and Kosher law—on Gentiles (Acts 15:1–35, NRSV). Because Gentiles can go on being culturally Gentile while following the Jewish Messiah, Paul never imposes Jewish culture on Gentiles. Hence, the existence of Gentile and Jewish believers implies a pluralism as a foundational feature of Christian faith.

[6] Mark Noll, "Keynote Address," *The Christianity and Communication Studies (CCSN) 2021 Unconference: Christian Persuasion in a Post-Christian Culture*, June 11–12, 2021, Zoom.

[7] Alan Jenkins, "Racial Equality and the U.S. Constitution: Scholars on Shortcomings That Need to Be Addressed," *Detroit Today with Stephen Henderson*, July 20, 2021, accessed November 9, 2021, https://wdet.org/2021/07/20/racial-equality-and-the-u-s-constitution-scholars-on-shortcomings-that-need-to-be-addressed/.

[8] Matthew 25:31–46, NRSV.

[9] Matthew 13:24–30, NRSV.

[10] Calvin Troup, "Humility and Hospitality: Two Conditions Necessary for the Possibility of Civility," in *Humility and Hospitality: Changing the Christian Conversation on Civility*, eds. Naaman Wood and Sean Connable (Pasco, WA: Integratio Press, 2022), 12.

[11] Ibid., 19.

[12] Ibid.

[13] Martin Luther King Jr., "Letter from Birmingham Jail," *The Atlantic*, April 2018, https://www.theatlantic.com/magazine/archive/2018/02/letter-from-a-birmingham-jail/552461/.

[14] Simone Cinotto, "'Everyone Would Be Around the Table': American Family Mealtimes in Historical Perspective, 1850–1960," *New Directions for Child and Adolescent Development* 111 (Spring 2006): 17.

[15] Ibid., 23.

[16] Tim Muehlhoff and Richard Langer, *Winsome Conviction: Disagreeing without Dividing the Church* (Downers Grove, IL: IVP Academic, 2020), 165.

[17] Ibid., 165–66.

[18] Abraham Joshua Heschel, "The Reasons for My Involvement in the Peace Movement," in *Moral Grandeur and Spiritual Audacity*, ed. Susannah Heschel (New York: Farrar, Straus & Giroux, 1996), 225.

[19] Ibid.

[20] Abraham Joshua Heschel, *The Prophets* (Peabody, MA: Hendrickson, 2007), 3.

[21] Ibid., 4.

[22] Hebrews 11:1, KJV.

[23] Hebrews 11:6, NRSV.

[24] English translations usually lock this passage into a limited meaning. The New Revised Standard Version (NRSV) translates this passage as "to till it and keep" the land,

Endnotes

while the New International National Version (NIV) renders it "to work it and take care of it." In the rest of the Bible, the Hebrew term rendered as "till" or "work" often appears in reference to servants and masters. For example, in Genesis 15:13–14, God promises Abram that his "offspring shall be aliens in a land that is not theirs, and shall be *slaves* there, and they shall be oppressed for four hundred years; but I will bring judgment on the nation that they *serve*" (emphasis added). The number of these types of references implying subordination occurs dozens of times throughout the Old Testament. Because Hebrew is a poetic language, these overtones can rightly be brought from these passages into Genesis 2. Part of what God calls humans to do is to serve the good creation God has made for us. Because our lives depend on what comes from the land, serving the land is a way of caring for each other and the gifts God provides us.

[25] Quoted in M. F. Wiles, "The Unassumed is the Unhealed," *Religious Studies* 4 (1968): 47.

[26] Matthew 19:30, 20:16; Mark 10:31; Luke 13:30, NRSV.

[27] Matthew 19:16–30; Mark 10:17–31, NRSV.

[28] Matthew 19:27; Mark 10:28, NRSV.

[29] Matthew 19:23b–26, NRSV.

Index

acquiescence from guests (hospitality), 48–49, 58
acting "as if," 104–05
action/speech, 118–20
African Americans, as subhuman, 137
Ahmari, Sohrab, 203n50
Alexander VI, Pope, 87
Alfonso V, King of Portugal, 87
Alvarez, Julia, 77–78, 91
Ambrose, 26–27
America
    cultural and economic dominance of, 64
    founding racism of, 166–67
American Methodist Episcopal Church, 103
Andrews, Edward E., 67
Anselm, 183n15
anti-abortion movement, 150–51
Anti-Oppressive Practice (AOP), 48, 53–56
Anzaldúa, Gloria, 188n28
Apostles' Creed, 7, 162
appearance of civility, 162–73
Aristotle, 20, 156
Armey Amendment, 150
Armstrong, Tonya, 54
Arterbury, Andrew, 72
Asmussen, Hans, 115, 197n67
Augustine, xxi, 20, 34, 42–43, 46, 91, 129, 145
    on city of man, 144
    on civility and virtue, 22
    on commonwealth, 11, 23–24, 26, 147, 166

    on empire, 11
    on founding violence of Rome, 81
    on free will, 183n11
    on households, 11, 25–26
    on Israel taking gold and silver from Egypt, 204n70
    on justice, 35
    on limits to virtue, 77–78
    on localities, 11, 26
    on lust for power, 43–44
    on ordered loves, 24, 147
    on power through weakness, 156
    on reality, 34, 35
    on right conditions for civility, 112
    on speaking truth with humility, 157
    on substance and appearance, 13
    on substance of justice, 182n8
Austin, J. L., 118
authority, and hierarchy, 34

Baldwin, James, 83
Barmen Declaration, 15, 111–26, 175, 193n1, 197n67
Barth, Karl, 111, 115, 120, 121, 122, 197n67
Basseline, Timothy J., 134
Bielefeld Confession, 115
BIPOC (Black, Indigenous, and other people of color), 12, 170
Black Lives Matter protests, 3
Boesak, Allan A., 188n26
Booth, Wayne C., 131
Bradley, Anthony B., 140
Brown, Austin Channing, 169
Brown, Peter, 183n11

Index

Brueggemann, Walter, 15, 144, 145, 146–49, 153
Bryant, Mary K., 15, 175
Butler, Judith, 188n24
Bytwerk, Randall, 116, 121

Cahn, Jonathan, 131
Cain and Abel, 145–46, 170–71
Cappadocian Fathers, 70
Carter, Stephen L., 112, 117–119
Castile, Philando, 3
Chaput, Charles, 133
charity, 34
Charles, Mark, 89–90, 91
Chaves, Mark, 98
Childers, Charles, L., 10
Christendom, 132
Christian Amendment Movement, 22
Christian America, 144
Christian incivility, benefits of, 101–04
Christian nationalism, 173, 175, 176
Christian persecution complex, 97–101, 204n2
Christian Reformed Church of North America, 14, 86–91
Christian Right, 132, 149–53
Christianity, negativity of, 123
Christians
  bear legacy of injustice and violence, xxii
  conversation on civility, 11
  as "counterpublic," 6, 164
  inhospitality of, 13
  as persecuted minority, 174
Chumash Christians, 66
Church
  boundaries, in the life of the church, 196n48
  as communal and countercultural, 133
Cicero, 20, 24
Cinotto, Simone, 169–70
civic laws, 26, 28
civil public square, 7–8
civil religion, 126
civility
  appearance of, 162–73
  calls for hospitality, 27–28
  conditions for possibility of, 8–10, 11–12
  depends on humility, 27
  Guinness on, 7–8
  and integrity, 112
  Mouw on, 5–6, 129–30
  Muehlhoff on, 6
  not a technique or method, 19, 29
  substance of, 162–63
  and suffering, 128–29
  unilateral conditions for, 104–05, 174
  as virtue, 130
Civitate Dei (city of God)
  and earthly city, 37–38
  loves of, 39
Cochrane, Arthur C., 114, 193n1
Cockenoe, 67
colonial empires, 66
colonialism, 14, 64, 78, 91, 173, 176
common ground, 131
commonwealth, 23–24, 60, 147, 150
  Augustine on, 11, 23–24, 26
Communications Studies, 21
compromise, 117, 195–96n41
Cone, James, 120, 122–23, 138, 140
Confessing Church, 111–12, 116, 119–20, 122
confessional beliefs, 7
Constantinianism, 15, 132
consumerism, 128, 130, 132, 141, 186n36
convict leasing, 137
"convicted civility" (Mouw), 5, 117, 129
Corbett, Steve, 71
core values, 7
Cornelius, offered hospitality to Peter, 72, 165
Costello, Damian, 189n52
covenantal hospitality, 13–14, 64, 73–76
Craddock, Fred B., 10
creation, care of, 205–06n24
Critical Race Theory, 140
Crouch, Andy, 135
cruciform witness, 149
crusaderism, 130
Crysdale, Cynthia, 84–85, 91, 186n1
cultural attentiveness, 20
cultural encounters, arrogance in, 63–64

Index

culture
  as local, 26–27
  retreating and hiding from, xxii
culture Protestantism, 126
Cyrus, 131, 152

Daniel, civility of, 28
de Brébeuf, Jean, 68
de Minaya, Bernardino, 67
Derrida, Jacques, 54–55
Descartes, René, 180n19
desired ends, 7
diakonia, 141
dichotomies of difference, 81–82
disagreement, within households, 21
discernment, 118–20, 125, 196n59
discourse, and substance, 46
Doctrine of Discovery, 14, 78, 86–91
"double consciousness," 96
Dreher, Rod, 133
Du Bois, W. E. B., 96
Dum Diversas, 87

early Christians, hospitality of, 70
earthly city, loves of, 39
Egede, Hans and Gertrude, 68
Eliot, John, 67
Ellul, Jacques, 20
Elshtain, Jean Bethke, 25
Emerson, Michael O., 136, 169
empire, 11, 13, 23–24, 47–48, 174
  and hospitality, 47, 50, 56
Erasmus, George, 92
eschatology, as diverse in covenantal hospitality, 13–14
covenantal hospitality, 13–14
ethos, 156
evangelicals, support for Trump, 15, 100, 131, 133, 144–45, 149–53
experience, 9

faithful discipleship, 15
Falwell, Jerry, 132
Falwell, Jerry, Jr., 203n50
family, 25
family meals, 21, 169
family values, 149–50
Fanon, Franz, 188n25

Fea, John, 132–33
Ferngren, Gary B., 70
Fikkert, Brian, 71
Finke, Roger, 102
fire analogy, 10
fixed roles (host and guest), 64, 69
Floyd, George, 175
fluid identities (host and guest), 13, 48, 53–56, 69
Forum 4:15 Unconference, xxi, 4, 12, 144, 166
foundational colonial violence, 80–81
Founding Fathers, racism of, 166–67
founding violence of North America, 14, 80–81
fratricide, 23, 145
freedom, 34
French, David, 152–53, 203n49

Galli, Mark, 118, 125
Garces, Julian, 68
Garver, Eugene, 131
Gates, Henry Louis, Jr., 137
German Christians, 112, 121
German Evangelical Church (*Deutsche Evangelische Kirche*), 111–112, 114, 116
Gingrich, Newt, 99
Ginsburg, Ruth Bader, 87
Girard, René, 15, 144, 145–49
Gleichshaltung, 114
God, as stranger, 53
"good grief," 84
goodness, 42–43
Gorski, Philip S., 98, 191n10
Gospel Coalition, 155
Graham, Billy, 99
Graham, Franklin, 99
Grant, Ruth W., 119
Greco-Roman notion of hospitality, 70
Green, Joel, 10
Gregory of Nazianzus, 175
Grim, Brian J., 100
Grim, Melissa E., 100
guidelines for conduct, 7
Guinness, Os, 7–8, 11, 163, 164, 166–67, 179n18
Hahn, Gerhard, 196n61

209

Hall, Catharine, 83, 90
Harper, Stephen, 79
Harris, Jaime, 14, 174, 204n2
Hatch, John B., 15–16, 175
Hauser, Jerry, 21, 181n4
Hegel, Georg, 82
Heschel, Abraham Joshua, 163, 170–72
hierarchy in love, 34, 39–40
Hitler, Adolf, 113–14, 195n39
Hochschild, Arlie, 183n1
Homer, 82
homeschool movement, 150
homogeneity, 163, 164–65, 172
honesty, 117
hospitable discourse, and substances, 44–45
hospitality, 129
  action of empowerment and disempowerment, 60
  in Christian mission, 64–69
  as condition for civility, xxi, 9, 12, 27
  earthly and heavenly, 35
  and empire, 47, 50, 56
  as interaction, 48, 56–59
  as reciprocal, 64
  as recognizing and valuing the guest, 54
  spaciousness in, 58–59, 60
hosts and guests, fluidity of, 13, 48, 53–56, 69
household, 58
  Augustine on, 11, 25–26
humility, 130
  as condition for civility, xxi, 9, 12, 27
  in Greco-Roman world, 25
Hunter, James Davison, 198n1, 198n18

Iannoccone, Laurence R., 102
"identity theologies," 6
image of God, xxii, 6, 70
Incarnation, 175
incivility, xxi, 58
indifference to injustice, 163, 166–73
Indigenous Americans, 150
Indigenous hospitality, 66–68
individualism, 128, 130, 132, 141
injustice, 170–71. *See also* indifference to injustice

integrity, 125–26
  and civility, 112
  as directing meta-virtue, 112, 117–120
  in practicing hospitality and civility, 15
intellectual pride, 20
Inter Caetera, 87
interfaith dialogue, 6
Isocrates, 20

Jennings, Willie James, 161–62, 188n27
Jesus Christ
  bodily suffering of, 175
  concern for the city, 10
  form of a servant, 28
  interaction with rich man, 176
  lament over Jerusalem, 148, 158
  received hospitality, 71
  self-emptying of, 141
John of Goch, 85
Joseph, 146
Judeo-Christian values, 150
Jüngel, Eberhard, 122
justice, xxii, 24, 34
  apparent and substantive, 38
  Augustine on, 35–36
  as hope for marginalized, 106
  and love, 14, 34, 38–39
  and reality, 34
  as the substance of virtue, 36

Kant, Immanuel, 9, 180n19
kenosis (self-emptying), 141
Killinger, Barbara, 117
King, Martin Luther, Jr, 14, 97, 106, 107–08, 124, 168–69
Kluth, Brian, 192n27

La Mousee, Ignace, 67
labor of guests (hospitality), 48, 49–51, 58
lack of shared trust in culture and polity, 130–33
lament, 153–57, 203n58
Langer, Richard, 5–6, 164, 170
Las Casas, Bartolomé de, 67
"Letter from a Birmingham Jail" (King), 124, 168
Lewis, C. S., 27

Index

LGBTQ+ community, 12, 14, 101, 104–06, 123, 174
Limbaugh, David, 99
living sacrifice, 149
local partnerships, 74
localities, Augustine on, 11, 26
logos, 156
Logos (divine Word-made-flesh), 158
love, 34
  Augustine on, 11
  entangled with violence, 90–91
  for God, 25
  just and unjust, 39–40
  and justice, 14, 34, 38–39, 97, 107–108
  for neighbor, 25
  as substantive, 38–39
  Troup on, 130
Luke, Gospel of, 9–10
Lupton, Robert, 74
lust for power (*dominandi cupidate*), 43–44, 46
Luther, Martin, 85
lynching, 137, 150

McCaulley, Esau, 169
McCracken, Paul D., 22
McKerrow, Raymie, 124–125
MacIntyre, Alasdair, 25
Majority World, stereotypical impressions of, 63, 69
Manasseh ben Israel, Rabbi, 184n4
marginality, embracing of, 153, 154–55
marginalized, 106, 123
  as contributors and givers, 64
Markus, R. A., 182n4
marriage, 25
Marshall, John, 87
martyros, 157
Marxism, 140
Massachusetts Bay Colony, 65
mercy and peace, xxii
mestizo, 82
Métis, 82
#MeToo movement, 4
mimesis, 145–46
mistrust, 136, 174
modesty, 130
Moral Majority, 132

moral mandates, 7
Morris, Leon, 9–10
Moss, Candida R., 99, 100
Mouw, Richard, 5–6, 11, 117, 129–30, 163, 165
Muehlhoff, Tim, 5, 11, 163, 165, 170
mulatto, 82
Müller, Ludwig, 115–116
multiple interpretations, 84–85
mutual friendship, 74
mutual trust, 74
mutuality, in hospitality, 51–53, 64, 74
mutually constituted identities, 83–85, 88, 92
Myers, Bryant, 71

Narayan, Deepa, 74
National Church (*Reichskirche*), 112
National Emergency Termination Bill ("Enabling Act"), 113
natural law, 26
Nazi worldview, 114, 119, 121
neocolonialism, 14, 64, 68–69, 71
new heaven and new earth, 23
Newcomb, Steven T., 189n52
news media, precludes civility, 21
Nicene Creed, 7, 162
niceness, 21
Nicholas V, Pope, 87
Niebuhr, H. Richard, 22, 92
Niebuhr, Reinhold, 22
Niemöller, Martin, 116, 120, 195n39
Nietzsche, Friedrich, 199n18
Nieves, Alvaro L., 76
Nkrumah, Kwame, 68
Noll, Mark, 65, 67, 132, 166–67, 198n1
nonprofit organization leadership, 13

obedience to truth, 129
Obomsawin, Alanis, 187n13
Occom, Samson, 67
Oden, Amy, 72
oppression, xxii, 55, 101, 108
ordered loves. *See* well-ordered loves
orthodox/heretical Christian identity, 89, 92
orthopraxy, 162–63
Osborn, Robert T., 113

Index

otherness, 96, 108
Ott, Craig, 68

pathos, 156
Patrick, Susangeline Y., 13–14, 174
Paul
 civility of, 28
 conversion of his imagination, 205n5
 on speaking the truth in love, 117
 on suffering, 135–36
Paul III, Pope, 68
Paul, Tillie, 67
Pavlovitz, John, 155–56
peace, 9–10
Pearl (fourteenth-century text), 85
Pemberton, Glenn, 154
Pence, 152
Perlman, Janice, 71
perpetrator trauma, 89
Petesch, Patti, 74
Plato, 20, 37, 46, 89, 182n5
pluralism, 5, 164
 as problem to be solved, 164–65, 204n2
Pohl, Christine D., 53–54
poverty, reimagining of, 70–71
power, through weakness, 156
Presbyterian Church in America (PCA), 139–40
pretense, 20
private life, 33
privilege and oppression, 55
prophetic imagination, 145, 146–48, 152, 154
prophetic witness, as cruciform, 149
prophets, on injustice, 170–71
Puritan settlers in North America, 65, 66
Putnam, Robert, 74

Quintilian, 20

racial justice, 128
racial reconciliation, 128
 and suffering, 136–40, 174–75
racism, as foundational to America, 166–67
Rah, Soong-Chan, 154

Rational Choice Theory of religion, 101–02
reciprocal society, 74
reconciliation, 88
Reed, Ralph, 202n47
Reformed Presbyterian Church of North America, 22
Rehoboth Christian School, 86, 87–91
relevance, 20
religious "nones," 98
religious traditions, 129
repentance, 139, 153
Requerimiento, 65
Residential Schools (Canada), 78–80, 86, 174, 187n13
ressentiment, 199n18
reverse hospitality, 13–14, 64, 70–73, 76
righteousness, 35
Robert, Dana, 66, 74
Romanus Pontifex, 87
Romulus and Remus, 23, 81, 145
royal consciousness, 144, 146–47, 149, 151, 152, 153–57

Sackreiter, Amanda, 54
sacrifice, 130
same-sex marriage, 6
Sanford, Mark L., 130, 131
Sarah, Amma, 70
Saul, rise to the throne, 152
saying openly, 118
scapegoat, 144, 145, 146–49, 150
Schaeffer, Francis, 132
Searle, John R., 118
secularization, 98, 132
segregation, 137
self-critical examination, 122
self-determination, 49
self-righteousness, 20–21
Serequeberhan, Tsenay, 68–69
Serra, Junipero, 65
service, 141
sexual assault, 4
Shadrach, Meshach, and Abednego, 28
shalom, 71, 73, 76, 88
Shepherd, Andrew, 54
Shockness, Michelle, 13, 14, 175

Index

short-term missions, covenantal hospitality in, 75
Silo, Kimi, 75
Sixties Scoop, 14, 78–81, 83–84, 90, 91, 174, 187nn12–13
Skreslet, Stanley, 72
Smith, Christian, 136, 169
Smith, Linda Tuhiwai, 188n31
social justice, 106, 107
social media, 21, 130
socialism, 140
spaciousness in hospitality, 58–59, 60
speech, 118–120
Spencer, Greg, 118
Stark, Rodney, 102
Steiner, Mark Allen, 15, 64, 174
Sterling, Alton, 3
Stevenson, Brian, 125
stewardship of creation, 74–75
Stillman, Todd, 105
stranger, 53–54
Strauss, Stephen J., 68
substances, 34, 36–38, 41–45
substantive Christianity, 173–77
substantive justice, 37, 38
substantive truth, 43
suffering, 15, 128, 133, 163
  of the Black American community, 137–39
  evangelical resistance to, 141
  as faithful discipleship, 135–36
  as flourishing, 135
  as ontological condition, 134
  and racial reconciliation, 136–40, 174–75
  of White evangelicals, 200n54

Tatamy, Moses Tunda, 67
Tennent, Timothy C., 68
third-person effect, 20–21
Thomas Aquinas, 85
Thorowgood, Thomas, 184n4
"those people," 95–96
Thurman, Howard, 138, 140
Tisby, Jemar, 120, 123–25
trauma, 89
tribalism, 131, 132, 134, 136, 174
triumphalism, xxii, 133, 135, 154, 164

Troup, Calvin L., xxi, xxii, 164, 173
  on conditions for civility, 5, 8, 11, 34, 58, 112, 117, 129–30, 144
  on justice, 35, 106
  theory of hospitality, 69, 104
  unintentional indifference to injustice, 166–68
Troup, William E., 21–22
Trujillo, Rafael, 77
Trump, Donald
  call for removal from office, 118, 125
  election of, 3
  evangelical support for, 15, 100, 131, 133, 144–45, 149–53
Truth and Reconciliation Commission of Canada, 86
two great commandments, 25

unidirectional hospitality, 69
"Unite the Right" rally (Charlottesville, VA), 3

Van Til, Cornelius, 6
Van Tol, Deanne, 186n1
Varro, 78
violence, 23–24
  decried by lament, 155
  making unintentional room for, 165–66
virtue, 9
  forces that limit, 78
  not a technique or method, 19, 29
Vitoria, Francisco de, 67
vulnerability, 135

Ward, Annalee R., 15, 175
weakness, 156, 158
Weinstein, Harvey, 4
well-ordered loves, 23, 35, 58, 147, 150
Westerners, as saviors, 82
Whipple, Henry Benjamin, 68
White, Melanie, 104, 106
White supremacy, 123
Wilkens, Steve, 130, 131
Williams, Mark A. E., 12–13, 14, 162
Williams, Robert A., Jr, 82
wisdom, 118
witness, 157

Index

Wood, Naaman, 14
Wolfe, Alan, 141
Worcester, Samuel and Ann, 68
words, severed from substance, 43
woundable, 135
wounded victims, healing and justice for, 85
Wright, Daunte, 175
Wytsma, Ken, 139

Yancey, George, 99, 100–101
Yong, Amos, 71–72

www.ingramcontent.com/pod-product-compliance
Lightning Source LLC
Chambersburg PA
CBHW030434010526
44118CB00011B/629